LESSONS IN HOPE

LESSONS IN HOPE

My Unexpected Life *with*
St. John Paul II

GEORGE WEIGEL

BASIC BOOKS

New York

Basic Books
Hachette Book Group
1290 Avenue of the Americas, New York, NY 10104
www.basicbooks.com
Printed in the United States of America

First Edition: September 2017
Published by Basic Books, an imprint of Perseus Books, LLC, a subsidiary of Hachette
Book Group, Inc.

The Hachette Speakers Bureau provides a wide range of authors for speaking events.
To find out more, go to www.hachettespeakersbureau.com or call (866) 376-6591.

The publisher is not responsible for websites (or their content)
that are not owned by the publisher.

Print book interior design by Jack Lenzo.

Library of Congress Control Number: 2017948323
ISBN: 978-0-465-09429-5 (hardcover)
ISBN: 978-0-465-09430-1 (e-book)

LSC-C

10 9 8 7 6 5 4 3 2 1

For

Joan

William, Claire, and Lucy

Contents

A Dinner of Consequence

I N EARLY DECEMBER 1995, I FLEW FROM WASHINGTON TO ROME TO give the keynote address at an international conference on secularism and religious freedom. One of the oddities of European academic conferences is that the "keynote address" is sometimes the finale of the proceedings, so my paper was slotted at the end of a three-day meeting. This curiosity of scheduling set the table for something even stranger, however. For the chairman of the conference's closing session, Cardinal Agostino Casaroli, former secretary of state of the Holy See, devoted his remarks to a refutation of me and of the analysis of the Church's role in the collapse of European communism I made in a 1992 book, *The Final Revolution*.

The cardinal's suggestion—that I didn't *quite* understand Pope John Paul II and ought not be taken *quite* so seriously as an interpreter of the Pope's thoughts and actions—was more than a little ironic. And the irony turned on a dinner conversation in the Vatican the night before, of which Cardinal Casaroli, the Pope's "first collaborator" for more than a decade, was completely unaware.

The previous day, as the conference's postlunch session was about to begin, I had slipped into the back row of a large auditorium and sat down beside my friend Father Richard John Neuhaus. As was often the case, we were thinking the same thing: the moment called for a nice winter's nap, our heads enclosed in earphones as if we were paying close attention to the simultaneous translation while several colleagues droned on. There would be no napping that day, however. For no sooner had I muted the earphones than a seminarian, somewhat excited, began tapping me vigorously on the shoulder. I looked around, removed the headset, and heard him say several times, "Don Stanislao is on the telephone for you." He spoke in slightly awed tones, for my caller was Monsignor Stanisław Dziwisz, John Paul II's highly competent secretary and the man to whom few people in Rome wanted to say no.

I took the call and Dziwisz, as usual, got straight to the point: "Come over for dinner tonight and bring Father Neuhaus with you." I returned to the auditorium, where Richard was fast asleep, and gave him a gentle nudge. When he came to, I leaned over and said, "If your calendar permits, we're dining with the Holy Father tonight." Richard allowed as how that might be fitted into his social schedule.

So at 7:15 that evening we presented ourselves at the Portone di Bronzo, the Bronze Doors of the Apostolic Palace, and were duly led to the Terza Loggia, the third floor, and the papal apartment. We waited a bit in one of the apartment's small parlors, which, like the rest of the apartment, conjured up "middle-class Italian family," not "Borgia decadence." Then, without any ceremony, John Paul II and Msgr. Dziwisz came in, greeted us, and led us into the dining room, where Fr. Neuhaus and I were seated across from the Pope. John Paul said his usual rapid-fire Latin grace before meals and we tucked into an antipasto followed by roast chicken with a local red wine.

Conversations at John Paul II's table typically covered a lot of territory. The Pope was insatiably curious and used his mealtimes to keep himself abreast of new arguments, new books, trends in the world Church, and people his guests thought he should meet. But the table talk seemed disjointed this time, as if the Pope's mind were elsewhere. At one point, Fr. Neuhaus raised the issue of whether a thorough biography of the Pope wouldn't be a good idea and whether I should do it—an idea I had broached with John Paul's press secretary, Joaquín Navarro-Valls, seven months before and had talked over with Richard more recently. The Pope immediately changed the subject, as if this were something he didn't want to discuss. So the conversation drifted into other matters, with John Paul looking into the distance from time to time as if pondering how to say something.

Then, completely out of the blue, the 263rd Successor of St. Peter abruptly and forcefully said to Fr. Neuhaus, while glancing at me, "You must force him to do it! You must force him to do it!" "It," of course, was the biography, and "him" was me. Richard said that he didn't think that any force was going to be required. I simply exhaled. John Paul II smiled.

Later that night, after we had shared a scotch or two with Monsignor Timothy Dolan, the rector of the Pontifical North American College and our host during this Roman excursion, Richard said, "You know, this is going to change your entire life." I told him I didn't think so; I'd do the biography over the next few years and then return to the life I was leading at the Ethics and Public Policy Center, the Washington think tank that had been my professional home since 1989. "No," Richard insisted, "this is going to change everything."

He was right, if in that slightly exaggerated way that was one of his trademarks and one of his charms.

Becoming John Paul II's biographer didn't change *everything*. But it did become the pivot of my life. I began to see a lot of what had gone before in a new perspective, and I gradually came to understand that I had taken on a responsibility that would define me in the future, in ways I could not have anticipated that December afternoon in Rome when a nap seemed in order.

This album of memories is one unanticipated consequence of that dinner and what flowed from it.

When the second volume of my John Paul II biography, *The End and the Beginning*, was published in 2010 and I was promoting the book in its various language editions, I discovered that what my audiences most wanted to hear were stories: stories about the man who had gone home to the Father's house in 2005, stories that would make him present again by rekindling memories or illuminating previously unknown aspects of his rich personality. That yearning to get to know more personally a saint who bent the course of history in a humane direction, and to know him in ways that didn't quite fit the genre of serious biography, struck me as the impulse that inspired the informal "lives of the saints" over the centuries. Responding to that curiosity seemed another way to honor the pledge I made to John Paul II at the end of his life: that I would complete the task I accepted at his dinner table on December 6, 1995.

Doing so, however, requires widening the anecdotal lens and exploring how it was that someone who never expected to become a papal biographer became just that. When I finished *The End and the Beginning*, I had devoted two large volumes, totaling some sixteen hundred pages, to chronicling the life of the emblematic figure of the second half of the twentieth century—and I thought there was no more to be said. My readers and my audiences taught me I was wrong about that, just as I was wrong in dismissing Fr. Neuhaus's prediction that writing the Pope's biography would change everything.

John Paul II thought he was finished with poetry when he wrote his valedictory to Kraków, the poem "Stanisław," en route to Rome for the conclave that elected him pope. But toward the end of his life, he discovered there were things he wanted to say that could only be said in poetry, and the result was *Roman Triptych*. I thought I was finished with the making of John Paul books in 2010. But like the Successor of St. Peter who unexpectedly became a friend and the defining personality in my life's work, I now find that there are other things to be said and other stories to be told.

So, like him, I now look back on a remarkable journey by making a triptych: in this case, a third panel to flesh out the portrait of John Paul II, and of many of the notable people around him, that I offered in *Witness to Hope* and *The End and the Beginning*.

COINCIDENCE AND PROVIDENCE

Arriving at the Marian shrine of Fátima on May 12, 1982, on a pilgrimage of thanksgiving for his life having been spared when he was shot a year before, John Paul II said, "In the designs of Providence, there are no mere coincidences." That brief remark summed up his view of God's ways with the world and with history.

Much of what happens to us over the course of a lifetime can seem mere happenstance or coincidence. Some might view the fact that Mehmet Ali Agca's bullets tore into the Pope on the liturgical feast of Our Lady of Fátima as coincidence. It didn't seem that way to John Paul II, for whom salvation history was world history read in its fullest dimension. In salvation history—that inner core of world history in which God's purposes are worked out through the action of divine grace on individual lives—there are neither happenstances nor coincidences. Rather, what appears to be sheer happenstance or coincidence is an aspect of Providence we don't yet grasp.

Karol Wojtyła, the man who became John Paul II, thought about coincidence and Providence for a long time. In his vocational memoir, *Gift and Mystery,* he remembered a fellow underground seminarian, Jerzy Zachuta, with whom he used to serve Mass for Archbishop Adam Stefan Sapieha during the Nazi occupation of

Kraków in World War II. One day Zachuta didn't show up. Wojtyła went to his friend's home after the early morning Mass and discovered what had happened: the Gestapo had come the night before and arrested Jerzy Zachuta, who was later shot. As John Paul wrote more than a half century later, "Sometimes I would ask myself: so many young people of my own age are losing their lives, why not me? Today I know it was not mere chance."

That same conviction—that nothing is mere chance—explains why John Paul II came to Fátima a year after he was shot in his front yard, St. Peter's Square. Some might have thought it mere coincidence that a professional assassin, shooting at point-blank range on May 13, 1981, the day the Church's liturgy commemorated Our Lady of Fátima, failed to kill his target. But John Paul had come to a different understanding of his life and of history. As he put it more than once, "One hand fired, and another guided, the bullet." Providence acting through Our Lady, not ballistics, guided the bullet that missed his abdominal aorta by a few millimeters. He was spared, and for a reason. There was a mission to complete, and the Lord of history would see that he was given the opportunity to complete it.

The experience of learning John Paul II and his life taught me a new way of looking at events in my own life that might once have seemed happenstance or mere coincidence but that I came to see as remote preparation for being the Pope's biographer. The first of these non-happenstances came early, when I was a little short of nine years old. Others unfolded over the next three decades. Each is a piece of the puzzle of how I came to know Pope St. John Paul II and became his biographer.

Lent in the Third Grade

BALTIMORE, 1960

In September 1957, I entered the Cathedral School in downtown Baltimore. The granite-faced redbrick building at 7 West Mulberry Street was built in 1830, and the school was an adjunct to the Cathedral of the Assumption, a Federal-period masterpiece designed by the great Benjamin Latrobe, one of the first architects of the US Capitol.

The cathedral's eight-grade elementary school was conducted by the School Sisters of Notre Dame, a religious community founded in Bavaria that had flourished in the United States since the mid-nineteenth century. When I arrived, the oldest of these black-gowned and white-wimpled ladies was Sister Mary Grace, thought to be the resident Methuselah because she had been at the Cathedral School since the days of Cardinal James Gibbons, who had died in 1921—meaning that her temporal relationship to the great cardinal was the same as mine, today, to Jimmy Carter and Ronald Reagan. In any event, and despite the thrashing religious sisters frequently take in popular culture, my memories of the sisters at the Cathedral School are happy ones. My first-grade teacher, Sister Mary Moira, was a gentle soul who could teach a rock to read, and I maintained contact with my second- and third-grade teachers for decades.

It is none of these fine religious women, though, whom I remember when thinking about the remote anticipations of my life with John Paul II. It's the school's principal, Sister Mary Euphemia.

Ash Wednesday in 1960 fell on March 2, and a few days prior to our being marched into Latrobe's cathedral for penitential ashes, Sister Euphemia announced that each grade would pray for the conversion of a communist dictator throughout the impending six weeks of Lent. We third graders hoped we would draw Soviet premier Nikita Khrushchev as our designated prayee; he was the only communist dictator any of us had ever heard of. But Khrushchev must have been reserved for the lordly souls of the eighth grade. So there was disappointment, quickly giving way to puzzlement, when, on Ash Wednesday, Sister Florence wrote the name of our guy on the blackboard in block letters, absent the proper Polish orthography: W-L-A-D-Y-S-L-A-W G-O-M-U-L-K-A. I doubt that even my classmates of Polish extraction knew of this miscreant. And while I can't remember how we pronounced his name during the next month and a half of prayer for his conversion, I'm sure we pronounced it incorrectly.

Had anyone told me that, some thirty years later, I would write books in which Władysław Gomułka's complex role in postwar Polish history figured prominently, I would have thought the prognosticator mad. Yet there it is. And please don't tell me those weeks of Lenten prayer in 1960 for Comrade Gomułka's conversion—seemingly unanswered—didn't have something to do with planting in me a seed that would finally flower in a passion for Polish history and literature—and a determination to tell the story of a then-forty-year-old auxiliary bishop of Kraków whom Gomułka and his associates foolishly thought a mystically inclined intellectual they could manipulate.

First Steps in Philosophy

T HE FIRST FULL-SCALE BIOGRAPHY OF JOHN PAUL II IN ENGLISH, written by veteran journalist Tad Szulc, suffered from numerous defects, one of which was a marked lack of interest in John Paul's intense intellectual life. But perhaps Szulc, who died in 2001, should be granted a measure of posthumous absolution on this point: Karol Wojtyła, the philosopher, was not easy reading, and getting inside his philosopher's mind was virtually impossible for someone without some formal training in the discipline. Which brings me to St. Mary's Seminary College, the liberal arts undergraduate division of St. Mary's Seminary and University in Baltimore, where I studied from 1969 to 1973, taking a philosophy degree on graduation.

I wasn't enthusiastic about studying philosophy when I entered the college in the fall of 1969. But I was a seminarian, philosophy was a prerequisite to the graduate study of theology, and in any case a degree in philosophy was the only degree St. Mary's offered when my parents drove me to 711 Maiden Choice Lane in Baltimore's Catonsville neighborhood to begin my baccalaureate studies. So, for better or worse, philosophy it would be.

For better, as it turned out.

It took me about two weeks in the required introduction to philosophy course taken by all freshmen—Philosophy of Man, as it was known in that politically incorrect age—to discover the intellectual excitement of abstract thought. There were two texts in the course, both written by a Dutch Augustinian priest, Father William Luijpen, who would not rank, then or now, as a great philosopher. (Some of his more exuberant and grating phraseology sticks in my mind more than four decades later, eruptions such as "Ah, the call of the Absolute Thou!") To his credit, though, Fr. Luijpen, who was in close touch with contemporary currents in philosophy, never lost a tether to the conviction that reason could get at the truth of things. Out of that heady mix of the classical and the modern, Luijpen created what he called "existential phenomenology": a way of getting at the truth not from the top down, as classical philosophers had done, but from, so to speak, the bottom up.

Whatever his rank among modern Catholic thinkers, his impact on me was like an intellectual electric jolt. Were I to reread them today, I might laugh, at least discreetly behind my hand, at his books. But it would be a friendly chuckle, not a mocking one, for Fr. Luijpen opened up to me a world of adventure I had never before imagined: the adventure of disciplined abstraction. That excitement was stoked by some fine teachers, for the study of philosophy at St. Mary's Seminary College, which closed a few years after my graduation, was like a light bulb that glowed most brightly at the end.

Father Thomas "Butch" Leigh, SS, one of the sweetest of men, led us neophyte philosophers through Luijpen, thereby getting me hooked on philosophy. James Anderson took us into, and out of, Plato's cave and into the bright, sunlit uplands of Aristotle. A freshman-year seminar in the philosophy of mathematics made me enjoy math in a way I had thought impossible since getting befuddled by Algebra II in high school.

Two men stand out as teachers whose work on me, and for me, yielded major dividends when it came to drilling into the mind of Karol Wojtyła.

Francis Kane introduced me to the modern Continental thinkers who had such an impact on Wojtyła, including Edmund Husserl, the founding father of phenomenology. His teaching ranged all over the history of philosophy, though, so it was Kane with whom I read the British empiricists, the contemporary linguistic analysts, and political philosophers from Plato and Aristotle to Hegel, Marx, and Mill, with pit stops along the way at Augustine, Hobbes, and Rousseau. His metaphysics course also introduced me to the "pleasures" of reading Immanuel Kant.

John Donovan taught me Fichte, Schelling, and Hegel, but above all he got me acquainted with Thomas Aquinas, who was rapidly being jettisoned in many post–Vatican II philosophy programs as impossibly old hat. In my senior year, Donovan gave me a good grounding in the thought of the Angelic Doctor, a lifelong respect for Thomas's intellectual achievement, and thus some understanding of the foundations on which John Paul II's philosophical project rested.

While I was getting intellectually excited by philosophy, the same thing was happening in theology, which I chose to pursue in graduate school as a layman on deciding that my vocation lay elsewhere than the priesthood. These two intellectual interests were connected, I came to understand. There are theologians who write as if they never studied philosophy at all—and it shows, usually in confusion. I was fortunate enough to learn as a young man that philosophy is the essential prerequisite to doing theology seriously, and has been since the first synthesis of biblical and Greek thought was forged in the late second century AD. Then there are theologians who are indeed formed, although ill-formed, by philosophy—and their attraction to inadequate (or false) philosophical approaches or systems also shows up in their theology, to bad ends.

Understanding this linkage between philosophy and theology—between sometimes unarticulated presuppositions and theologizing—was more than a matter of good intellectual hygiene for me. For there is no way to understand John Paul II's magisterium—his teaching as pope—without understanding the rudiments of his philosophical position and his general philosophical instincts. Nor is there any way to grasp John Paul II's critique of certain modern and contemporary theologians without grappling with his philosopher's critique of the philosophical positions that underwrote what he thought were their defective theologies. This was obviously true, for example, in John Paul's challenge to those forms of liberation theology he thought dependent on a Marxist philosophy of history. But it was just as true in his critique of certain trends in post–Vatican II Catholic moral theology, which he thought false philosophically before they led to trouble, theologically and pastorally.

None of these applications of what I had learned at St. Mary's could have been imagined when Cardinal Lawrence Shehan handed me my bachelor's degree on May 20, 1973. But the foundations had been laid. And looking back, I am immensely grateful that my adolescent skepticism about philosophy and its utility in the contemporary Church was overcome so quickly in September 1969, and so decisively in the four years that followed.

Contesting the Council

M Y GRADUATE STUDIES AT THE UNIVERSITY OF ST. MICHAEL'S College in Toronto, from the fall of 1973 through the spring of 1975, took place when the Second Vatican Council and its immediate implementation were regarded as insufficiently radical by most of the principal personalities in theology in Western Europe and North America.

I don't believe we ever read a document of Vatican II in my Toronto classes; the Council was regarded as a good thing but an incomplete thing, thanks to what most of my colleagues thought was Pope Paul VI's timidity. According to the prevailing view, that timidity then overflowed into disaster in the 1967 encyclical *Sacerdotalis Caelibatus* (which reaffirmed Latin-rite Catholicism's commitment to a celibate priesthood) and in the 1968 encyclical *Humanae Vitae* (which reaffirmed the Church's classic teaching on marital chastity). There were some reverberations along Lake Ontario of the 1972 split among prominent theologians that led Hans Urs von Balthasar, Henri de Lubac, Joseph Ratzinger, and others who would play large roles in John Paul II's pontificate to found the journal *Communio* as an alternative to what they deemed a rigidly enforced progressive Catholic party line in *Concilium*, the journal they had helped establish during Vatican II. But this effort to maintain pluralism in Catholic theology was largely dismissed as irrelevant, even craven, in the world of Toronto theology.

Thus the idea that there was an alternative view of Vatican II— that the Council was a good thing but John XXIII's intention to dialogue with the modern world for the sake of converting the modern world had too often become a wholesale surrender to an increasingly incoherent modern world—was notably absent in Toronto. As for the possibility that the Council might be getting its most thorough pastoral implementation in an ancient diocese in the south of Poland, well, that was quite unimaginable.

Despite this hothouse atmosphere of progressive or liberal Catholic self-certainty, I learned important things in Toronto, especially from a gifted teacher, Father Daniel Donovan. I read a lot of what was known as "Transcendental Thomism" with Fr. Donovan, especially the Christology of Karl Rahner, on which I wrote my master's thesis. And if I later came to understand the limits of Rahner's theological project, that dissertation taught me something important for a then-unimagined future: that philosophical anthropology—the idea of the human person that animates a theologian's work—has a lot to do with how that theologian does theology.

The most famous and mediagenic member of the St. Michael's faculty in those years was Father Gregory Baum, the Berlin-born son of a Jewish mother and a Protestant father, a war refugee who had made it to Canada in the nick of time, a multilingual scholar who had become a Catholic, then an Augustinian priest. During Vatican II, Baum was recruited to the staff of the conciliar Secretariat for Christian Unity, the liberal counterbalance to the more conservative conciliar Theological Commission. Thus "Gregory," as everyone called this friendly and gregarious man, was at the epicenter of the internal struggles of Vatican II.

Gregory was a man of pyrotechnic intellectual dexterity who discovered one new disciplinary interlocutor for theology after another: different forms of philosophy, psychology, and so forth. I was his teaching assistant in a 1974–75 undergraduate course on the sociology of religion, then his newest fascination. He was a brilliant lecturer, if not the deepest of thinkers, and I enjoyed working with him. But what sticks in my mind from our time together is a casual remark he made at a party while regaling us with tales of Vatican II intrigue— secretly printing documents and covertly distributing them; lobbying the bishops (assumed by the progressive periti, or Council theologians, to be a little dull); battling the retrograde Roman theologians and their intransigent ways. All in all, Gregory smiled, "it was a theologian's paradise." The implication was that, were we lucky, we nascent theologians would have a similar opportunity in the future.

Over time, however, I came to understand that what Gregory Baum was referring to that night was not the clash of great ideas in the service of great causes; he was talking about power. And by that I don't mean to suggest something necessarily dishonorable. Gregory and those like him truly believed that the power they wielded—especially over those sometimes-dim bishops—was in aid of noble objectives: ecumenical reconciliation with other Christian communities, a new dialogue with Judaism, an openness to modern intellectual culture, an intensified focus on work for justice in the world. The point, though, is that they really *liked* that power and the purposes to which it could be put. And they were not hesitant to use the whip hand to keep the theologians' guild in line. In their view, the ratchet of theological and ecclesial history turned only one way, and they were prepared to enforce that conviction by exercising their power to quell deviations from the guild's line.

Shortly before I left St. Michael's there was a North American challenge to this liberal theological hegemony in the 1975 Hartford Appeal for Theological Affirmation—quickly dubbed (and dismissed) by many in Toronto as the "Hartford Heresies." The *Concilium* versus *Communio* fracas was an intra-Catholic affair. The Hartford challenge to the dominant liberal way of doing late-twentieth-century theology was thoroughly ecumenical. It began one night over the kitchen table at Peter Berger's home in Brooklyn, when that eminent sociologist of religion and Richard John Neuhaus, then a Lutheran pastor, spent a postprandial evening smoking cigarillos and sketching on a pad of paper the things that most annoyed them about contemporary theology. That list of dubious propositions became the basis for a much more considered exploration of what was afoot in North American theology, held at Hartford Theological Seminary in January 1975. Among the signatories of the refined Hartford statement, which was a frontal challenge to much of what was in the Torontonian air in my days there, were men with whom I would work closely in the years ahead: the two instigators, Berger and Neuhaus; Father Avery Dulles, SJ; philosopher Ralph McInerny of Notre Dame; patristics scholar Robert Wilken; and moral theologian Stanley Hauerwas.

As I later discovered, the Hartford Appeal spoke to many of the discontents I began to experience in Toronto as one theological fad followed another: liberation theology, then the black theology subset of liberation theology, then feminist theology, and so forth and so on, in each case the guild following the lead of the ambient public culture. It took me some time to figure out just what was wrong with all that. But in time, I, too, would become a "Hartford Heretic," if of the second generation. Doing so prepared me to encounter the thought of John Paul II, which was not so much against the dominant liberal consensus of the post–Vatican II years as it was far beyond the progressive Catholic versus conservative Catholic civil war.

One more image from my Toronto years sticks in my mind as remote preparation for understanding a man who spent thirty-two years as priest and bishop battling communism in Poland. It was the night of April 29, 1975—the twenty-fourth anniversary of my baptism—and after having supper with some friends who were living in a convent near St. Michael's, I went with them to the convent's common room to watch the evening news. There I saw the helicopters of Operation Frequent Wind lift off from the roof of the US embassy in Saigon, frantic refugees hanging onto the landing skids and even more desperate men and women abandoned on the roof below. Something, it seemed to me, was very, very wrong here.

Like most of my college and graduate school classmates, I thought the war in Vietnam a grave mistake, although I understood that the heirs of Ho Chi Minh were unlikely to bring a workers' and peasants' paradise to Vietnam. The full awfulness of the American scuttle shocked me that night, however: this was not how a great nation treated those who had trusted it, callously leaving them to what they believed would be a terrible fate. It would be another five years or so before the anticommunism with which I had grown up reemerged in mature form, shaped by readings of Aleksandr Solzhenitsyn's epic *The Gulag Archipelago* and his gripping novella *One Day in the Life of Ivan Denisovich*, James Billington's *Fire in the Minds of Men*, and Leszek Kołakowski's *Main Currents of Marxism*. But once those readings sank in, I entered the lists in what would turn out to be the last decade of the Cold War, working for human rights in communist lands while battling the anti-anticommunism then rife in liberal American political circles. That work was another brick in the foundation of my study of the life of John Paul II. It began to be forged in Toronto on that terrible evening, watching my country dishonor itself and asking how such a thing could happen.

Apprentice Wordsmith

MY WIFE JOAN AND I, NEWLY MARRIED, MOVED ACROSS THE country in the summer of 1975. I had been offered a job as a very junior faculty member at St. Thomas Seminary School of Theology, located just outside Seattle in Kenmore, Washington; I would also teach adult education courses for the Religious Education Office of the Archdiocese of Seattle. Joan, who had earned a master's degree in education, was offered a position at Forest Ridge School of the Sacred Heart, where in addition to her teaching she would create an innovative community service program for high school students. The two years I spent at St. Thomas were its last, as the bishops of the Pacific Northwest decided in 1977 to close the school. It was a shock at the time, yet it turned out to be a crucial turning point in my life, with major consequences for my becoming John Paul II's biographer.

At St. Thomas, I was the faculty's utility infielder, teaching everything from Introduction to Systematic Theology to Introduction to the Old Testament to Catholic Social Ethics to something called Critical Thinking (a meager substitute for the philosophy requirement the Northwest bishops ignored in their program of priestly formation). In the archdiocese, I was a roving catechist, offering various adult education courses—most of them having to do with overviews of the faith or US Catholic history—in parishes from Tacoma to Bellingham and at numerous points in between. It was a bit of a scramble, but looking back on it I can see that I was being taught an invaluable lesson: you really don't know what you think about something until you try to teach it, persuade others of it, or engage others in it. And what I discovered was that the theological approach in which I had been immersed in Toronto didn't make much of an impression on seminarians or adult laypeople. It didn't translate, so to speak, that Rahnerian theology; it left my seminary students and the people who attended my adult education courses cold.

During this period I also read David Tracy's seminal essay, "A Social Portrait of the Theologian: The Three Publics of Theology—Society, Academy, Church," and realized that the dominant forces in contemporary theology thought like some of the critters on George Orwell's fictional farm: there may have been three publics, or audiences, for theology, but some publics were more equal than others, and the really important public was the academy. Where this would lead had been identified by the "Hartford Heretics": to theology being held prisoner in an academic hothouse often characterized by boredom with the very mystery of being, skepticism about the human capacity to know anything with certainty, and moral relativism.

That those who occupied the commanding heights of North American theology refused to recognize this Babylonian captivity was another important lesson for me, and later helped me embrace John Paul II's view that theology is always an ecclesial discipline that learns from the Church and ought to serve the Church, even as it ought to take seriously its duties to the world and the canons of genuine scholarship.

With the seminary's closing in June 1977, I found myself three thousand miles from my Baltimore roots and without a job—for the Archdiocese of Seattle, perhaps sensing the beginnings of my dissent from the progressive consensus that then ruled the roost, declined to offer me a position when the seminary was shut down. Fortunately, though, the archdiocese was not my only professional option when St. Thomas shut its doors. During the 1976–77 academic year I had come into contact with the Seattle office of an improbably named organization, the World Without War Council, whose executive director, Stephen Boyd, proposed that we apply to the Washington Council on the Humanities for a grant that would fund me as WWWC's Seattle scholar-in-residence. Just as improbably—although, as I now see it, providentially—the grant came through.

And so I definitively left the world of the academy (and Church bureaucracy) for the world of think tanks and, eventually, the world of the scribes, journalistic and scholarly. In those interconnected worlds,

I was taken under the wings of two men who left an indelible mark on my life and, without realizing what they were setting in motion, spiffed me up intellectually and stylistically and set me on the course that led to John Paul's II dinner table.

The first of these extraordinary mentors-become-friends was Robert Pickus, who died at ninety-two in 2016 after a life that could only have happened in America. Born in the Midwest of Jewish immigrant parents, he studied under Hans Morgenthau at the University of Chicago in its glory days before serving in the Office of Strategic Services during World War II. Returning to Hyde Park and Robert Maynard Hutchins's university after postwar study on a Fulbright scholarship at the London School of Economics and a trek through the Middle East and India, he worked with Mortimer Adler on the latter's *Syntopicon*, which purported to be an index of all the world's great ideas. While he never finished the dissertation that would have gained him a doctorate, Pick, as he was known to one and all, took from the University of Chicago a profound reverence for classic liberal learning, a thorough grasp of political theory from Plato through the moderns, and a vocational commitment to work for peace, which he defined as work for a law-governed world safe for democracies.

That commitment took him first to the American Friends Service Committee. But when the Quakers' principal peace organization took a hard left turn into anti-anticommunism, which he regarded as a violation of historical Quaker pacifism and elementary political common sense, he struck out on his own, founding a variety of organizations, of which the most substantial was the World Without War Council. The Council was more think tank than activist agency, and, over time, it became a sign of contradiction in the world of "peace organizations" for several reasons: Pick's unapologetic patriotism and his belief that the US should play a large role in world affairs, which challenged the regnant post-Vietnam left-wing isolationism of the peace movement; his anticommunism, which infuriated the anti-anticommunists; his stress on law as an alternative to mass violence in settling conflict, which few took seriously; and his devotion to human rights and democracy, which made the anti-anticommunists nervous because it made the communists nervous.

The intellectual and moral framework Pick created for the Council made a lot of sense to me, so I fit readily into the basic cast of mind that shaped WWWC work around the country. But beyond offering me an institutional base in Seattle, the Council, meaning primarily Pick, became my personal doctoral program. I was unrewarded by a degree, but his tutelage was crucial in the development of my thinking—and, in time, to appreciating John Paul II in greater depth.

It was Pick, whose Judaism was idiosyncratic but serious, who reminded me, the Catholic, that Catholicism had long thought of peace as the product of law and politics: in Augustine's fine phrase, peace is *tranquillitas ordinis*, the "tranquillity of order."

It was Pick, a pacifist, who showed me, a Catholic in the just war tradition, how these two ways of thinking and these two moral commitments could work together when "work for peace" was focused on developing legal and political alternatives to war in resolving international conflict—a perspective that eventually led me to look closely, if with an occasionally critical eye, at Vatican diplomacy.

It was Pick who, by insisting that peace and freedom were inseparable, helped me to think about human rights in a disciplined, precise way, and who first showed me what John Paul II and Václav Havel later confirmed: that the robust defense of human rights behind the iron curtain was one crucial key to bringing down the Berlin Wall and liberating what Pickus understood full well were "captive nations."

It was Pick who invited me to fill in my theoretical anticommunism from literary sources—Arthur Koestler's *Darkness at Noon,* Ignazio Silone's *Bread and Wine,* André Malraux's *Man's Fate*—and thus helped me understand the human texture and context of Karol Wojtyła's life from 1946 through his election as pope.

It was through Pick that I came to know, and befriend, the first- and second-generation leaders of what came to be known as "neoconservatism," a largely Jewish network of thinkers who intersected at key points with Catholics and about-to-be-Catholics who had also broken with the American political left for a variety of reasons—including two men with whom I would later be closely identified, Richard John Neuhaus and Michael Novak. It was a heady mix, and while the polemics could get fierce, the relationships were warm and supportive as the first neocon generation was remarkably open to guiding and encouraging a successor generation, irrespective of formal academic credentials or former cast of mind.

Finally, it was Pick who suggested that I apply for a fellowship at the Woodrow Wilson International Center for Scholars in order to write a major study of American Catholic thought on war and peace. I thought the thing impossible: how could a thirty-two-year-old without a doctorate hope to win one of the most prized sabbatical positions in American academic life? But he insisted it could be done, and with some encouragement from Max Kampelman (an old friend of Pick's, then serving as the Wilson Center's board chairman), I won a full-year fellowship and moved back east in the summer of 1984 for a year at the Wilson Center, to be followed by establishing a WWWC sister organization, the James Madison Foundation, in the nation's capital.

The second large figure in my Seattle period, and the man who shaped me into an author, was David Brewster. The mid to late 1970s and early 1980s were the golden years of alternative journalism in the United States, when weekly newsmagazines in tabloid newspaper format—like the *Village Voice* in New York, the *Boston Phoenix*, and the *Figaro* in New Orleans—developed a generation of writers who were encouraged to break new ground in reporting and commentary. The Seattle iteration of this phenomenon was *the Weekly*, which became the unanticipated launchpad for several internationally known writers—including one of the world's premier espionage novelists, Alan Furst, and the biographer of John Paul II.

David Brewster was a dynamo of energy who came to Seattle with his wife Joyce after they had both done doctoral studies in English at Yale. Deciding that teaching at the University of Washington was not to his taste, David put his considerable talents into journalism, eventually launching *the Weekly* in 1976. We met by chance in late 1978, and shortly thereafter Brewster asked me if I wanted to do "sermon reviews" for his paper—a first hint that this was not your ordinary editor. David's idea was that religion was an important part of any cityscape and that a city's cultural health could be measured in part by the quality of the preaching its people heard; I thought that the local clergy, among whom I numbered many friends, would not take kindly to having their homiletic skills dissected the way David, the most respected and feared restaurant critic in the Pacific Northwest, analyzed the merits and defects of various chefs. So I told him that, while I was interested in writing, I thought it advisable that I stick to foreign policy matters, thus combining my day job at WWWC with some journalism.

David agreed, but it wasn't long before he had me on the religion beat, if in a different way than first proposed. John Paul II had created something of a media storm in the United States with his speech to the bishops of Latin America at Puebla, Mexico, on January 29, 1979; there, he had critiqued politicized forms of liberation theology that, as their proponents put it, used Karl Marx the way Thomas Aquinas used Aristotle. The Pope's critique was given the usual thrashing from the usual progressive Catholic suspects, one of whom wrote in the *Washington Post* that the Pope's address had given comfort to the Latin American regimes that were persecuting Catholic liberation theologians for their political dissent. I knew enough about the Polish-born pope at this early stage of his pontificate to know that this was rubbish. And so with David's editorial pencil hovering over my shoulder (much to my benefit, and our readers'), I tried to explain that the difference between using Marx as a theological interlocutor and using Aristotle lay in the fact that Marx was wrong and Aristotle was right on more than a few crucial points. I also used that March 1979 article to unpack key themes of Christian personalism in John Paul's first encyclical, *Redemptor Hominis* (The Redeemer of Man), which had just been published and which I found very exciting.

My debut as a public intellectual/theologian/columnist in *the Weekly* had several effects. As I continued to write about John Paul in favorable terms, the gap between my thinking and the anti–John Paul II consensus rapidly emerging among Catholic progressives soon became something akin to a chasm, which deepened when the Seattle archdiocesan newspaper, the *Catholic Northwest Progress*, offered me a slot as a regular columnist. Thus even as I was learning the journalistic parallel to what I had learned from teaching—that a good way to figure out what you really think about something is to try to write about it in a coherent way—I was also learning that H. L. Mencken's description of the exposed position of the magazine editor—"a man who lives on a sort of spiritual Bataan, with bombs of odium taking him incessantly from the front and torpedoes of obloquy harrying him astern"—was also true of the columnist. And while I didn't much like the brickbats at first (why couldn't these people see how reasonable I was?), I became more or less inured to them over time, thanks in part to the example of David Brewster, who caught his own share of flak and handled it with aplomb.

Even as I was writing myself into Catholic neoconservatism in *the Weekly*, David remained an honest, old-fashioned liberal, committed to open discussion conducted with civility and whatever measure of elegance was to be found in journalism. I don't think I was an awful writer when he began to whip me into shape, but I certainly retained some of the unpleasant traits of graduate school writing, especially among those influenced by German theology. David firmly and kindly sharpened my authorial steel, let me write about whatever I wanted (including baseball, one memorable summer), and never once suggested that I modify my views to accommodate the nascent political correctness of a Seattle that was moving steadily to the left.

Two other *Weekly* moments in the early 1980s were crucial mileposts on my path to writing John Paul II's biography. In December 1981, I penned an elegy for the Solidarity movement, which I had celebrated in *the Weekly*'s pages since the first Solidarity Congress in September 1980, and which the Polish communist regime had just tried to bludgeon to death via martial law. The *Weekly* pieces I wrote in those days were the first in which I explored John Paul II's grand strategy for the victory of freedom in Central and Eastern Europe: the robust defense of human rights, anchored in religious freedom, as a nonviolent weapon that communism could not match.

Then there were the murders of Mike Hammer and Mark Pearlman. Both men worked for the AFL-CIO–sponsored American Institute for Free Labor Development (AIFLD), and through WWWC connections I met Mike Hammer in Washington in late December 1980. Three weeks later he and Pearlman, a Seattle native, were gunned down in a San Salvador hotel along with a Salvadoran colleague, Rodolfo Viera. I wrote a memorial piece in the January 14, 1981, *Weekly*, "Our Martyrs for Democracy," which AIFLD reprinted and distributed nationally. It was my first, but not last, immersion in the bloody politics of Central America in the 1980s, which John Paul II would later confront and try to temper.

Front Row Seat

IF ACADEMIC LIFE OFFERED THE SECURITY OF A STEADY SALARY AT the price of department meetings, paper-grading, and other forms of tedium, life in the world of think tanks and journalism, while not so financially secure, offered a lot more freedom. It was a freedom I thoroughly enjoyed, and one of my first exercises of it took me to New York and Washington in October 1979 to write about John Paul II's first papal pilgrimage to the United States for *the Weekly* and the *Catholic Northwest Progress.* The logistical circumstances under which I worked—writing my stories and columns longhand and dictating them over the phone back to Seattle—seem almost primeval in a world of laptops, cell phones, text messages, and e-mail. But I was twenty-eight years old and it was all a great adventure—despite such hassles as the US bishops' conference press office misplacing my credentials on three separate occasions.

I skipped Boston, the starting point of John Paul's US tour, and began my work in New York. Amazingly, the credentialing process worked well at the UN and it was a breeze to walk into the great Secretariat Building on First Avenue and pick up a set of credentials that gave me the run of the whole UN headquarters. I was a rank amateur as a journalist but some inner voice told me that, as I could go anywhere in the complex, I ought to scout out the fastest route to where the Pope would enter the General Assembly building and the shortcuts from there to the balcony of the General Assembly Hall, where he would be speaking.

That intuition stood me in good stead the day John Paul II arrived at the UN. I quickly found my way to the foyer through whose doors he entered—and suddenly there he was, striding purposefully a foot or so away from me. There was no opportunity for a word, but I vividly remember my first impression of Karol Wojtyła, the man: he was a little shorter than I expected and he walked with a slight tilt to his shoulders and head, but his robust physique and powerful stride struck me as not dissimilar to those of an NFL linebacker. It was thrilling to be up close and personal, but there was no time to dawdle; the Pope's entourage and the UN bigwigs swept him away to meet-and-greets that preceded his address to the General Assembly, and I hightailed it to the General Assembly Hall balcony along the route I had traced the day before.

Remarkably, it was all open seating, and as I was an hour early I planted myself in the front row—later to look behind me and wave to Senator Daniel Patrick Moynihan, who, if memory serves, was escorting Jacqueline Kennedy Onassis into seats far less desirable than mine.

John Paul gave a stunning speech that I would analyze in detail twenty years later. And I like to think I remember the uncomfortable looks on the faces of the delegations from communist Central and Eastern Europe when the Pope made his powerful plea for religious freedom as the first of civil rights; but any such memory may be influenced by reading Pat Moynihan's comments to that effect later. In any event, it was an unforgettable morning, and after I left the UN I walked down First Avenue to the home of Richard John Neuhaus, then Pastor Neuhaus, to get his take on the speech. He was, as usual, lucid and eloquent in what would be our first conversation about the proper interpretation of a John Paul II text: the keys, he insisted, were the Pope's locating human rights at the center of any humane world politics, religious freedom at the center of human rights, and a biblically informed notion of human dignity as the foundation of the whole edifice. In addition to giving me numerous quotes for my stories and columns, Richard and I shared a laugh—the first of what must have been hundreds—over the fatuousness of the *New York Times*, which involved a headline to the effect that "Trip Will Determine Whether Pope Is a World Leader."

In the Washington phase of the visit, the US bishops' conference credentials, which I had finally acquired, got me onto the North Lawn of the White House, where I watched in fascination as the born-again

Southern Baptist president of the United States warmly welcomed the Polish-born Bishop of Rome. The Pope's encounter with religious sisters in the vast National Shrine of the Immaculate Conception was another event for which I was in the press pool. That meeting was later remembered for Sister Theresa Kane's challenge to John Paul on the ordination of women; what sticks in my mind, though, is that the sisters who stood in protest during the Pope's formal remarks were often the ones climbing up on the pews to take pictures of him when he made his way out of the Shrine down its long center aisle. Then there was the papal Mass on the National Mall later that Sunday afternoon: it was a windy day and the visual takeaway was the Pope's green chasuble whipping around him in the brisk breeze as he preached a stirring homily, during which he cited Thomas Jefferson in defense of the primordial right to life.

As John Paul II made brief stops in Philadelphia, Des Moines, and Chicago, I played hooky and went to Baltimore, where I managed to get to the first game of the 1979 American League Championship Series, in which my beloved Orioles were playing the California Angels. That postseason would end in grief for the O's, thanks to Willie "Pops" Stargell and the "We Are Family" Pittsburgh Pirates, but the first game of the ALCS couldn't have been better for a lifelong Orioles fan and a rising John Paul II fan. I ended my coverage of the papal trip for *the Weekly* on that note:

> Will this remarkably gifted man make a difference, not only to his Church, but to the world? My hunch that the answer is yes came into focus . . . in Memorial Stadium. . . . As I sat there . . . and later watched John Lowenstein's pinch-hit home run slither over the corner of the left field fence to send 54,000 maniacs into an uproar, I suddenly thought to myself, "The Pope ought to be here." Somehow . . . I knew he'd enjoy it. That curious thought gives me confidence that, in time, John Paul II may just be the kind of religious leader we've all been instinctively awaiting for, a man who thoroughly enjoys being alive, who believes unabashedly that there is greatness in us—and who could eat crab cakes and drink beer on Wednesday night in Baltimore.

Later experience taught me that among John Paul's few cultural lacunae was a marked lack of interest in baseball. The intuition that John Paul II would relentlessly summon his Church and the world to live more nobly than many imagined possible turned out to be correct, however. And the nascent desire to know him better, born in those few seconds when he strode by me in the UN General Assembly building on October 2, 1979, full of purpose and confidence, would lead me into relationships and adventures I wouldn't have thought possible when I was a newbie columnist on the fringes of the papal media tsunami in October 1979.

In the Castle

ONGRESS ESTABLISHED THE WOODROW WILSON INTERNATIONAL Center for Scholars in 1968 as the official national memorial to the twenty-eighth President of the United States. Today, it's one among many Washington think tanks, with no particular focus or character. Things were different in 1984–85, when I spent a year there. The Wilson Center was then housed in the old Smithsonian Castle on the National Mall; the Castle had been modeled on a medieval Norman monastery by that gifted architectural copycat, James Renwick, and under the direction of James H. Billington, later the Librarian of Congress, the Wilson Center had a certain monastic quality about it.

Part of that had to do with the fellows' small offices, reminiscent of monastic cells, and the refectory-like dining room. The greater part of the monastic ambience was created by Jim Billington, though. This distinguished historian of Russian culture and twentieth-century revolutionary thought had the singular ability to walk into any discussion and ask the one question that got almost everybody thinking about the matter at hand in a new, fresh way. Thus, without making a big deal about himself, Billington fostered something resembling a true academic community: a fellowship that reverenced the truth. Jim Billington was also a man of deep Christian faith, and he quietly made it his business to put a little leaven into the Wilson Center mix by offering fellowships to scholars with theological and religious interests. Thus one of my predecessors as house Catholic was none other than the great Fr. Avery Dulles.

During my first month as junior subaltern in this gathering of the far-more-credentialed, I befriended five men who would decisively shape my future thinking and work.

Bohdan Bociurkiw from Carlton University in Ottawa was the world's leading expert on the world's largest illegal and underground religious community, the Ukrainian Greek Catholic Church. Bohdan had survived the Flossenbürg concentration camp and after emigrating to Canada had taken his doctorate at the University of Chicago. With significant contacts behind the iron curtain, he was well-informed about his underground Church, which the Soviet secret police tried to liquidate in 1946 with the connivance of the Russian Orthodox Church. We became fast friends, and he gave me a yearlong tutorial in Ukrainian Catholic history that later proved invaluable.

Menahem Milson, a native-born Israeli scholar who specialized in Arabic language and literature, served in Ariel Sharon's famous Unit 101, and, after the Six-Day War, was briefly civil governor of the West Bank, where he tried to implement an imaginative plan to develop a Palestinian political leadership with which Israel could make peace. Three years after we became friends in the Castle, Menahem invited me to Jerusalem, where I gave a few lectures at Hebrew University and made a host of contacts who later became important in helping me get inside the dramatic story of John Paul II's efforts to establish full diplomatic relations between the Holy See and the Jewish state, and in facilitating my writing on John Paul's epic Holy Land pilgrimage of March 2000.

Father Joseph Komonchak's work on Vatican II helped hone my understanding of the Council in which Karol Wojtyła played a significant role and that John Paul II would spend his entire pontificate trying to explicate. Komonchak's view of Vatican II and mine did not always coincide, but he made me think through the Council, its effects, and its implementation at a deeper level. Joe was also a great collector and retailer of hilarious clerical stories, and we spent more than a few lunches together swapping tales of ecclesiastical folly.

Then there was Columbia historian István Deák, another émigré scholar, in this case from Hungary. One afternoon he floored me by climbing into my cell in the Castle tower (which had a great view of the Mall on three glass-paned sides) and showing me a court-martial record he had unearthed in the Library of Congress. István was writing a book about the Austro-Hungarian army's officer corps as the world's first true multinational organization—a book I read with great

interest when sketching a portrait of Captain Karol Wojtyła, father of
the future pope, in *Witness to Hope*. But that payoff wasn't on my radar
when he gleefully showed me the court-martial record of a Lieutenant
Augustin Weigel (no relation, fortunately), who had been cashiered
from the Habsburg army: not for being blind drunk, and not for getting into a brawl with a peasant while blind drunk, but for failing to
redeem his officer's honor by killing said peasant in said brawl.

Finally, there was James Childress of the University of Virginia,
a distinguished ethicist whose work helped me understand how the
just war tradition had become distorted in the hands of certain theologians, with powerful impacts on the US Catholic debate on war and
peace and on Vatican thinking about world politics and the pursuit of
peace. Jim Childress certainly disagreed with my take on his take on
just war thinking, but he was a true gentleman and friendly interlocutor with whom I enjoyed interacting during that year in the Castle.

My year at the Wilson Center also saw the beginning of my friendship and collaboration with Congressman Henry Hyde, which was
entirely accidental but nonetheless providential. In September 1984, I
went up to the Capitol to have lunch in the House dining room with
Joel Pritchard, a Seattle-area congressman with whom I had worked
on arms control issues in my WWWC days. Joel was recovering from
chemotherapy, and Henry, walking through the dining room, came
over to ask how he was feeling. Joel introduced me and Henry politely
asked what I was doing in town. I explained that I was at the Wilson
Center, studying Catholic thought on war and peace.

Hyde smiled and went off to his own lunch. A few minutes later, he
came back to our table and asked me whether I'd written anything on
Church-state issues, then a hot topic in the 1984 presidential campaign.
I said that I had and would arrange to get copies of those articles and
columns to him. A few days after that, Henry called and asked me to
stop by his Rayburn Building office. It seems that he had been asked
by the Thomas J. White Center at the Notre Dame Law School to come
to South Bend and deliver an address on the Church-state debate as a
response to New York governor Mario Cuomo's recent disquisition on
that subject. Would I draft a speech for him to consider? I said I'd be
delighted to do so.

That was the beginning of a twenty-two-year collaboration, during which I did most of Henry's major speechwriting. Fascinating in itself, that experience also had important consequences for my work on John Paul II. The first was that working with Henry deepened my understanding of the ideas of the pro-life movement, to which I had always been committed but, pre-1984, in a friendly-bystander sort of way. Now I found myself working with the undisputed congressional leader of the pro-life community, helping craft arguments for both Congress and the public debate. So by the time I came to write about John Paul's pro-life teaching and his 1995 encyclical, *Evangelium Vitae* (which Henry himself influenced, if indirectly), I was well schooled in the intellectual architecture of the pro-life cause and experienced in trying to explain its reasoning to a secular audience.

The second effect of my collaboration with the remarkable Henry Hyde on my John Paul II work would involve the impeachment and trial of the President of the United States. But that is a tale for later.

During my year at the Wilson Center I wrote a very fat manuscript on a Kaypro 4 computer that I didn't realize I ought to back up until after I had ground out something like eight hundred pages of copy. Luckily there were no crashes, and with the able editing of Cynthia Read of Oxford University Press, my first major book, *Tranquillitas Ordinis: The Present Failure and Future Promise of American Catholic Thought on War and Peace* was published in September 1987.

The book made three large arguments: that there was in fact a tradition of US Catholic thought on war and peace, inherited from Augustine, Aquinas, and other just war theorists and developed in a distinctive way in America; that this tradition had been largely forgotten in the post–Vatican II years; and that, reclaimed and developed, this tradition could help shape a more morally and politically coherent public discussion of international security issues. John Paul II's rich, subtle, and complex thinking about the human person and human rights, I suggested, would be at the center of any such reclamation and development.

Writing the book was my first experience in making an extended set of arguments over hundreds of pages, which stood me in good stead when it came to telling John Paul II's story. I also learned that giving books Latin titles in late-twentieth-century America was asking for trouble, in that most of those who interviewed me about the book had no idea of how to pronounce *tranquillitas ordinis,* much less grasped how those two words encapsulated the main motif of my proposal: that what Augustine had called the "tranquillity of order" in *The City of God* could be "translated" in modern terms into a compelling idea of peace—peace as the fruit of freedom and the democratic political process. In retrospect, I should have called the book *Peace Through Freedom: US Catholics and World Politics*, but Bob Pickus insisted that the Latin title was perfect, and as I was dedicating the book to him (along with the late American Catholic theologian and political theorist John Courtney Murray, SJ) I took his advice—for the last time, in the matter of titles.

Tranquillitas Ordinis was perhaps the first book to suggest that John Paul II's robust, evangelically grounded defense of human rights might provide a key for resolving the Cold War in peaceful terms. That point was, I think, vindicated by the events of late 1989 in Central and Eastern Europe. And my fascination with the idea and experience of societies liberating themselves by "living in the truth" would lead me in short order to a deeper exploration of how that had happened—and into the company of John Paul II, who had begun to come into clearer focus as a radically converted Christian disciple who could not be pigeonholed on some conventional liberal-conservative spectrum.

Cold War Endgame

I SPENT THE FOUR YEARS AFTER MY WILSON CENTER SABBATICAL launching and leading WWWC's sister organization, the James Madison Foundation, which involved me in enterprises that would shape my work on John Paul II.

The first of these, which involved prying Lithuanians out of the gulag, was made possible in part by a Seattle friend, John Miller, who had won Joel Pritchard's old seat in the US House of Representatives in 1984 and who, like me, thought that effective human rights advocacy on behalf of dissidents behind the iron curtain was a key to resolving the Cold War in favor of the forces of freedom. John asked me to do part-time consulting work with him, and I suggested that we focus on his human rights concerns. Here, another seeming happenstance in my Baltimore upbringing turned out to be providential.

When I was a boy, Baltimore had a small but vibrant Lithuanian-American population, whose communal life was centered on St. Alphonsus Church, a few blocks from the Cathedral School. The leading figure in the Lithuanian-American community in those days was Father Casimir Pugevicius, who served the parish at St. Alphonsus while working on the archdiocesan newspaper, the *Catholic Review*. I first met "Father Cas," as he was universally known, in the 1960s, and he must have planted in me a seed of interest in Lithuanian affairs. That seed would flower twenty years later, when I convinced a Jewish congressman that he should try to do something about Lithuanian Catholic priests and nuns doing hard time in Siberia.

With the six hundredth anniversary of Lithuania's conversion to Christianity on the horizon in 1987, I suggested to Congressman Miller in 1985 that we put together a Lithuanian Catholic Religious Freedom Caucus in the US House of Representatives. The object was to provide congressional support for Lithuania's Catholic Committee for the Defense of Believers' Rights, whose heroic work I had become familiar with since the *Chronicle of the Catholic Church in Lithuania,* the longest-running samizdat publication in the history of the USSR, began to circulate in the United States—thanks to the work of Fr. Casimir Pugevicius, who was by then working full-time with Lithuanian Catholic Religious Aid, a nongovernmental organization headquartered in Brooklyn.

With John Miller's encouragement, I met with Father Cas for the first time in years and told him of our hope to get a caucus in support of religious freedom in Lithuania established in the US House of Representatives. Father Cas was enthusiastic, so the next step was to find a Democratic partner for Congressman Miller in establishing the group. A quick study of voter demographics suggested that a Cleveland-area congressman named Edward Feighan might be naturally sympathetic. So after John Miller called Ed Feighan and outlined the plan, I met Feighan's chief of staff—a then-obscure young Democratic activist named George Stephanopoulos. George agreed to assign someone to work with me, and the Lithuanian Catholic Religious Freedom Caucus was born.

At the time, three of the principal figures in the Lithuanian Catholic Committee for the Defense of Believers' Rights were behind barbed wire in, if memory serves, Perm Camp 36: Sister Nijolė Sadūnaitė, Father Alfonsas Svarinskas, and Father Sigitas Tamkevičius, SJ. So the caucus focused some of its attention on giving visibility to their cases in the Congress and urging the Reagan administration to pressure the Gorbachev regime in the USSR for their release—a goal that was achieved before the collapse of the USSR. Congressmen Miller and Feighan also sponsored, and I drafted, House Resolution 192, on "the denial of freedom of religion and other human rights in Soviet-occupied Lithuania." H.Res.192 was cosponsored by forty-four members of the House of Representatives and was passed in time to mark the six hundredth anniversary of Lithuanian's conversion. On that occasion, the caucus sponsored a large reception and rally in the US Capitol; various congressmen and senators spoke in defense of Lithuanian religious freedom and Lithuanian independence, and the entire program was broadcast to Lithuania by Radio Liberty and Radio Free Europe.

A decade later, with Lithuania self-liberated from the collapsing Soviet Union, I came to understand how influential John Paul II had been in inspiring the Lithuanian Catholic Committee for the Defense of Believers' Rights, which was formed shortly after his election. It was a piece of the John Paul II story virtually ignored by others. But it was crucial in grasping just how significant an impact John Paul's election had had on what had been the "Church of silence," and how a no-longer-silent local Church could reassert itself as the safe-deposit box of national memory and identity—and in doing so, help give Lithuania a new birth of freedom. I doubt that I'd have been alert to this when I was preparing *Witness to Hope*, had not another "happenstance" made me into an advocate for these heroes of modern Catholicism.

Then there was the 1988 millennium of Christianity among the eastern Slavs, during which the Soviet Union and the Russian Orthodox Church intended to highlight the changes inaugurated by Mikhail Gorbachev's glasnost and perestroika while rewriting (and in some cases airbrushing) the history of Christianity in today's Belarus, Russia, and Ukraine. Blunting that intention, putting pressure on the Gorbachev regime to realize its promise of openness and restructuring, and providing ideas for President Ronald Reagan's summit meeting with Gorbachev in Moscow seemed to me worthy goals for the James Madison Foundation to pursue. Thus was born the *Appeal for Religious Freedom in the Soviet Union on the Occasion of the Millennium of Christianity in Kievan Rus'*.

I drafted the *Appeal*, which was addressed personally to Mr. Gorbachev, with an invaluable assist from my Wilson Center fellow fellow, Bohdan Bociurkiw, who knew the relevant parts of the Soviet constitution, pan-union Soviet religious law, and the criminal codes of the various Soviet "republics" inside and out. The *Appeal* was both discursive, describing what religious freedom in full in the USSR would look like, and quite specific, identifying what should be changed at the various levels of the complex Soviet legal system—including the legalization of the Greek Catholic Church in Ukraine, then in the forty-second year of its underground existence. Jim Billington, by then the Librarian of Congress, made some useful suggestions, and the *Appeal* was translated into Russian and Ukrainian. With the help of WWWC and Madison Foundation colleagues around the country, and my Madison Foundation program officer, Amy Sherman, we rustled up signatories, and by the time we finished the *Appeal* was signed by virtually every major religious leader in the United States and a plethora of scholars, activists, journalists, businessmen, labor leaders, and public officials: Catholic, Orthodox, Protestant, Jewish, and Muslim; liberal and conservative (theologically and politically); Democrat and Republican.

Ten thousand copies of the *Appeal* were distributed in North America and on both sides of the iron curtain in Europe; more than a few pilgrims to the USSR during the millennium celebrations took copies with them to circulate privately. We also got word that the *Appeal,* having penetrated the USSR, was being copied and distributed in samizdat form. The *Appeal* was sent to John Paul II through the Vatican embassy in Washington, and on April 25, 1988, I presented a copy to President Reagan in the Oval Office. Themes from the Appeal would later resonate in the president's May 30 address at the Danilov Monastery in Moscow, and in others of his speeches in the USSR.

At the time, I thought of the *Appeal* as the culmination of the work for religious freedom in communist lands that I began in Seattle in the late 1970s. That turned out to be quite wrong, for the *Appeal* also helped prepare me to understand in greater depth the circumstances in which Karol Wojtyła had worked as priest and bishop in communist-dominated Poland, the lengths to which communist legal systems went to circumscribe religious activity, and the role of communist bloc intelligence services as agents of state-sponsored atheism. The project also accelerated my study of Mikhail Gorbachev, which began in another unexpected "happenstance" at a Wilson Center dinner on March 10, 1985.

A visiting delegation of Soviet scholars was in town; Jim Billington hosted a dinner for them in the Smithsonian Castle and, in addition to the usual congressional and executive branch types, invited those of the Wilson Center fellows he thought might ginger things up a bit at the dinner tables scattered throughout Renwick's great hall. I spent the evening probing my Soviet dinner companions' sensibilities and views on religious freedom and other human rights matters. Then, around dessert, there was a flurry of comment in Russian, within and among tables. Suddenly, the entire Soviet delegation got up, left, and boarded buses to be transported back to the Soviet compound on Mount Alto in northwest Washington. This weirdness, it quickly became clear, had to do with the unexpected death that night of Konstantin Chernenko and the imperative of getting these Soviet academics and officials out of circulation while the official line on What It All Meant and Who Was Coming Next was worked out.

The next afternoon, after Mikhail Gorbachev had been named General Secretary of the Communist Party of the Soviet Union, I asked Jim Billington what difference he thought Gorbachev might make. The difference, he said, was generational. Unlike his three predecessors—Leonid Brezhnev, Yuri Andropov, and Chernenko—Gorbachev hadn't seen his friends dragged into the basement of the Lubyanka and shot in the back of the head, as had happened during Stalin's 1930s purges. "They all had that cold-blooded, reptilian look," Jim recalled, "and that's why: they saw their friends liquidated." The conclusion: Gorbachev had not been permanently dehumanized by such an experience, and he'd be different because of that. It was another insight on my long list of debts to Jim Billington. And that image of a "cold-blooded, reptilian look" was in my mind when, a dozen years later, I was putting together the pieces of another great Cold War puzzle, the assassination attempt of John Paul II on May 13, 1981.

EPPC, Diplomacy, and *Centesimus Annus*

O N June 1, 1989, I became the second president of Washington's Ethics and Public Policy Center, succeeding the founding president, Ernest Lefever. EPPC had a well-deserved reputation for serious public policy research that fit well within the neoconservative consensus. I enjoyed my seven years at EPPC's helm, working with an ecumenical and interreligious group of colleagues who shared my conviction that John Paul II was *the* religious figure of consequence on the world stage. In those years, EPPC sponsored conferences and symposia on the history of Catholic social doctrine and on the thought of John Paul II. From those conferences, we published a book of commentaries on the social encyclicals, another book on John Paul's 1991 encyclical, *Centesimus Annus,* and yet another on the future of public Christianity in the United States in the last years of the twentieth century.

In those conferences I insisted that EPPC try to re-create a real dialogue across the usual ideological divides; it was not easy going, given the passions of the day, but it seemed worth the effort. Alas, that effort was rarely reciprocated, further confirming my judgment that something had gone wrong with progressive Catholics (and Protestants, and Jews): a certain intellectual brittleness that made it impossible to understand John Paul II in anything other than the tired left/right terms in which he couldn't be understood. At the same time, however, EPPC brought me into much closer contact with evangelical Protestant and Jewish thinkers about Church and society, many of whom had keen insights into John Paul.

The fall of the Berlin Wall in November 1989 was celebrated with satisfaction at EPPC, for we believed that our defense of human rights and our insistence on the moral superiority of imperfect democracies over pluperfect tyrannies had been vindicated. A month and a half later, I was having lunch with my friend Charles Krauthammer, who asked, "What are we going to do with the rest of our lives?" I told him that I imagined there would be plenty to keep us occupied, as I didn't buy Francis Fukuyama's "end of history" thesis and was confident that "history" had a few surprises left in her pocket. In my case, the immediate impact of the wall coming down was my first and only experience as a diplomat of sorts.

The Conference on Security and Cooperation in Europe was established by the 1975 Helsinki Final Act to periodically review the condition of, well, security and cooperation in Europe, east and west of the Berlin Wall. In the last decade of the Cold War, CSCE conferences were occasions to hold the Soviet Union's toes to the fire on the human rights commitments it undertook in 1975. But with the Cold War over, what was CSCE to do, especially in terms of securing democracy in the old Warsaw Pact countries?

Max Kampelman, who was helpful in getting me to the Wilson Center and who had a lot of CSCE experience under Presidents Carter and Reagan, was appointed by President George H. W. Bush as head of the US delegation to the first post–Cold War CSCE review conference, to be held in Copenhagen in June 1990. Max invited me to become a public member of the US delegation: meaning, essentially, that I would pay my own way but be fully a part of the US team. I agreed and spent two weeks in the Danish capital, writing speeches for Max, acting as US liaison to the Vatican delegation, listening to hour after hour of diplomatic rhetoric, and observing Max's skill in handling both his diplomatic interlocutors and his bosses in the State Department. The US goal at the meeting was to get the strongest possible agreement on what the "rule of law" meant in the post–Cold War world. We largely succeeded, although we made no headway on getting the Soviet delegation to concede that the Baltic states deserved the independence that Stalin had stolen from them in 1941. And when we left, there were still unresolved issues about certain Soviet prisoners of conscience, whose cases I had tried to press.

It was quite a scene, that conference. Several of the delegations from the new democracies east of the Elbe River were composed of men who had served the old communist regimes and were clearly lost, substantively and rhetorically—a good experience, for me, of *Homo sovieticus* and, in retrospect, another unanticipated bit of learning that would serve me well in understanding the world from which Karol Wojtyła had emerged to become Pope John Paul II. Many of these delegates spent hours shopping: discounted consumer goods were available in one section of the vast conference center where the CSCE meeting was held, and I saw dozens of TVs, stereos, VCRs, and other electronic goodies being carted out by the ex-comrades. Some of these boys were also laggards in moving beyond communist-era self-presentation and haberdashery; one head of delegation always had a suspicious bulge under his jacket, while another wore business suits that looked as if they had been dry-cleaned in vichyssoise.

Our hotel was on one of Copenhagen's many quays and one evening I spotted a huge yacht tied up there. On inspection it turned out to be *Freedom*, owned by my friend and benefactor William E. Simon, former secretary of the treasury. I wrote him a note and a few days later received an invitation for drinks aboard *Freedom* the following evening, accompanied by Max Kampelman and John Evans, our deputy head of delegation. So there we were, sitting on the fantail, sipping gin and tonics, when an unmistakable voice accosted me from below decks: "What are *you* doing here?" Up the stairs bounced William F. Buckley Jr., who was crewing *Freedom* with his friend Bill Simon. The two Bills, Max, John, and I had a serious conversation for the next hour about the post–Cold War situation in Europe before the three landlubbers left *Freedom* (which was larger than any Danish navy vessel we saw in the harbor) and returned to diplomacy.

Ten months later, John Paul II issued his greatest social encyclical, *Centesimus Annus*, and I took another step along the path to becoming the Pope's biographer.

I had continued to write steadily about John Paul since that first *Weekly* piece in March 1979, and by 1991 I was likely one of the pope's principal interpreters in North America. John Paul had an efficient personal intelligence network and was aware of what I was doing in trying to explain him to an American audience. None of this made my stock rise higher among those who insisted that Karol Wojtyła was a conservative Pole with a premodern mind, but I had come to the settled view that he was a thoroughly modern intellectual with a very different read on modernity—one that deserved serious attention. That judgment was amply confirmed when *Centesimus Annus* was published at the beginning of May 1991.

That there would be a social encyclical commemorating the centenary of Leo XIII's *Rerum Novarum*—the first of the modern papal social encyclicals—was obvious. The real question was, who would help shape the draft with which the Pope would work? John Paul, I later learned, was still dissatisfied with the work done on his previous social encyclical, the 1987 document *Sollicitudo Rei Socialis*, by the Pontifical Council for Justice and Peace, and was even more unhappy with the draft for a centenary encyclical that Justice and Peace composed—especially after the Italian philosopher Rocco Buttiglione reviewed the Justice and Peace draft and told the Pope, in so many words, "This is not the way the economy works today and it isn't the way it will work tomorrow." Rocco then helped John Paul, who never had a bank account and had long lived outside everyday economic life, understand that there might be economic laws roughly analogous to the natural moral law: meaning that some things worked economically because those things cohered with human nature, and some things didn't work economically because they cut against human nature.

Discarding the Justice and Peace draft, John Paul crafted an encyclical that brilliantly described the threefold free and virtuous society of the future as one composed of a democratic political community, a free economy, and a vibrant public moral culture. And, he insisted, the culture was the key to all the rest, because it took a certain kind of people, culturally tutored in certain virtues, to make the machinery of free politics and free markets work so that the result is genuine human flourishing. Truth, he argued, and especially the truth about the human person, had everything to do with living freedom well and building prosperous economies. And the central truth that the free societies of the future had to own was the truth about the human person, which we can know by both revelation and reason.

There was a lot more in *Centesimus Annus*, of course, including a crisp analysis of the communist crack-up, a sharp critique of dependency-inducing welfare states, and a plea for social-welfare programs that stressed the empowerment of the poor. But what shocked the Justice and Peace bureaucracy in the Vatican, much of the world press, and the liberal Catholic establishment was the Pope's endorsement of what he called the "free economy": markets regulated by law and a robust moral culture. I was less interested in that than in his analysis of the Revolution of 1989 and his insistence that democracies had to recognize certain moral truths about the human person if they were to survive; so less than a quarter of my article on the encyclical, "The New 'New Things,'" was dedicated to questions of the economy. But it was the economic stuff that caused the first of many *Centesimus Annus* flaps, as the liberal establishment, gobsmacked by the encyclical, kept insisting that the Pope had not written what the Pope had, plainly, written (one Jesuit in Rome claimed that the kind of regulated market the Pope endorsed could only be found in fantasy or in textbooks).

I was given an advance copy of the encyclical in English by the US ambassador to the Holy See, Thomas Melady, and sent copies of it to my colleagues Richard Neuhaus and Michael Novak. The pieces we published immediately on the encyclical's release—in the *Wall Street Journal* (Richard), the *Washington Post* (Mike), and the *Los Angeles Times* (me)—framed its immediate reception and upset those who were eagerly anticipating something other than what John Paul II had delivered. Thus Richard, Mike, and I were accused for the first time, but certainly not the last, of expropriating the Pope for our partisan purposes, ecclesiastical and political—an accusation that any sensible person would recognize was false from the fact that John Paul, no fool, maintained close contact with the three of us until his death, wrote one of his oldest friends of his appreciation for our interpretation of his work, and encouraged one of us to write his biography, none of which seems very likely if he had thought we were distorting the meaning of his teaching.

Whatever the slings and arrows of opprobrium that came flying my way over *Centesimus Annus*, they were minor irritants compared to the exhilaration of learning from and writing about a pope whose teaching, it seemed to me, had brilliantly scouted the terrain on which the battle for the twenty-first century would be fought in the West—a man I thought I would like to know better.

NEW WORLDS

In early September 1990, I received a letter from the editor of the *Washington Quarterly,* the journal of the Center for Strategic and International Studies, which had published my first major article on John Paul II and what I had begun to call "the Catholic human rights revolution." Brad Roberts quickly got my attention: "Now that you've unpacked your bags from Jerusalem, how about repacking them for Moscow?"

I had made my second visit to the Holy City the previous month to participate in the last meeting of the Jerusalem Committee, an international advisory board to the Jerusalem municipality created by Mayor Teddy Kollek. Saddam Hussein invaded Kuwait on August 2, a few weeks before we were to meet, and tourists fled Israel in droves. Teddy, however, was of the view that "we don't arrange our meetings according to the whims of totalitarians"; the committee agreed with this democratic tough-mindedness, so we met for several days in a Jerusalem deserted by just about everyone but its residents and us. The tourist scuttle made it possible for me to tour Masada virtually alone, accompanied by my friend Yigal Carmon, former adviser on counterterrorism to two Israeli prime ministers. The only other visitors exploring that striking memorial to Jewish courage on September 1, 1990, were about a dozen fundamentalists from the up-hollows of the old Confederacy; they had stayed in the Holy Land, evidently thinking that, with war on the short-term horizon because of Saddam, they had just won a front-row ticket to the Battle of Armageddon.

During that week in Jerusalem I deepened the conversations I'd begun in Israel in 1988, which would later play a large role in facilitating my research on John Paul II's efforts at Catholic-Jewish reconciliation and his drive to establish full diplomatic relations between the Holy See and Israel. Now, Brad Roberts was inviting me to fill in for Harvard's Samuel Huntington at a three-day seminar CSIS was sponsoring on democratization in the Soviet Union, right in the belly of the beast. I quickly accepted and another remarkable week ensued, which would decisively bend my work toward an ever more intense study of John Paul II and his impact on contemporary history.

As our group flew back to New York from Moscow's Sheremetyevo airport on October 10, I tried to sleep, but the extraordinary experiences of the previous five days swirled through my mind. After years of fighting communism from outside, there I had been, in the middle of the Soviet capital, fomenting nonviolent revolution in a series of discussions with men and women who called themselves the democratic opposition to Mikhail Gorbachev, whom none of them considered much of a democrat. It was exhilarating and frustrating, appalling and encouraging, the entire exercise given a sharper edge by the self-evident fact that we were under KGB surveillance from the time we arrived at Sheremetyevo until the moment we left the country.

As I turned the experiences of Moscow over in my mind, the same question kept recurring: How had this happened? How was it that American scholars and human rights activists were in the capital of Lenin's and Stalin's communist empire, discussing with Russians the intellectual, cultural, and institutional prerequisites for its replacement by a democracy? What had happened to the communist project, and why was it crumbling right before my eyes, at its epicenter?

Then the thought occurred: "The Pope and the Church must have had something to do with this."

The next day, I called my editor at Oxford University Press, Cynthia Read, and as we met over drinks that evening I made a proposal:

John Paul II and the Catholic Church must have had something to do with the communist crack-up; I wanted to figure out what that something was; and I thought it would make a good book for OUP. Cynthia was sold on the spot.

Thus a late-night thought on a plane returning to America from a place I'd never imagined I'd visit launched me on fifteen years of work that would eventually lead to a two-volume biography of John Paul II. In order to pursue that life-transforming thought, though, there were new worlds to learn, and that recent Muscovite experience to ponder more deeply.

In the Belly of the Beast

MOSCOW TODAY, OR AT LEAST THE PARTS OF IT IN WHICH WESTerners do business, is the bustling capital of the authoritarian kleptocracy that replaced communism after a brief democratic experiment. At the end of the Soviet period in 1990, however, it was showing the effects of decades of deferred maintenance: broken sidewalks and streets, nonpotable water, broken-down taxis, the fug of old tobacco and unwashed interiors everywhere. The most negotiable form of "currency" for basic consumer goods was a pack or two of Marlboros (each member of our CSIS group was advised to bring several cartons). The tourist rubles we bought were worth less than one-third of what the dollar brought on the ubiquitous black market. The work ethic was notable by its absence, especially in what Westerners thought of as the "service industry."

We were housed in the Hotel Belgrad near the foreign ministry, a gargantuan structure of Stalinist provenance that looked vaguely like a sinister wedding cake. Members of our group decided to meet in the evening to review that day's discussion and plan strategy for the next day. And as it was obvious that our rooms were bugged, we decided to get together in the hard-currency saloon in the hotel's basement, which you could only enter by showing wads of US dollars or deutschemarks; its shrill rock music seemed likely to discourage any eavesdroppers.

The air in that dive was thick with smoke; East German prostitutes lined the walls, eyeing the clientele for potential business; one heavily made-up fraulein plopped herself onto the lap of Leszek Kołakowski and was promptly if politely batted off by the world's leading intellectual historian of Marxism. The scene was not quite Hieronymus Bosch, but it was close enough to Edvard Munch.

Subsequent events demonstrated that the damage done by communism to *Homo sovieticus* was so severe that the kind of democratic political culture our group was sketching during conversations with our Russian colleagues couldn't achieve critical mass quickly enough to prevent a return to authoritarianism. But if our mission to Moscow was a failure in that respect, I took away from that week two indelible memories that shaped my future thought and work.

The first involved Leszek Kołakowski, whom I was meeting for the first time, years after profiting enormously from his masterwork, *Main Currents of Marxism*. One morning, Leszek, Brad Roberts, and I took a walk through Red Square down to St. Basil's; nearby, a squalid tent city had been erected by Russians who had come from the countryside to petition Mikhail Gorbachev for a redress of their grievances—which, by the look of things, included severe poverty. Leszek spoke fluent Russian from his days in Stalinist Poland, and as we walked through that sad village of the dispossessed, I was profoundly touched by the courtesy and kindness with which he engaged these poor people.

Leszek's example reminded me of the empathetic capacities of another Pole, Karol Wojtyła. Here were two men of about the same age (Wojtyła was seven years older); both lived through the horrors of the Nazi occupation and both fought an intellectual battle against the communist usurpation of Poland's liberties. Yet they were also men of a rare compassion, with an ability to engage others' suffering that offered the sufferers a measure of hope. Kołakowski's compassion was rooted in a philosopher's finely etched perceptions of the human condition. Wojtyła's compassion grew out of his cross-centered Catholic faith. Yet both were Poles, which suggested that there was something distinctive in Poland's history of national suffering: it could engender fellow feeling and empathy rather than bitterness and hatred. This was a national experience worth exploring in greater depth.

The second Moscow experience that stuck with me resulted from some unpleasantness caused by the secret police goons lurking about our hotel lobby. The hotel staff was all surly, all the time, but the ferrets were the worst. Brad Roberts and I noticed that they constantly hassled a young man we kept meeting in the lobby, who obviously wanted to practice his English with Anglophones. Having several free hours one day, Brad and I decided to stick it to the goons, and do ourselves a favor, by hiring this young man as a tour guide after he assured us that he knew his way around the main sites in the Kremlin.

We got there on the Moscow subway—its famously elegant stations inaugurating my lifelong distaste for socialist realist sculpture—and walked around that vast enclave for a while before going into one of the three "cathedrals" inside the Kremlin walls. The building had been magnificently renovated for the 1988 millennium of Christianity in Rus', and as we came up a stone staircase we found ourselves looking at a very large restored fresco of the Last Supper. It was obviously the Last Supper; it couldn't have been anything else. Yet our young Russian friend turned to Brad and me and asked, with complete sincerity, "Please tell me: who are those men and what are they doing?"

I had read about the effects of state-sponsored atheism but here they were, right in front of me: a bright twentysomething, well-educated and open-minded, with absolutely no idea what one of the most familiar of Christian images was communicating. This young man had been culturally lobotomized by the hatred for religion deep in communism's DNA; that lobotomy had denied him part of his patrimony. His simple yet somehow plaintive question undoubtedly shaped how I thought about Karol Wojtyła's war against communism in Poland and his intuition that that war was best fought with the weapons of a revitalized national culture and identity.

Rookie Vaticanista

I HAD BEEN TO ROME FOR A FEW DAYS AS A BOY AND RETURNED IN 1988 with Peter Berger, Michael Novak, and Richard John Neuhaus on a weeklong visit that taught me a lot about the touchiness of certain mid-tier Vatican officials when they encountered even friendly criticism of their work. That 1988 excursion was also the occasion for my first extended conversation with Cardinal Joseph Ratzinger, who would prove unfailingly helpful when I was preparing *Witness to Hope*. It was in May 1991, however, that I began my career as a sort of Vaticanista while looking for Roman clues to John Paul's role in the collapse of European communism.

The timing was determined by an academic seminar marking the centenary of *Rerum Novarum,* held at the Centro Nazareth and sponsored by the Pontifical Council for Justice and Peace. The conference papers and conversation made it abundantly clear that the Vatican bureaucrats in the Roman Curia, who were responsible for disseminating Catholic social doctrine, and the Catholic social thought professoriate in the Roman universities hadn't begun to understand, much less come to terms with, the dramatic developments in the social doctrine represented by *Centesimus Annus.*

The things that most engaged me about the new encyclical—its empirical sensitivity, its insistence on culture as the primary driver of history, its linkage of freedom and moral truth, its emphasis on civil society as essential to democracy, and its description of creativity as a principal source of wealth in the postindustrial world—went completely unremarked at the conference. That likely reflected the fact that not a single American had been invited to offer a paper, although the

United States was arguably the place where Catholic social doctrine had been taken most seriously over the previous century and where the liveliest debate over *Centesimus Annus* was underway. This was disappointing, but it taught me two important lessons: the Church in the United States was not taken seriously as a source of ideas in the Roman Curia and the Roman universities; and in those universities, the exhaust fumes of liberation theology and its Marxist understanding of the dynamics of history were still befogging the atmosphere. From these lessons I drew a conclusion that stood me in good stead as I began to grasp the essentials of Vaticanology 101: Don't assume that what we think is important in the US, or even what the Pope thinks is important, is necessarily going to be thought important by the curial bureaucracy or by the Roman academic establishment.

The two-day seminar ended with an official commemoration of the *Rerum Novarum* centenary in the Synod Hall inside the roof of what everyone in Rome called "the Nervi": the hypermodernist audience hall built by Paul VI inside the Vatican walls. At one point, the caterwauling of the Sistine Choir caused John Paul II to hold his head in his hands, to protect his hearing from the noise; and I thought, if he can cover his ears, so can I. So I did.

Over the course of eight days, I met a dozen or so major and minor figures in the Roman Curia and a bevy of Rome-based journalists. The most important conversation in shaping my perceptions of John Paul II's role in the communist crack-up was with then-archbishop Jan Schotte. Schotte had helped draft John Paul's bracing address to the United Nations in 1979, and his star had been rising in the curial firmament ever since. In 1991, he was General Secretary of the Synod of Bishops but still retained a keen interest in Vatican diplomacy, and the fact that he was not part of the Vatican diplomatic service gave him a certain critical distance from its default positions and idées fixes.

One of these set-in-stone defaults (especially among Italian papal diplomats) was that 1989 was the cash-out of the accommodating, soft-spoken *Ostpolitik* (Eastern policy) that Pope Paul VI and his chief Eastern bloc diplomatic agent, Agostino Casaroli had adopted toward the communist nations of the Warsaw Pact. Schotte was having none of that and at the outset of our discussion gave me an important piece of information: the first thing John Paul II did on assuming the papacy was to ask for the archives on the *Ostpolitik*. That review, Schotte suggested, helped convince John Paul to follow his instincts and to be more forthright and "undiplomatic" in his defense of religious freedom and his unmistakable challenge to communism from the very beginning of his papacy.

Schotte also told me a great story about John Paul's shrewdness in turning the Vatican and its sometimes inscrutable ways to his purposes. Poland's communist leaders knew that their state-run television could not ignore the inaugural public Mass of the first Polish pope, so they allotted four hours for coverage of the events of October 22, 1978. The ceremony would normally take two and a half hours, which would give communist spin doctors ninety minutes to explain that all of this meant nothing. John Paul called in the papal masters of ceremonies and told them to devise an inaugural Mass program that would last exactly four hours, thus outwitting the communist spinmeisters at their own game.

Schotte seemed to have intuitively grasped John Paul II's culture-driven approach to historical change, in which the truth, spoken clearly and winsomely enough, has the power to forge cultural tools of resistance to oppression. Thus Schotte understood how the Helsinki-CSCE process and its capacity to link human rights activists behind the iron curtain to their Western counterparts had helped set the stage for John Paul II's revolution of conscience. Schotte also recognized how important the two US radios aimed behind the iron curtain, Radio Free Europe and Radio Liberty, were in providing real information amid the communist culture of the lie.

I next spoke with Cardinal Joseph Ratzinger, then in his ninth year as Prefect of the Congregation for the Doctrine of the Faith and John Paul II's chief theological collaborator. When I first met Ratzinger in 1988, he subtly indicated, during an hour's conversation with Peter Berger, Richard Neuhaus, Mike Novak, and me, that he agreed with some of our criticisms of the Curia's way of thinking about Catholic social doctrine. Now, he spoke forcefully about the "moral and human incredibility" of communism and about the damage that communism had done to the human ecology of Central and Eastern Europe. The most serious, near-term challenge for postcommunist countries, he insisted, would be rebuilding a "culture of conscience" capable of sustaining democracy and the free economy.

The journalists I met during this period were more inclined than many curial officials to recognize that, with John Paul II, things had changed dramatically in the Vatican approach to communist countries, and less inclined to accept Team Casaroli's claim that speaking softly without carrying any sort of stick was the prudent modus operandi behind the iron curtain. *Time's* Wilton Wynn and Rome's longtime Associated Press bureau chief, Victor Simpson, were also more willing than the Vatican bureaucracy to credit John Paul with highly developed political skills. Wynn understood that John Paul II could have "lifted a finger" in Poland in June 1979 and "the regime would have been overthrown." But the Pope also knew that would have brought in the Soviet tanks. So he opted for working through the Solidarity movement, the kind of movement for social renewal he intuited might come out of his June 1979 pilgrimage to his homeland. It would have been nice to have heard these acknowledgments from the Vatican diplomats, but as Victor Simpson pointed out, the Italians in the Curia were still in shock over the election of a non-Italian pope, and "to protect Casaroli is to protect the Italian link to the papacy," which to some Italians seemed a matter of divine right—a crucial fact to remember in analyzing the pontificate of John Paul II in greater depth.

The points made by Wynn and Simpson were echoed by John Paul's press secretary, Joaquín Navarro-Valls, with whom I began to forge a friendship. Navarro, a Spanish layman and medical doctor, had practiced psychiatry before turning to journalism: his psychiatric background, he often suggested, was the perfect preparation for dealing with swarms of Vaticanisti—some of whose grip on the difference between fact and fiction was not altogether secure—in his role as papal spokesman. Navarro pointed out that John Paul II's election not only "changed the cards on the table" in Poland; it also had a dramatic effect in Czechoslovakia. Navarro also emphasized the sharp difference between Paul VI and John Paul II in their readings of the Yalta accords, which divided Europe at the end of World War II: Paul VI saw Yalta and its division of Europe as a political fact, while John Paul II rejected Yalta and all it represented on ethical, historical, and cultural grounds—which was why his method turned out to be "much more subversive" in undermining the Yalta system than an overtly political approach would have been.

Finally, it was Joaquín who planted the first seeds of my conviction that, while communism would have collapsed from its own implausibility at some point, the fact that the crack-up came in 1989 (rather than 1999 or 2009 or 2019), and that it came nonviolently, was largely due to the John Paul II Effect during the 1980s. The Pope wasn't the only one preaching the imperative of living in the truth, or "living as if one were free," in those days; I would meet some of the Polish, Czech, and Slovak exponents of that strategy of anticommunist resistance later in the year. But John Paul had the biggest megaphone, and without him, Navarro suggested, what happened during the 1980s, and the way 1989 unfolded, would have been impossible.

I left Rome confirmed in the conviction that John Paul II had played a singular role in the collapse of European communism, the final act of which would be played out in the USSR in a few months. And while it was clear that the Pope had political skills that he had deployed with considerable dexterity, I had also come to understand that his primary impact on what became the Revolution of 1989 would be found in the realm of the human spirit.

That first extensive foray into the curial maze also made me deeply skeptical of the widespread assumption that the Vatican operated like the US Marine Corps: the commandant (pope) issues an order and everybody down the chain of command staples a salute to their forehead and gets with the program. It clearly didn't work that way along the Tiber. The lesson that the Curia had its own ways of doing business was an important one for the future, both for understanding John Paul II's way of governing the Church and for getting my biographer's work done.

That week in Rome intensified my eagerness to get to Poland and Czechoslovakia to explore the Revolution of 1989 on the ground. Before I could do that, though, I had to go to Denver, where my friend Archbishop J. Francis Stafford had invited me to address an archdiocesan convocation. I was staying in the archbishop's home and his dinner guest the first night was Cardinal Joseph Bernardin of Chicago, another convocation speaker whom I had first met in the run-up to the US bishops' peace pastoral of 1982. In the course of dinner, Stafford mentioned that I had been in Rome investigating John Paul II's role in the events of 1989, which I was prepared to argue was quite important. "What do you think, Joe?" the archbishop asked Bernardin—who answered, "I think Gorbachev had more to do with it."

That was the conventional view at the time, and perhaps the cardinal ought not be blamed for sharing it. But Bernardin's lack of interest in what I had unearthed thus far was a harbinger: certain prominent Catholics were not going to abandon their disinclination to give John Paul II much credit for anything, or to see him in something other than the liberal/conservative terms in which they analyzed everything. This meant missing a lot of the story of a man who, I was becoming convinced, could only be understood as a genuine Christian radical.

Another trip to Rome in the spring of 1992 deepened the conversations I had begun the previous year and gave me further insights into the complexities of the Vatican, the intricacies of John Paul II's task, and his approach to his work.

It was my first time in Rome with Richard Neuhaus since his reception into full communion with the Catholic Church and his ordination as a priest by Cardinal John O'Connor. The high point of the visit for Richard was a Mass with the students of the North American College in the old Matilda Chapel of the Apostolic Palace, at which John Paul was the principal celebrant and Richard concelebrated and read the Gospel. There was a brief moment of greeting after the Mass, but the serious conversations with the Pope would begin later that year.

The most curious encounter during that Roman work period was with the Father General of the Jesuits, Father Peter-Hans Kolvenbach, SJ, which had been arranged by Fr. Avery Dulles. Richard and I spent the hour before our lunch appointment with Kolvenbach at the Congregation for the Doctrine of the Faith, speaking with Cardinal Joseph Ratzinger about the ecumenical initiative that Richard and I were just launching with Chuck Colson and Kent Hill, "Evangelicals and Catholics Together." Ratzinger encouraged us in this work. More than most Vatican officials, Ratzinger understood that there were different kinds of evangelical Protestants and that the fierce criticism of "the sects" by

Catholic bishops in Latin America was crudely undifferentiated and an obstacle to serious ecumenical conversation with the growing end of world Protestantism. As we were leaving Ratzinger's office to walk the few blocks up the Borgo Santo Spirito to the Curia Generalizia of the Jesuits, one CDF official murmured, "You're going into the heart of mission territory."

Our lunch with Father Kolvenbach took an instructive turn when he spoke of the future of his own religious order, which John Paul II had taken into a kind of papal receivership a decade earlier. Musing on what was permanent and what was transitory in the Church, Kolvenbach said that what was utterly permanent was the triad bishops/priests/people; but it also seemed likely that there were permanent religious charisms or forms of consecrated life in the Church. There would always be something like the Benedictine form of religious life, he thought, and there seemed a certain permanence to the distinctively Dominican and Franciscan ways of living the vows of poverty, chastity, and obedience. But what powerfully struck Richard and me was that the twenty-eighth successor to St. Ignatius Loyola as General of the Society of Jesus didn't argue that the Jesuit charism was a permanent fixture in the Church.

The best stories of the week came from Cardinal Jozef Tomko, then running the Congregation for the Evangelization of Peoples, which everyone in Rome still called by its pre–Vatican II name, Propaganda Fide (Propagation of the Faith), or simply "Prop." Tomko was a Slovak and, in those days, part of the John Paul II inner circle. He told us that the emir of Dubai had told him that "John Paul II was chosen by Allah to be *the* figure shaping world history" at that moment. And then he said something arresting about John Paul's management style and his confidence in Providence. They had been discussing some intractable problem or other, about which Tomko was evidently at his wit's end. The Pope's response? "Jozef, we're just supposed to keep doing our jobs."

"Do You Have Some Polish Ancestors?"

T HE MOST OBVIOUS PLACE TO SEARCH FOR CLUES TO JOHN PAUL II's role in the Revolution of 1989 was his native Poland, which I visited for the first time over twelve days in June 1991. The answer I got to my most important question—"When did the events that led to 1989 begin?"—was the same, no matter who I asked: Solidarity activist, government official, journalist, academic, priest, bishop, cardinal, housewife, believer, nonbeliever, liberal, conservative, or radical. Without exception, everyone said that "all of it" began ten years earlier, during John Paul II's epic June 1979 pilgrimage to Poland, the Nine Days that changed the history of the twentieth century.

There were certainly complexities in the great historical upheaval of 1989. It made a considerable difference to the way the 1980s worked out that Mikhail Gorbachev was running the Soviet Union, not one of his reptilian predecessors, who would have rolled tanks into Poland without a second thought. It made a great difference that Ronald Reagan was president of the United States, not Jimmy Carter, and that Margaret Thatcher, not James Callaghan or Michael Foot, was living at 10 Downing Street. By linking human rights activists on both sides of the iron curtain, the Helsinki process surely played its role, as did the first phase of the IT revolution and the new economics of globalization. Like any great historical inflection point, 1989 happened because of the confluence of multiple forces.

Yet 1989 had a special human and moral texture that set it apart. The twentieth century's normal method of effecting massive social change was violence and bloodletting on a colossal scale; 1989 was different. That difference, my Polish conversation partners confirmed in June 1991, was the John Paul II difference.

During my year at the Woodrow Wilson Center, I had been fortunate to draw as my research assistant a Georgetown senior, Rodger Potocki, who later won a Kosciuszko Foundation fellowship for graduate study in Poland; there, he got a good grip on the language and met his future wife, whose parents lived in Nowa Huta, near Kraków. In 1991, Rodger was working part-time at the National Endowment for Democracy while doing his doctoral coursework at Georgetown, and he quickly accepted my suggestion that he accompany me to Poland as translator and guide.

Our first three days in Warsaw coincided with the last three days of John Paul II's fourth Polish pilgrimage, which taught me a lesson for the future. Rodger and I spent Sunday at the closing papal Mass in the city's Agrykola Park and visiting the grave of the Solidarity martyr Father Jerzy Popiełuszko. The warm day involved a lot of walking and by the time we got back to our hotel we were parched, so I proposed watching the Pope's departure on the TV in the hotel bar. But when I tried to order a beer, I was informed that the city was dry until the Pope left—a precaution taken by the local authorities to prevent things from getting out of hand among already amped-up Poles. My somewhat exaggerated plea for mercy—"I'm a friend of the Pope; he *wants* me to have a beer!"—got me the universal stare that says, "I've heard *that* one before," and no sustenance. I resolved not to be caught in a similar situation again.

Twenty months after Tadeusz Mazowiecki became Poland's first noncommunist prime minister since World War II, Warsaw retained much of its communist-era feel. The city had been flattened after the Warsaw Uprising of 1944, and if there is anything worse than having your capital destroyed by Nazis, it's having it rebuilt by communists and then allowed to crumble during decades of neglect. The city was very grey and the skyline was dominated by the Palace of Culture and Science, another massive, ugly Stalinist wedding cake; according to the oft-repeated local joke, the best view of the Polish capital was from inside the Palace. (Years later, it would be remarkably improved, even humanized, by the addition of Big Ben–like clocks to its central tower.) I wasn't in Warsaw to admire or deplore Stalin-era architecture, though, but to deepen my understanding of how John Paul II triggered a revolution of conscience in his people, with epic consequences.

The most moving moments in my first visit to Warsaw came at the Church of St. Stanisław Kostka in the Żoliborz neighborhood, just off Woodrow Wilson Square (a name recently restored from the communist-era "Square of the Defense of the Paris Commune"). It had been Fr. Popiełuszko's parish, where his monthly "Mass for the Fatherland" had drawn thousands, and he was buried in the churchyard under a huge polished granite cross. The church was a shrine to Solidarity's martyr-priest, a museum of the struggles of the martial law period in the early 1980s, and a poignant reminder of the truth that freedom is never free.

When I first arrived in Kraków on June 11, 1991, I certainly didn't know that I would spend, all told, more than two years of my life there. But the combination of that remarkable Polish hospitality (in this case, offered by Rodger Potocki's in-laws, Fred and Danuta Chrobok), the charms of the city itself, and the intensity of my conversations with its people quickly turned the city John Paul II called "my beloved Kraków" into a place close to my own heart. Kraków then was not the vibrant, multicolored jewel it is in the twenty-first century: dirt and grime still muted the brightness of its Main Market Square; many people wore the plastic shoes that were an emblem of consumer life under communism; there was only one passable restaurant in the Old Town. But one could sense the architectural and decorative vitality waiting to be reborn, as the city's people had been, in the first freedom they had enjoyed since 1939.

My first conversation in Kraków was the most important. Cardinal Franciszek Macharski, Karol Wojtyła's successor as archbishop of Poland's cultural capital, welcomed me on June 12 to the archiepiscopal residence and offices at Franciszkańska 3, an address I would get to know well over the next two and a half decades. Macharski did not have the vibrant public personality of his predecessor, but that he came from a family of heroes became clear when he told me about his experiences on September 1, 1939, when he was twelve years old. His father was a prosperous merchant and the family lived in a flat above their store on the Rynek Głowny, Kraków's Main Market Square. As Luftwaffe bombs fell on the city, Mr. Macharski telephoned the aged Archbishop Adam Stefan Sapieha and asked, "What are you going to do?" "I stay!" Archbishop Sapieha replied forcefully—at which point Macharski's father turned to his family and said, "We stay, too!"

Macharski had been a bold, courageous defender of Solidarity under martial law, which he understood as part of his job description. For centuries, he told me, the local bishop was the *defensor civitatis*, the ultimate defender of the city and its people against those who would deny them their liberties. It was a tradition born in the eleventh century with the martyr-bishop of the city, St. Stanisław, and it had continued through the centuries as Cracovian bishops defended their people against one invader, occupier, or partitioning power after another. Archbishop Sapieha, he said, had exemplfied this tradition for Wojtyła and Macharski when they were young men.

So Kraków was especially well prepared by its history, he continued, to appreciate Vatican II's Declaration on Religious Freedom, *Dignitatis Humanae*. Religious freedom makes everything else possible: it puts a check on state power because it declares the inner lives of men and women out-of-bounds to state coercion. The cardinal also insisted that *Dignitatis Humanae* led to the kind of Church that Karol Wojtyła fostered in Kraków: an open Church that could, as Macharski put it, "open its space" to everyone, believer or unbeliever, who was "honest to man." That openness was the tool with which Wojtyła built coalitions that proved crucial in stitching together the national movement of social renewal called Solidarność.

Two days later, I met in the offices of *Tygodnik Powszechny* (Universal Weekly) with its longtime editor, Jerzy Turowicz, and Father Józef Tischner, the distinguished Polish philosopher who, like Turowicz, was a good friend and longtime collaborator of Karol Wojtyła.

Under communism, Turowicz was responsible for the only reliable newspaper in the country, and *Tygodnik Powszechny* became an outstanding example of Catholic journalism, a platform for anyone willing to think outside the box of communist orthodoxy. It was also the paper in which a young priest named Wojtyła began to flex his wings as a commentator and to publish his poems pseudonymously. It was

Turowicz who taught me that Karol Wojtyła, John Paul II, had become a European and a world figure *because* he was a Pole and a Cracovian. No one is a "European" in the "abstract," Turowicz insisted; you become a "European" through your roots in one of the national cultures that make up the European heritage. John Paul II embodied universal truths about the human person he had learned from being a Cracovian: the son of a city of encounter and genuine pluralism, a city of cultures in conversation. It was a striking comment from the editor whose columnist had become pope, and a keen insight into what made Kraków, which made the man who became John Paul II, different.

Tischner, a big, bluff son of the Górale, the Polish highlanders of the Tatra Mountains, combined robust Góral humor with a first-rate philosophical mind. His sermon at the first Mass of the first Solidarity Congress in Gdańsk in September 1981 was one of the greatest homilies of the twentieth century, and it was Tischner who coined the finest image of Solidarity: "a huge forest planted by awakened consciences." Communism, he insisted, was a culture of lawlessness masquerading behind a façade of legality. The façade began to crack when, during John Paul II's June 1979 pilgrimage, people said to themselves and to each other, "Let's stop lying," meaning "Let's stop pretending to believe what 'they' tell us is true." It was John Paul II, Tischner said, who had shown people that living in the truth was a "new way of being a partisan." Poles had long been fierce partisan fighters; now, Tischner suggested, they had learned that there were ways to be a partisan that involved not swords and rifles but the weapons of the human spirit.

On Sunday afternoon, June 16, another Polish priest, Father Kazimierz Jancarz, gave me a lesson in how hope was kept alive at the grassroots level in the 1980s, during and after martial law. We met at his parish, the Church of St. Maximilian Kolbe in the Mistrzejowice neighborhood of Nowa Huta. Fr. Jancarz described himself as "just a proletarian" and in fact was built like the New York Yankees' fearsome closer Goose Gossage. Under his leadership, the Kolbe parish in Nowa Huta became a piece of free Poland when the regime tried to stamp out Solidarity and what it represented: free space for free associations of free people who could think freely about themselves and the future. An underground university was formed for the steelworkers, the professors coming from the Jagiellonian University and the Kraków Polytechnic; some four hundred workers "graduated" after four semesters (including their "proletarian" parish priest). "Evenings of Polish culture"—political cabarets, theatrical performances, musical programs—replicated Karol Wojtyła's own experience in the cultural resistance during World War II: people in touch with their own culture can never be completely occupied, whether by a Nazi occupation force or by communist usurpers.

It was all exhilarating, meeting these people who had made a different kind of revolution, and I must have bubbled over with stories when Rodger Potocki and I returned to his in-laws' apartment in Nowa Huta at night to review the day. Living in one of those great apartment blocks in the steel-milling town built on the eastern outskirts of Kraków as Poland's first "city without God" was itself an education. The blocks had been organized to facilitate secret police surveillance: there was no access from one apartment to another along the long axis of the building; if you wanted to visit a neighbor, you had to go downstairs, exit the building, and enter by another door, all the while being watched by the ubiquitous ferrets. Still, Fred and Danuta Chrobok had made themselves a handsome and friendly apartment, and one night, over vodka and steak tartare, Fred said to me, "Do you have some Polish ancestors?" And while the family tree didn't yield a positive answer to Fred's query, I decided that, as old-school Thomists might say, I had a "connatural" affinity for Poland and Poles.

A brief visit to Gdańsk, the Baltic seaport where Solidarity, the "independent, self-governing trade union," was born, introduced me to its intelligent and open bishop, Tadeusz Gocłowski, another great defender of Solidarity during its hardest years. Like Cardinal Macharski, Gocłowski was noticeably free of the clericalism that is not unknown among Polish bishops, and he spoke without hesitation about what the Church had gotten right, and what it had gotten not-so-right, during Solidarity's crisis years and in the immediate postcommunist period.

His cathedral in Oliwa boasted a most remarkable organ, its bellows animating a large cast of mobile angels holding stars, suns, trumpets, and bells in addition to the pipes, but impressive as that organ was, it was the bishop's linkage between 1989 and Vatican II that made a lasting contribution to my work on John Paul II. Like Cardinal Macharski, Gocłowski stressed the importance of Vatican II's defense of religious freedom as a fundamental human right. But he also underscored the importance of the Council's Pastoral Constitution on the Church in the Modern World (*Gaudium et Spes*), on which Karol Wojtyła had worked to great effect. It was *Gaudium et Spes*, Gocłowski said, that defined an "integral humanism" across the fields of politics, economics, and culture. And it was that all-in, Christ-centered humanism that gave the Church the weapon it needed to resist what he called "administrative atheism": not the atheism of personal intellectual conviction but a state-enforced atheism that sought to occupy every available space in society.

Two days in Tarnów initiated my friendship with Józef Życiński, the youngest bishop in Poland and a man deeply versed in the philosophy of science, who was full of penetrating observations. Życiński, a new type of Polish prelate, nonetheless he went out of his way to praise the old primate, Cardinal Stefan Wyszyński, for deliberately "maintaining the spiritual tension" in Polish society under communism, by which he meant stirring things up when the dead weight of the regime might have proven crushing. Like Cardinal Macharski in Kraków, Życiński proudly showed me the place in his home's tile stove where one of many secret police bugs had been hidden and told me how the ferrets tried to recruit his predecessor's driver as an informant.

There were other memorable moments during that first visit to Poland: praying at the cell in Auschwitz where Maximilian Kolbe died; visiting the "Wojtyła sites" in Kraków, including the St. Leonard Crypt of Wawel Cathedral, where the young priest the world would know as John Paul II said his first Masses on November 2, 1946; making a first pilgrimage to the Black Madonna of Częstochowa, who would look over my desk for the next quarter century. But in addition to confirming my intuition that the Polish pope had played a large, if largely unrecognized, role in the Revolution of 1989, June 1991 in Poland taught me more about communism and how it had "worked" (and not worked) than I had learned from years of study and human rights activism.

I had read and reread Václav Havel's brilliant essay "The Power of the Powerless," and I knew, conceptually, that communism was a "culture of the lie" that could be resisted by people willing to risk living in the truth. To actually meet such people, though, made for a different kind of learning. An avid reader of history since I was a boy, I was now in conversation with people who had made history, and in a singular way: for had there been any other such moment in recent centuries when the good guys won cleanly and against great odds?

June 1991 also set me on a program of intense reading in Polish history and the classics of Polish literature. I began that crash course because sparks of intellectual and cultural curiosity were struck in my mind during twelve remarkable days. Those sparks would be fanned into a passion that would take me even deeper into Poland, and even deeper into the life of its greatest son.

Pilsner on Tap and Martyr-Confessors

I N ROME IN MAY 1991, JOAQUÍN NAVARRO-VALLS SUGGESTED THAT, when it came time to explore the Czechoslovak dimension of John Paul II's effect on 1989, I get in touch with Father Tomáš Halík, the secretary of the Czechoslovak bishops' conference, whom Joaquín described as an "archetypal figure": a priest ordained underground who had carried on a clandestine ministry for years before playing word-smith for the octogenarian Cardinal František Tomášek during the Velvet Revolution of November–December 1989. I wrote Fr. Halík, explaining my project; he arranged for me to stay at the Prague seminary in October and indicated that he would be on hand to help arrange my interviews.

But when I arrived in Prague on October 18, 1991, there was no Fr. Halík, who had decamped for a few months to Rome. A driver from the bishops' conference met me, waving a Vatican flag; the ride into town was subdued, as we didn't share a word in common. The seminary had recently been recovered from the communists, who had turned it into a publication house for propaganda materials. I was given a large three-room suite, far larger than I needed, for the comrades had taken good care of themselves; but while its people were immensely hospitable, the seminary was desperately poor.

The rector, Father Karel Pilík, greeted me, saw me to the suite, and said he'd come and fetch me for dinner. Our conversation on the way to the meal was a bit stilted, as he had no English and my high school conversational French proved less than serviceable in carrying on a conversation in his one Western European language. I was seated at the head table with the faculty, many of them elderly men recently released from work camps, including uranium mines. They could not have been friendlier, and the seminarians were told that I was an honored guest who had come to Prague to learn their Church's story and then tell it to the West.

Then came the "honor," as I was presented with a platter of carp heads—not the whole fish, just the heads—from which dull, piscine eyes stared out at me. It was, I deduced, a local delicacy, and these good men were trying in their straitened circumstances to be generous. So I picked at the heads during the meal, while trying to carry on some sort of conversation in very bad French and remnants of Latin—and immediately repaired afterwards to a nearby hotel bar; there were ample bar snacks, and the draft beers included Pilsner Urquell and real Czech Budějovický Budvar (not to be confused with insipid American Budweiser). That bar became my evening refectory over the next nine days, and I lost a fair amount of weight on what I came to call the "Prague seminary diet."

My linguistic luck improved the next day when, looking for help in the offices of the Czechoslovak bishops' conference (also housed in the seminary), I had another coincidental/providential moment. First, I ran into a man Halík had recommended I see, Václav Vaško, the premier historian of the persecuted Church in communist-run Czechoslovakia; then I bumped into Ondřej Fischer, a seminarian with good English. Vaško gave me a multihour crash course in the history he knew so well, and Fischer became my tour guide in Prague. I was also fortunate in meeting, at the English-language Sunday Mass at St. Joseph's Church, the secretary of the new Vatican embassy to Czechoslovakia, Monsignor Thomas Gullickson, a son of South Dakota who helped arrange meetings for me and got me into a Mass and reception that marked the anniversary of John Paul II's visit to Prague. There, I met and arranged interviews with a remarkable cast of characters who had played large roles in the Catholic part of the Velvet Revolution.

In the early Church, persecuted (and often tortured) Christians who survived their ordeals were known as "martyr-confessors," and over a week of conversations I met such men and women in Prague and Bratislava: modern martyr-confessors, including underground priests and bishops, who had all done serious jail or labor-camp time. Their stories of John Paul II's impact on them in the 1980s deepened my conviction that the *Ostpolitik* of Pope Paul VI was a well-intentioned failure, even as I learned how Vatican efforts to appease communist regimes in the hope that they would play nicely were especially catastrophic in Czechoslovakia.

The basic story they told me was that the Catholic Church in Bohemia, Moravia, and Slovakia, having been laid low by the Casaroli *Ostpolitik*, was reborn in resistance, a rebirth that began on October 16, 1978. That afternoon, while he was receiving the cardinals' homage in the Sistine Chapel, the just-elected John Paul embraced the ancient Cardinal Tomášek, Archbishop of Prague, and somehow gave that hitherto timid figure a transfusion of spiritual energy. The result over the next decade was "this singular spectacle of the cardinal getting older *and tougher* at the same time," as former-dissident-become-parliamentarian Pavel Bratinka put it to me.

But the cardinal was not the only dramatic figure in the amazing, John Paul II–inspired story I learned over a week of intense conversation.

Cardinal Ján Chryzostom Korec, SJ, was clandestinely ordained a bishop in 1951 at age twenty-seven and conducted his episcopate underground while working as a warehouseman, elevator repairman, and night watchman—when he wasn't serving a dozen years in prison for his ministry.

Father Oto Mádr, an elfin figure who, like Tomáš Halík, had helped give words to Cardinal Tomášek's new toughness, spent a year wondering every morning whether the death sentence he had received in 1951 for being a "spy" would be carried out. The fifteen years he served in prison were, he said, "a very happy period of my life, with many conversions," because being in prison "gave the Church a new apostolate."

Václav Benda, a bear of a man wearing a Harvard sweatshirt, was a Catholic parallel to another Václav, Havel, although a philosopher rather than a playwright; Benda's underground writings gave intellectual depth to the idea of "living in the truth"—in this case, the truth of Christ—as the way to exercise Havel's "power of the powerless." An evening spent with him and his wife Kamila, who surreptitiously brought her husband Holy Communion in prison on the four times each year she was permitted a visit, was an experience of Catholic and democratic solidarity across national and linguistic barriers that left a deep impression.

Benda's Slovak counterpart, Silvester Krčméry, had done thirteen years in jail for "treason," meaning that he had catechized young people and translated the social encyclicals into Slovak. Like Fr. Mádr, Dr. Krčméry looked back on his jail time with wry affection, telling me that, in prison, meditation "was like spiritual weightlessness—you lost contact with the cell and the prison."

Then there was Father Václav Malý, another underground priest, who catechized his fellow stokers in a hotel boiler room before becoming the master of ceremonies at the Velvet Revolution's great demonstrations in Wenceslas Square. President Havel offered him a government post after the revolution, but Malý replied that he just wanted to be a priest, openly.

These men, and the Slovak parliamentarian František Mikloško, emphasized that the *Ostpolitik* of Paul VI had made matters worse, not better, irrespective of the Pope's intention to guarantee the sacramental life of Czech and Slovak Catholics. The persecution of real Catholics never let up, and in fact intensified. Under the *Ostpolitik*, the faux-Catholic collaborators with the regime were empowered, like the priests in the fake peace organization, Pacem in Terris, whom the dissidents called "pax terriers." What was left of the Church's institutions became, in effect, extensions of the state. And the regime, rather than acting more benignly, as the *Ostpolitik* assumed it would, cracked down with greater severity, sensing weakness in Rome and an unwillingness to defend the Church's most vocal proponents of religious freedom. Remarkably, the former dissidents weren't bitter. But they were puzzled—how could Paul VI and Agostino Casaroli have so mistaken the nature of communism and communists?

John Paul II changed all this. The change in Cardinal Tomášek accelerated after a 1982 instruction from the Vatican's Congregation for the Clergy banning priests' involvement in partisan politics. Widely deplored in the West as another attack on Latin American liberation theology, the instruction put paid to the pax terriers and gave Tomášek a weapon against clerical dissidents who were de facto agents of the regime. Then there was John Paul II's social teaching, which, Václav

Benda said, provided a bridge between Christian humanism and the idea of a "parallel polis" being developed by the secular people in Havel's human rights movement, Charter 77. John Paul II's openness also convinced Cardinal Tomášek that coalition-building with non-believers was not a trap for the Church but could strengthen Czech Catholicism. Thus by 1983, Benda said, Tomášek, at the ripe old age of eighty-four, was "fully engaged" with the Catholic resistance.

John Paul II's support gave the resistance such a new sense of security that there was even a revival in Catholic circles of that biting form of Czech humor embodied by the eponymous protagonist of Jaroslav Hašek's novel, *The Good Soldier Švejk*. In 1985, Bishop František Lobkowicz told me, there had been the usual argument with the communists over how many people had come to Velehrad to mark the 1,100th anniversary of the death of St. Methodius (with his brother, St. Cyril, one of the apostles of the Slavs). The Velehrad event was a major turning point in the history of the resistance Church, and Cardinal Tomášek's office said that 150,000 Czechs and Slovaks had attended; the state said there were 50,000. Then the Švejkist humor kicked in as the Catholic resistance said, "We're both right. We're counting ours and they're counting theirs."

On the evening of October 22, the martyr-confessors—and several thousand congregants—reassembled to commemorate John Paul II's pilgrimage to their recently liberated country, eighteen months before. The principal celebrant of the Mass was the newly created Cardinal Korec. Words of welcome were offered by the newly appointed Archbishop of Prague, Miloslav Vlk, a former window washer who had conducted a clandestine ministry at night. The Bendas were there and so was Václav Vaško, who, in a splendid (and perhaps providential) irony, now ran a Catholic publishing house from the office formerly occupied by the chief pax terrier. In our conversations, these sophisticated people described what had happened over the past two years to them, their country, and their Church as nothing less than a miracle.

I certainly wouldn't have quarreled with that point: their new president, Václav Havel, said as much when welcoming John Paul II to Prague in April 1990. What my Czechoslovak research taught me was that the miracle was accomplished through the John Paul II Effect.

In the Alps

B EFORE AND AFTER *CENTESIMUS ANNUS* WAS ISSUED, MICHAEL
Novak was in contact with the Italian philosopher Rocco Buttiglione, who had a considerable influence on shaping the encyclical
and its fresh approach to the classic themes of Catholic social doctrine. Rocco and Michael decided it would be useful to create a summer seminar for up-and-coming young Catholic thinkers from Europe
and North America, who were likely to carry John Paul II's teaching
on the free and virtuous society into the twenty-first century. Michael
recruited Richard Neuhaus and me for the core faculty, and it was decided to hold the seminar in Liechtenstein, where Rocco taught at the
International Academy of Philosophy, whose facilities we could use for
the academic part of the program.

Thus began a twenty-five-year exercise in international education
that, by 2016, had produced some eight hundred graduates, many of
whom were taking leading positions in business, the academy, the
Church, and politics in their respective societies: the United States,
Canada, and Australia; Chile, Colombia, and Mexico; Italy, Portugal, and the United Kingdom; Poland, the Czech Republic, Slovakia,
Lithuania, Latvia, Estonia, Germany, Hungary, Romania, Macedonia,
Croatia, Belarus, Georgia, Russia, Ukraine, and Moldova. After a second summer in Liechtenstein in 1993, we decided to move the seminar
to Kraków—a transition John Paul II encouraged, for the Pope was
keenly interested in our project, often sent a note of encouragement to
the students, and was eager to get news of what had happened in the
seminar after we completed each year of the program. In June 1994,
for example, John Paul wrote the Polish partner who had joined our

faculty team, Dominican Father Maciej Zięba, OP, asking Maciej to greet the student and faculty for him, thanking us for our work in promoting *Centesimus Annus,* and then musing that "in the old days (and even now) I never thought about seminars in July, only about how to tear myself away to get to the mountains or lakes."*

July 1992 in Liechtenstein gave me a much better idea of Rocco Buttiglione's mind. He had the striking ability—matched only by Joseph Ratzinger, Pope Benedict XVI, in my experience—to listen to a question, think, and then respond in complete paragraphs in what must have been his second or third language. Over dinner one night I told Rocco about my project on John Paul II and 1989, in which he expressed great interest. So I said I'd send him a set of page proofs when I got back home, for I had finished writing *The Final Revolution* and the book was well into production. In early September, Rocco called and said, "I just wanted to let you know that I'm taking your proofs to the Holy Father at Castel Gandolfo tonight."

"Those proofs are all marked up," I replied. "Can't it wait a week or so, when I can send you a clean copy of the book?"

Rocco was having none of it: "No, he has to see this *tonight.*"

So that was that. Later, I began to understand something of Rocco's sense of urgency. He had long thought that what he called a "bridge" should be built between John Paul II and the United States, where the vision sketched in *Centesimus Annus* might be taken seriously. *The Final Revolution* was another span in that bridge, and I imagine he was

---

* John Paul II's ongoing interest in the seminar led to an interesting moment twenty years or so later. Having taken over the leadership of the program from Mike in 1999, I would write John Paul a letter after each seminar, which was sent to him through the Vatican embassy diplomatic pouch. In 2001, some days after the letter had gotten to Rome, I was working at home and, feeling quite tired in the early afternoon, told my wife that I was going to take a nap and didn't want to be awakened "unless the house is on fire or the Pope calls." Fifteen minutes later, Joan came upstairs, walked into our bedroom, and said, "I know what you just said, but he's calling." It was Msgr. Dziwisz, calling from Castel Gandolfo and handing me over to John Paul, who wanted to talk about the letter he'd received and obviously just read of a summer's evening, Rome time. Needless to say, I took the call, which had caused considerable shock to the receptionist at my office when the switchboard at the papal villa first called there and announced that the Pope was looking for me.

also attracted by my argument that 1989 had been a revolution of the spirit, not just a political upheaval—indeed, that 1989 would have been inconceivable without a John Paul II–ignited revolution of conscience.

So thanks to some weeks in improbable Liechtenstein, the protagonist of my book was reading it, if in rather battered and marked-up page proofs. From this much would come: unknown, and indeed unexpected, at the time.

Così Giovane

AFTER *The Final Revolution: The Resistance Church and the Collapse of Communism* was published in September 1992, it seemed a good idea to present the book's arguments in Rome, so an evening lecture at the North American College, the US seminary up the Janiculum Hill from the Vatican, was arranged for November 18. Aside from the books that were to have been sold that night getting lost in the chaos of the Vatican post office—another lesson for the future—the event went well. But the far more important encounter that week was with John Paul II.

I arrived in Rome on November 14 and had dinner that evening with Rocco Buttiglione, who asked about my schedule. Rocco must have then called Msgr. Stanisław Dziwisz, John Paul II's secretary, because the following morning I received a note from the college porter instructing me in Italian to "present yourself tomorrow morning at 0630 at the Bronze Doors of the Piazza San Pietro to be taken to assist at the Mass of the Holy Father." Dziwisz had written me previously, thanking me for the published copy of *The Final Revolution* I had sent him and for my recent interview in *Tygodnik Powszechny*, laying out the argument of the book—an indication that, fourteen years after leaving Kraków, John Paul was still reading *Tygodnik Powszechny* every week, and closely.

Carrying an autographed copy of *The Final Revolution* for the Pope, I was at the Bronze Doors at the appointed hour and, with a group of about twenty or so, was escorted up to the Terza Loggia and the chapel of the papal apartment, where John Paul II was already immersed in prayer. The chapel, which had been redecorated by Paul VI, had one distinctively John Paul feature: an icon of the Black Madonna, mounted below the apse crucifix in the same position as the "M" on the Pope's coat of arms. I was seated in the back row, and after Mass the guests were taken into the formal library of the papal apartment and lined up along its perimeter bookcases; the Pope would walk down the line, shaking hands and dispensing rosaries. Msgr. Dziwisz had spotted me earlier and told me to put myself at the very end of the line.

The point was to give John Paul II some time with me as the others were leaving the library, without offending them by his spending time with someone in the middle of the queue. So when the Pope got to the tail end of the line, we shook hands, I offered him the autographed copy of the book (which he riffled through, pausing on the pictures of several of his friends), and, with a broad smile, he thanked me for what I had written. We spoke for about six or seven minutes; he asked how the book had been received, about my family, and about several mutual friends, including Richard Neuhaus, Mike Novak, and Rocco Buttiglione. Then, late for a breakfast meeting, he gave me his blessing, thanked me again, and asked me to stay in touch. I promised him I would.

Msgr. Dziwisz saw me out, thanked me again for the book and for "what you have done for Poland," and then said, "Ma così giovane!" (But you are so young!) It was the first of many gentle tweaks to come from the gatekeeper; yet it was said in such a friendly way that I sensed the gate would be kept as open as circumstances permitted.

Later that week, sitting outside a coffee bar near the Piazza Venezia, I pondered a photo of John Paul II and me looking at *The Final Revolution* and asked myself why this man, with a lot of other things on his mind, was so taken by my book and its analysis. I knew from study and from conversation with his friends that he had no use for flattery or sycophancy. Moreover, hadn't he told Cardinal Tomko that his responsibility was simply to do his job, like any other servant? That was how he thought of his role in the events of 1989: he was just doing his job.

What struck him, I decided, was that we had come by different routes to a common understanding of the inner dynamic of the overthrow of European communism. He had a well-developed theory of history: he thought that culture was the principal driver of history over the long haul, not politics and not economics. It was a deeply Slavic view of How Things Worked, and he had deployed it with analytic effect in *Centesimus Annus*. For my part, research in Poland and Czechoslovakia in 1991 had both confirmed and filled out my sense that much more was going on in the Revolution of 1989 than a rejection of communism's political cruelties and economic idiocies. Something had stirred in the souls of the people who made the revolution, and that something had made for a different kind of revolution: a "final revolution." It was not final in the sense of temporality (there would surely be other revolutions in the future), but it was final in the sense of "final causality" or destiny—the destiny of the human spirit liberated in the truth, be that the truth of revelation, the truth of reason, or both.

That was John Paul II's view of things, too, and that agreement was the beginning of the bond between us. He was grateful, not because I had made him the hero of this episode of history, but because I had explained that episode in a way he thought important, not least because it might be an alternative to the false views of history that had made such a bloody mess of the twentieth century.

After the Revolution

THE FOLLOWING TWO YEARS TOOK ME TO POLAND AND ROME several times, deepening my exploration of those now not-so-new worlds.

Academic conferences in Warsaw and Kraków in June and October 1993, plus conversations held on the sidelines of the *Centesimus Annus* summer seminar (which moved to Kraków in 1994), taught me that Poland had become what the people of the Solidarity revolution had said they wanted: "a normal society." And with normality came contention. The old Solidarity coalition fractured, and I found myself in the disconcerting position of knowing an increasing number of ex–prime ministers of postcommunist Poland, where holding together a governing coalition amidst the dislocations of economic "shock therapy" was proving a tricky business.

What was more disconcerting was the difficulty Poles of all sorts (including many Polish clergy) were having in making real John Paul II's vision of public Catholicism. In one corner of the ring there were secular people (like Adam Michnik) and some progressive Catholics who wanted Poland to resemble France in its *laïcité*. In another corner were those Catholics (including not a few clergy) who imagined a return to the close Church-state cooperation of the 1920s and 1930s. In yet another corner were those who really got John Paul II's idea of a culture-forming Church that shaped public life through an educated and engaged laity: a Church that was not identified with any political party but that taught a vision of the free and virtuous society that animated all of society. Yet the numbers in this third corner were smaller than one might have imagined—or hoped.

From all of this, I learned that a stringent interpretation of the idea of a wall of separation between Church and state was one of America's least admirable exports to the new democracies of Central and Eastern Europe. I tried to clarify what that phrase did and didn't mean at a Warsaw conference in June 1993 and in an article in the August 27, 1993, issue of *Tygodnik Powszechny*, "Fourteen Theses on Church and State," which reflected the idea of the public-but-not-partisan Church John Paul II outlined in *Centesimus Annus*. Two weeks later, a note from Msgr. Dziwisz assured me that the Pope had read my "valuable paper," which was being put to "good use."

I spent a week in Rome in June 1994. In addition to extending the conversations I had begun with Cardinal Ratzinger, Cardinal Edward Cassidy of the Vatican's ecumenical shop, and Joaquín Navarro-Valls, I began a multidecade conversation with Cardinal Francis Arinze, a native Nigerian then serving as President of the Pontifical Council for Interreligious Dialogue. Arinze helped me understand John Paul II's impact on, and fascination with, sub-Saharan Africa and opened for me a window into the fastest-growing part of the world Church.

I hoped to see John Paul and was encouraged to get in touch by Msgr. Dziwisz, but the broken hip the Pope had suffered a month earlier put a major crimp in his schedule. Dziwisz, unfailingly polite, called to explain the situation and went the extra mile by writing me a note, promising a get-together in September, when I would return to the city and, as he put it, "we should all feel stronger after a good vacation, which you surely deserve!"

The Pope's limited schedule did include a meeting with President Bill Clinton while I was in Rome. That session, on June 2, coincided with the announcement that Msgr. Timothy Dolan of St. Louis would become the new rector of the North American College later that summer. Dolan and I were old friends and as he and I were both staying at the College, we decided to tag along for the meeting the president and first lady would have with the college's students after Clinton met with the Pope.

The presidential motorcade, including special black vans ("HRC I" and "HRC II") for Mrs. Clinton and her staff, pretty well filled the Cortile di San Damaso of the Apostolic Palace. The majority of the seminarians did not seem thrilled to be meeting a man they regarded as hopelessly offside on core Catholic concerns, but former Boston mayor Ray Flynn, Clinton's ambassador to the Holy See, arranged the meeting and the college rector, Monsignor Edwin O'Brien, properly told the boys that if the President of the United States wanted to meet with them, they would meet with him, period. Flynn didn't improve the atmosphere when he announced to the president, the first lady, and the students that the seminarians were "all Democrats." (Paul Scalia, son of Justice Antonin Scalia, looked particularly unhappy with this bit of Bostonian blarney.) Then President Clinton described all the things that he and John Paul had discussed, while the first lady looked at him with a rapt smile, although without the black mantilla she wore to meet the Pope.

I was used to the Clinton spin machine, but this really took me aback. For I knew exactly what the Pope had talked about with the president, because I had discussed the matter with Vatican officials previously and developed, at their request, talking points for the meeting. And what the Pope had emphasized was the upcoming Cairo International Conference on Population and Development, where the Clinton administration was planning to get abortion on demand declared a fundamental human right. Yet POTUS 42 said not a single word about Cairo, the abortion issue, or any related matter in regaling the seminarians with tales of how he and John Paul agreed on just about everything they discussed.

Later that afternoon, I received a fax from Joaquín Navarro-Valls, who had quickly put out a statement challenging the administration's spin on what POTUS and the Pope had discussed: "The most important part of the meeting," the statement read, "was dedicated to the topic of the International Conference of the United Nations on Population and Development planned for Cairo in September and the serious ethical problems that are connected with it: defense and promotion of life, and defense and promotion of the family in particular. In this regard, the Holy Father made an appeal to the responsibility of a great nation such as America, whose origins and historical development [have] always promoted ethical values that are basic to every culture."

While the memory of Bill Clinton spinning the Pope remained with me, what was far more important for my work on John Paul II, and indeed for my learning the Vatican, was the friendship I began to form in those days with the head of the English section of the Vatican's Secretariat of State, Monsignor James Harvey. Over the next five years, Harvey, a Milwaukee native two years my senior, would become my closest friend in Rome, my tutor and consigliere in matters of Vaticanology, and a canny source of insight into how to get things done (and how not to get things done) inside the Leonine Wall.

In late July 1994, I sent John Paul a longish letter on my three most recent experiences in Poland, which had taught me a lot about the difficulties he was having in getting his teaching on Church, state, and democracy understood and implemented there. Msgr. Dziwisz wrote back on the Pope's behalf, thanking me and my colleagues for our "excellent work." I looked forward to seeing John Paul and Dziwisz in September, when I would be in Rome on one leg of a three-city tour arranged by the Mondadori publishing firm and my friend Leonardo Mondadori. I would be promoting *The Final Revolution*'s Italian edition, which was just appearing; Richard Neuhaus's book on *Centesimus Annus* had been published in Italian at about the same time, so he would be talking about that, with Mike Novak forming the third part of our team of Americans published by Mondadori and encouraged by Rocco Buttiglione. But as John Paul continued to have difficulties with his hip replacement, to the point where he was forced to postpone for a year a planned visit to the United States, it wasn't clear that we would be able to meet during our time in Rome.

Richard and I had useful meetings with Cardinals Ratzinger and Cassidy about our ecumenical work with evangelical Protestants. Ratzinger also encouraged me to get the book of commentaries on *Centesimus Annus* I had edited for the Ethics and Public Policy Center published in Central and Eastern Europe. Italian press coverage of the Mondadori-sponsored book presentation in Rome, held at the Collegio Teutonico inside the Vatican on September 27, taught me more important lessons about the porous border between fact and fantasy in Italian journalism: Italy's newspaper of record, the *Corriere della Sera*, described our press conferences and book presentations in Rome, Naples, and Milan as a nefarious plot to bolster Silvio Berlusconi.

On Saturday, September 24, Richard and I got a call inviting us to Castel Gandolfo for lunch with John Paul II the following day. So off we went to the Castelli Romani late Sunday morning, as our *pranzo papale* would take place immediately after the noontime Sunday Angelus with the Pope (which, during the summer, took place at Castel Gandolfo rather than in St. Peter's Square). Fr. Maciej Zięba was helpful in getting things organized and told us to meet him in the inner courtyard of the papal villa after the Angelus, after which the three of us would be taken upstairs to the Pope's quarters. It wasn't entirely clear how we were going to find Maciej in the mob scene at Castel Gandolfo, but once the crowds thinned out we spotted his white Dominican habit, exchanged greetings, and went inside the papal villa. There, a bit of opera buffa ensued.

Evidently, Ambassador Ray Flynn had shown up at Castel Gandolfo and was demanding to see the Pope. We only found out about this when the Prefect of the Papal Household, Archbishop Dino Monduzzi, chased Ambassador Flynn out of the villa through the parlor in which Richard, Maciej, and I had been parked before lunch. Ray would become a friend before his term in Rome expired, but that bizarre scene seemed at the time an apt metaphor for the Clinton administration's relations with the Holy See, two weeks after the showdown at the Cairo population conference.

Calm having been restored to Castel Gandolfo, we were brought into the dining room where John Paul II greeted us, dressed in papal summer casual: white cassock, no Roman collar, no sash, and no cuffed shirt beneath the cassock. He was obviously comfortable with us and didn't see any need to look pontifical. Still recovering from the hip-replacement operation, he was nonetheless full of robust conversation and striking comments over a ninety-minute *pranzo*.

Asked about his role in Central and Eastern Europe, he was crisp and shrewd: "Before 1989 they found the Pope useful; we shall see if they find him useful now." Pre-1989, he remarked, his had been a pontificate "facing East"; now it was "facing West." In that regard, he thanked us for our work in promoting *Centesimus Annus* and urged us not to back off in pushing the encyclical's teaching on the relationship between truth and freedom, virtue and democracy. He also said that he understood that, for some in Poland, he was a "dangerous radical."

His mind was already on what he would call the Great Jubilee of 2000, and he told the story of Cardinal Wyszyński saying to him, immediately after his election, "You should lead the Church into the third millennium." The recent Cairo conference, he said, had "vindicated" the Church's public role; after we talked about that for a bit, he said he knew that the radicalism of the Clinton administration's proposals at Cairo did not reflect public opinion in the United States. It was clear that he invested a lot of hope in America and spoke forcefully about the previous year's World Youth Day in Denver, which had been a "great consolation" to him—even as he smiled and cracked that it was a "big surprise" for the American bishops, who had insisted that a pope-centered youth festival built around the sacraments wouldn't work in the United States.

The three surprises of his life, he mused, were his election, the assassination attempt in 1981, and the fact that the communist crack-up had happened nonviolently. But what really struck Richard, Maciej, and me was the intensity of John Paul's insistence on ecumenical outreach. Ecumenism, he insisted, was "the great question of the third millennium"; he then said, flatly, that unity was "more important than jurisdiction" when it came to healing the breach between Rome and Eastern Orthodoxy, although he also noted that the Christian East had not disentangled itself from state power, as the Church in the West had done.

His sense of humor, always a bit wry, was evident throughout the meal. When Richard told him that he was "running ahead of history," he quickly shot back, "So maybe that's why I broke my leg?" He also laughed when musing on what Voltaire would have said about a pope as the world's premier advocate of human rights. He smiled at the irony of Americans explaining the importance of a Polish pope and his teaching to Poles, but shrugged and said, in a phrase he would use on other occasions when something struck him as amusingly strange or curious, "Ale co zrobić?" (What can you do?). At the end, seeing us out, he said, "Come back and visit me; I have lunch with the Pope every day."

Immediately after returning to Washington I flew to Grand Rapids to speak at Calvin College. The audience was composed of evangelical Protestants of one theological disposition or another. When word began to circulate that I had seen John Paul II five days earlier, everyone asked, "How is he?" The postponement of the US trip had set off the usual round of lurid media speculations; here was a cross section of the intellectual leadership of evangelical Protestantism in the US, deeply worried that the man they considered a premier Christian witness might be in distress, perhaps even on his way off the stage. I was happy to reassure them that the Pope was in good form and that ecumenism remained high on his agenda.

As for John Paul II, he dealt with his infirmity, which had caused him to start using a cane, with the medicine of humor. A week or so after our lunch, he noticed the bishops at a meeting watching him closely as he walked slowly to the dais. Turning toward them, he wisecracked in Italian, "Eppur' si muove" (And yet it moves)—the words Galileo muttered to his inquisitors on his way out of his trial, still insisting, sotto voce, that the Earth was not stationary but revolved around the sun.

The Biography That Wasn't

O N OCTOBER 19, 1994, JOHN PAUL II PUBLISHED *Crossing the Threshold of Hope*, a long-form interview with the Italian writer Vittorio Messori. The book was an instant bestseller in dozen of languages, and its searching exploration of some of the most profound questions of the human condition began to reconfigure the standard media stereotype of John Paul as a charming reactionary. *Threshold* was also the occasion for me to put into print for the first time the phrase "John Paul the Great," in an op-ed piece for the *Los Angeles Times*.

The first days of Lent 1995 found me in Rome to speak at a conference on "Development and Population in the Perspective of a New Humanism," in which Joaquín Navarro-Valls had urged me to participate. The conference was organized by some of his friends at the higher intellectual altitudes of Opus Dei, and the objective was to get clarified what the Vatican had done, and why, at the Cairo population conference the previous October. I spoke on the "New Cultural Imperialism," drawing on the article I wrote about the Cairo conference for *First Things*, the ecumenical journal of the Institute on Religion and Public Life, which had drawn a positive response from the papal apartment. So did my conference paper, for which Msgr. Dziwisz thanked me warmly in a letter of March 29; the letter suggested that he'd read the paper closely, for he ticked off all of its main points as if writing an exam.

Dziwisz also invited me to the Pope's morning Mass on Saturday, March 4. With his agreement, I brought along Mike Novak, in town for the same conference to build a bridge between *Centesimus Annus* and new approaches to economic development. After Mass, we spent a few minutes with John Paul in the formal library, where Dziwisz was effusive about these American *"amici veri"* (true friends). The Pope seemed more bemused than honored by being named *Time*'s Man of the Year, and most of our conversation was spent filling him in on our families and our mutual friends.

Crossing the Threshold of Hope was the far more important book, but it was Tad Szulc's *Pope John Paul II: The Biography* that took my relationship with John Paul to a new and unexpected level.

I got an advance copy of the book in the spring of 1995, and while I had been more skeptical about what Szulc was likely to produce than some of my Roman friends, I was appalled when I got down to studying it. When reading a book for review, I mark dubious passages or flat-out mistakes with an *x* in the margin. By the time I finished *Pope John Paul II: The Biography*, the book looked like a tic-tac-toe game in which I was playing *x*. And the thought occurred to me, "I can do better than this."

The first order of business, though, was to get a comprehensive response to Tad Szulc's errors, misapprehensions, and distortions into print. So I wrote a five-thousand-word review for *Crisis* magazine, where it appeared in late May. The review was called "The Biography That Might Have Been," and I summed up my indictment at the outset: "Szulc exhibits little understanding (and much misunderstanding) of Catholicism: its doctrine, its liturgy, its organizational and legal structure, its twentieth-century history. . . . Szulc's ready acceptance of the standard caricature of the Holy Father as socially progressive and theologically reactionary demonstrates a crippling incapacity to discriminate in weighing evidence, a lack of critical distance from the biographer's own presuppositions, and, indeed, a basic ignorance about key dimensions of the life of Szulc's subject." And that was before I got to the factual mistakes (such as the claim that Cardinal Eugène Tisserant presided over Karol Wojtyła's election as pope, when Tisserant had died six years earlier).

It was a very tough review. But what was one to do with a book that described John Paul II's clarion call to courage on October 22, 1978—"Be not afraid!"—as an assertion of authoritarianism? Or with a book that confused Augustine with Aquinas? Or with a book claiming that Aristotle's prime mover had something to do with the Pelagian controversy?

Yet for all that confusion, Tad Szulc saved his worst for his analysis of John Paul II's role in the Revolution of 1989. On close inspection, it struck me that Szulc's analysis of recent Polish history drew heavily on Mieczysław Rakowski, the last communist prime minister of Poland and one of the most unsavory of Polish political intellectuals—a faux-liberal opportunist whose combination of vanity and ideological shiftiness prompted Leopold Tyrmand to pen the greatest put-down essay in all of anticommunist literature, "The Hair-Styles of Mieczysław Rakowski." If Rakowski was Szulc's guide to public matters, a field in which the former *New York Times* foreign correspondent presumably had some competence, it was little wonder that Szulc would utterly miss John Paul II's call for a New Evangelization by describing it as a "crusade" aimed at imposing "iron discipline" on wayward theologians.

Advance copies of the review were widely distributed in the US, Poland, and Rome. Then my wife and I flew to *la Città Eterna* for our twentieth wedding anniversary.

On the morning of May 17, Joan and I participated in the Pope's morning Mass in the papal apartment chapel. Msgr. Dziwsz asked me to be the lector, and I found it hard to keep the tears from my eyes while reading Psalm 122, one of Scripture's great celebrations of Jerusalem. I knew how much John Paul II wanted to go there on pilgrimage, as I knew his frustrations at the diplomats' excuses as to why it couldn't happen just yet. So it was not easy to keep a steady voice when looking up from the lectionary during the antiphon and seeing him looking intently at me, just after I had read, "And now we have set foot / within your gates, O Jerusalem." But I made it through without incident, and after the Mass had the pleasure of introducing Joan to John Paul in the papal library. We had a brief talk about our family, and the Pope said he hoped to see us in the United States later that year. When I wished him a happy seventy-fifth birthday, which he would mark three days later, he gave me a wry look and asked me how old I was; when I replied "Forty-four," he informed me, with a smile and a shrug, that no one my age could possibly know what a birthday meant.

The weekly General Audience was being held that morning, and while Joan wanted to attend, I thought my time was better spent elsewhere, so she went to St. Peter's Square while I popped into the Holy

See Press Office, the Sala Stampa, to have a chat with Joaquín Navarro-Valls. Joaquín had seen my review of the Szulc book, with which he evidently agreed, so I came straight to the point: "This is ridiculous. We're almost seventeen years into the pontificate, 2000 is getting closer, and there still isn't a reliable biography of the Holy Father." There was no disagreement with my insistence that "something has to be done," and we spent some time considering who might be better positioned than Szulc to get the job done properly.

I insisted that it had to be someone who not only knew the outside history (and wouldn't lean on dubious sources like Rakowski) but was also prepared to take the Pope seriously as a man of ideas—which meant an author who had some familiarity with philosophy and theology. That criterion, it seemed to me, eliminated certain possible candidates. It also had to be someone who understood the Catholic situation from the inside, and in something other than the good progressives versus bad conservatives stereotypes of the post–Vatican II years; and that criterion eliminated other possible candidates. We discussed several names, and I offered reasons why I thought none of them worked. And then I said, "I think I could do this." We discussed that possibility for a while and agreed to think about it some more.

Judging from what happened over the Pope's dinner table six months later, it seems that Navarro's thinking about it involved some conversation with John Paul II and Stanisław Dziwisz.

Meeting Joan after the audience ended, we walked back up the Janiculum to the North American College and passed the Jesuit headquarters on the Borgo Santo Spirito. Catholic buildings all over Rome were flying the papal flag in anticipation of the Pope's birthday. But the flag on the Curia Generalizia seemed off, somehow. On closer inspection, it was flying upside down: the universal distress signal, which seemed an appropriate, if inadvertent, metaphor for many Jesuits' thinking about John Paul II. I took a picture for the record and then called the senior American at the Jesuit HQ, saying with as flat a voice as I could muster, "I think there's something wrong with the flag outside your building."

A month later, Msgr. Dziwisz sent me the longest letter I had gotten from him to date, a kind of book review of my review of the Szulc biography. He was obviously happy with it and I could only assume John Paul was, too. In the course of dissecting my "excellent review," Dziwisz, whose anticommunism was gut-level intense, took particular pleasure in my having nailed "the monstrosity of quoting Rakowski as crown witness" and told me that I had gotten the story of John Paul versus the old Casaroli *Ostpolitik* just right: "You know our Pope."

Parsing Freedom

M Y FRIENDSHIP WITH MSGR. JAMES HARVEY, HEAD OF THE SEC-
retariat of State's English section, which helped prepare texts
when John Paul II was visiting Anglophone countries, had developed to the point that, in the summer of 1994, he asked me for some
thoughts about the Pope's homily in Baltimore that coming October. I
sent him some suggestions but then the trip was deferred until the fall
of 1995. In the summer of that year, after Joan and I had returned from
Rome, Harvey asked me again if I had any further thoughts on a papal
homily in Baltimore, as well as suggestions for what the Pope might
say to a meeting of civic and religious leaders at the Cathedral of Mary
Our Queen, my old parish. I drafted some suggestions and sent them
off by fax, then the fastest means of communicating by written word
between Washington and Rome.

Things took a more dramatic turn when Msgr. Harvey asked me if I
had considered what the Pope might say to the United Nations General
Assembly on October 5. I sent suggestions based on my understanding of
Centesimus Annus and my analysis of 1989 in *The Final Revolution*: the
drama that had unfolded in Europe since John Paul's last UN address
had been triggered by a revolution of conscience; there were lessons from
that experience that applied to all of world politics, especially in terms of
recognizing the instinct for freedom built into the human person, which
was the foundation of any notion of universal human rights; religious
freedom was crucial to turning difference into conversation and community; the exercise of liberty must be linked to moral truth.

In early September, Harvey sent me the draft of what others in the
Vatican were proposing for the Pope's UN address and asked me for

an evaluation of it. After reading it I told him it would put the General Assembly to sleep after the third paragraph. I also asked why, with the memory of 1989 still fresh as a paradigm for something good in modern history, the Curia was proposing that the Pope deliver a dull academic lecture on international law when he had a chance to do something special from what the world imagined to be its premier pulpit, with the world's eyes riveted on him.

By mid-September, the two dueling drafts—the one reflecting my suggestions to Harvey and the one being pushed by the curial mandarins—had been presented to the Pope, and Harvey reported that John Paul liked ours, found it "stimulating," and joked of me, en passant, "He knows the Pope's mind better than the Pope." That was classic John Paul II raillery, but I may have developed a way of presenting John Paul's thought that he found accurate and helpful in an English-speaking context.

In any event, it seemed that the draft Harvey worked up with my suggestions was going to prevail, while being amplified by concerns the Pope had expressed about his defending the "rights of nations." Then a colleague of Harvey's in the English section, Father J. Michael Miller, a Canadian Basilian who had been privy to what was afoot, called and asked, "Why are we avoiding the J-word?"—meaning *Jesus.* I said that I thought confessional reticence was de rigueur in texts like the one being developed. But after discussing it briefly, Mike and I agreed that that needn't be the case and made some suggestions that eventually became the peroration of the Pope's address, in which he called himself a "witness to hope" and confessed that, "as a Christian, my hope and trust are centered on Jesus Christ," because of whose "radiant humanity . . . nothing genuinely human fails to touch the hearts of Christians."

Having agreed to provide television commentary on the papal visit to the UN for the Faith and Values Channel, I went to New York on October 4. Meeting Harvey that night at the Waldorf, where the papal party was staying, he introduced me to Archbishop Giovanni Battista Re, the *Sostituto* of the Secretariat of State and thus the de facto papal chief of staff. Re was aware of my contributions to what was going to happen the next day and thanked me "for [my] collaboration." After dinner, Harvey asked me to come to his room briefly, where he presented me with a booklet of the papal UN address; John Paul II had autographed it with a personal dedication and asked that it be given to me.

After doing more television in New York the next two days, I took the train back to Washington in anticipation of meeting John Paul in Baltimore on the last day of his US visit, October 8. The Pope specifically asked to meet Joan and the children, so Cardinal William Keeler of Baltimore arranged for the five of us to come to the archbishop's residence downtown that Sunday afternoon, where John Paul would greet various people before going out to the Cathedral of Mary Our Queen. We decided to watch the papal Mass at Camden Yards at my parents' home, an extraordinary experience because no one but Joan knew of my involvement in the preparation of the visit and the papal addresses in New York and Baltimore. I was sufficiently nervous that I decided to watch the homily of the Camden Yards Mass on the small television set in my parents' bedroom—where I almost had a stroke. The homily was crafted around the Mass texts for the day, but when it came time for the choir to sing the responsorial psalm, I found to my horror than someone involved in the Baltimore liturgical preparations had substituted another psalm in place of the one prescribed for that day in the lectionary, to which the homily made reference. Happily, no one seemed to notice, and the paper I grew up reading, the *Baltimore Sun*, printed the entire text of the homily in its Monday edition; it's been framed in my study ever since.

While bringing the family into the archbishop's house, I ran into Msgr. Dziwisz and Joaquín Navarro-Valls having lunch on an outdoor patio while the Pope rested upstairs in the house. (Or was supposed to be resting; Cardinal Keeler told me later that John Paul spent most of his time in the residence chapel, praying.) Both Dziwisz and Navarro thanked me for my help and promised that we'd get together in Rome on my next trip. Joan and I, with our children Gwyneth, Monica, and Stephen, were then seated along the perimeter of one of the house's first-floor parlors, which the Pope would walk through, a room at a time, greeting Keeler's guests.

By that point, John Paul II was using a cane all the time in private. On spotting us, he grinned, turned the cane into something like

G. K. Chesterton's sword-stick, and, like a man practicing his fencing moves, gave Stephen, then just short of eight years old, a gentle poke in the tummy before drawing him into a big embrace—which everyone else got, too. John Paul and I talked briefly about how the trip had gone thus far; he thanked me for my suggestions and said that we'd meet in Rome soon.

And so we did, eight weeks and three days later, over a dinner of consequence.

THE WITNESS,
FROM INSIDE

On the evening of March 7, 1996, John Paul II mused about other biographers and their attempts to tell the story of his life: "They try to understand me from the outside, but I can only be understood from inside."

There was neither anger nor hostility in the remark; the Pope's comment was wistful, almost sad. Which was quite in character, I learned. Throughout the quarter-century of his papacy, he never played the demagogue and never lost the pastor's touch: that passion for the care of souls. John Paul II wanted to be understood, not for his own sake, but so that others could experience what he had experienced as the power of God working through him. Thus at Castel Gandolfo in 1994, he said over lunch, as if it were the most obvious thing in the world, "Like Peter, the pope is a weak man; but the Holy Spirit works through him."

How to probe into that rich interior life, and then relate it to his teaching and his action in the Church and the world, was the challenge involved in preparing his biography.

Hiking through the Polish mountains with his lay friends, Karol Wojtyła would be full of conversation, joking and singing throughout the day. But as the sun began to set, he would drift to the end of the line of hikers by himself. No one resented this; everyone understood that the man they called "Wujek," their "uncle" who was both pastor and friend, needed to spend time with God. It was the time that made the rest of the hours of his day possible.

Getting "inside" that rich interior life was going to be interesting and not without its challenges, for it meant probing into areas that others writing about him had never explored and that he might, reasonably enough, be reluctant to discuss. In September 1996, over dinner at Castel Gandolfo, I told him that I knew he had a sense of privacy, which I respected. But, I said, I was going to spend the next several years systematically trying to violate his sense of privacy. If I went too far, he would let me know and I would understand. He nodded and that was the end of the matter.

As it happened, there were no questions I asked that he did not answer. Moreover, it was John Paul who pushed me to explore areas of his life that might otherwise have gotten biographical short shrift, such as the friendships he formed with university students in the early years of his priesthood: I couldn't understand him, he insisted, unless I understood his friends and their mutual friendship. Over time, of course, I learned that there were aspects of John Paul's interior life that I couldn't describe because he couldn't: they took place, like all mystical experiences, in a dimension before words, or beyond words, or however one describes the ineffable experience of contemplative communion with the Thrice Holy God.

He could also joke about this "getting inside" business. After one of our dinner conversations in the papal apartment—John Paul always insisted that we meet over a meal, so he could relax and focus on our conversation—he walked me out through the chapel, where two of the household sisters were setting up for the next morning's Mass. They were the soul of discretion, but John Paul II, whose mischievous streak had not been extinguished by a decade and a half in the papacy, stopped, pointed to one of the sisters, and said, in an audible stage whisper, "You should talk to her; she knows *a lot!*" The poor sister looked horrified, the Pope laughed, I winked at the sister; then we went into the main part of the chapel to pray together.

The conversations with John Paul II that began when I presented him with *The Final Revolution* in November 1992 continued for the next twelve years. Those encounters also took me into conversation with many others who could help me understand Karol Wojtyła's multitiered and richly textured personality "from inside." Here, I want to revisit the conversations and adventures that led to *Witness to Hope*, the first volume of my John Paul II biography. Those adventures put me in mind of a scene toward the end of Larry McMurtry's *Lonesome Dove*. There, the dying Gus McCrae says to Woodrow Call, his oldest friend and fellow veteran of the Texas Rangers, "By God, Woodrow, it's been quite a party, ain't it?" I hope no one will be offended if I say that that's exactly how I feel about the three and a half years that led to the publication of *Witness to Hope*.

The Mandatum Scribendi

O N RETURNING TO WASHINGTON AFTER THE CONSEQUENTIAL *cena papale* of December 6, 1995, I wrote Msgr. Dziwisz, thanking him and John Paul II for dinner and asking if I might have a written indication of the Holy Father's will in the matter of my writing his biography. In late January, a plain grey envelope with a Vatican postmark arrived at my EPPC office. There was no reason to think it anything special, as correspondence from the Pope or Dziwisz normally came through the Vatican embassy in Washington. So I opened the envelope, not knowing what to expect or from whom—and found the letter that unlocked the door to the next three and a half years.

It was not written on the watermarked, cream-colored stationery of official papal correspondence but on simple white paper with the papal crest in the upper left-hand corner—as if one friend were writing another, with no need for display. The typing suggested an old-fashioned manual typewriter and there were a few typos (reproduced here). What counted, of course, was the handwritten signature at the end:

January 19, 1996
Dear Professor Weigel,

Thank you for your letter of December 19, 1995. Of course my response to your kind offer to write my biography and the history of my pontificate was positive.

You are in a very good position to write it, since you have already studied one aspect of them in the "Final Revolution", and then you have experienced the sadness of "The Biography that could have been", while studying assiduously the more important Encyclicals—and also meeting me often.

I am aware what a demanding work this would be for you and how it would hamper your other important activities. Still, since you write you are ready to "give yourself to this work with whole-hearted enthusiasm" and that it gives you joy, since your life "has been a preparation for this work"—I can only answer with my wholehearted thanks and encouragement.

I am very grateful for your prayer and that of your dear Family, and send my blessing to you, Professor Weigel, to your Wife and each child.

Joannes Paulus II

Msgr. Tim Dolan quickly dubbed this the *mandatum scribendi,* the mandate to write, playing on the *mandatum docendi,* the mandate to teach, that instructors in theology in Catholic universities are supposed to request. Whatever it might be called, it was the clear indication of John Paul II's intentions that I had requested, a vote of confidence, and a pledge of John Paul's cooperation. All of which was needed, I knew, if I was to get the support for the project I needed. I was not an unknown author, but walking into a publisher's office and announcing that John Paul II had agreed to cooperate with me on a biographical project that would also be a comprehensive history of his pontificate would have raised editorial eyebrows, and with good reason.

I also needed a literary agent, and on Richard Neuhaus's advice I settled on Loretta Barrett—who, in another providential coincidence, turned out to have been the founding editor of Doubleday Anchor Books, whose publications were staples in my undergraduate philosophy courses. Loretta brought me to HarperCollins and Diane Reverand, who bought the book for her Cliff Street Books list. Foreign rights went to Leonardo Mondadori, with whom I had already discussed the possibility of such a project.

The next order of business was to arrange an orderly succession at the helm of the Ethics and Public Policy Center, as I knew I couldn't lead an institution and do this massive project in the time frame we had all tacitly agreed upon: the book was to be available in as many major European languages as possible in the months immediately preceding what John Paul II was already calling the Great Jubilee of 2000. So I spoke with my board chairman, Admiral Elmo "Bud" Zumwalt (the former Chief of Naval Operations), and the most influential of EPPC's board members, Richard Neuhaus; both Bud and Richard agreed with my suggestion that my old friend Elliott Abrams would make a fine president of EPPC, and that I would become a senior fellow of the Center, which would remain my institutional base for the John Paul II project. And so it was.

"THAT'S OBVIOUS . . ."

I RETURNED TO ROME AT THE BEGINNING OF LENT 1996 TO DISCUSS procedures with John Paul II and see what resources and materials were available at the Polish Home on the Via Cassia: a kind of a warehouse of John Paul documents and memorabilia, including a huge collection of Black Madonna icons given to the Pope by visiting Polish groups over the previous seventeen and a half years.

The Pope was on his annual Lenten retreat when I arrived, so I spent my first days constructing a timeline of the pontificate, using back issues of the Vatican daily, *L'Osservatore Romano*, in the North American College library. Finishing the timeline took several months. My capable assistant, Ann Derstine, became the world's foremost Mennonite authority on the late-twentieth-century papacy by turning the timeline into a seven-column, two hundred-page spreadsheet that allowed me to see what was going on in the pontificate, the Church, and the world on any given day since John Paul II's election on October 16, 1978: what political leaders John Paul met, what teaching documents he issued and major speeches he made, where he went in Italy or the world, whom he canonized or beatified, and what bishops' groups he saw, all set against the global events of the day. With this invaluable tool (regularly updated by Ann and her successor, Ever Horan) I was able, over the next two and a half years, to "see" the pontificate unfold in the multilayered yet linear fashion in which I wanted to describe it.

My most important meeting that week was with John Paul II, over dinner on the night of March 7. Msgr. Dziwisz was present as usual, as was a new junior secretary, Father Mieczysław Mokrzycki. There were procedural matters to clarify before I started work on the biography in earnest in the fall and ground rules to get established. So after thanking the Pope for the *mandatum scribendi*, I said, "Holy Father, two things are necessary to make this work. The first is that I have to have access to you, your friends and associates, and to some documentation that might ordinarily be unavailable until long after your death—and I have to be the one to decide what those documents are. The second is that you can't see a word of what I write until I hand you the published book."

John Paul II looked at me and, without missing a beat, replied, "*That's* obvious. Now let's talk about something interesting."

It was quintessential John Paul. He understood perfectly well that a vetted biography would rightly be regarded with skepticism. But this wasn't just a matter of shrewd tactics on his part. He had spent his adult life challenging and encouraging others to moral responsibility and he wasn't about to change that. The book was my responsibility. He would be as available and cooperative as possible. But I would make the judgment calls and no one would be looking over my shoulder making suggestions.

John Paul II's openness in this matter was not universally appreciated in the Roman Curia, I would discover. I would also learn that the Pope's wanting me to have what I thought I needed didn't necessarily mean I was going to get what I needed without curial foot-dragging. So I had to develop my skills in Vaticanology, an exercise in which the double or triple bank shot is often more effective than the direct approach. Which was itself was an invaluable education, for it helped me understand problems that my subject had to solve to get done what he wanted to do.

The ground rules I insisted on, and to which John Paul readily agreed, meant that what became *Witness to Hope* and *The End and the Beginning* would not be an "authorized biography," which in the usual parlance means a biography vetted (and edited) by the subject or his or her heirs in exchange for access to persons and materials. My biography would be as authoritative as unprecedented access to the Pope, and to previously unavailable and unpublished materials, could make it. But it would not be "authorized"—a point I would have to explain over and over again.

Having gotten the ground rules out of the way, our dinner conversation ranged over matters great and small. The Pope suggested that the book be pitched at the level of *The Final Revolution*, saying that he hoped my "gift for writing and explaining" would make his life, and especially his thought, accessible to others. He also urged me to look closely into his spiritual life as he had explored it in his poems and plays, and into his philosophical work, recommending that I get in touch with his chief philosophical disciple, Father Tadeusz Styczeń, and with his old friend and philosophical collaborator, Marian Jaworski, then serving as Archbishop of L'viv for Latin-rite Catholics.

John Paul was still enthusiastic about his October 1995 visit to the US and about the "strong Church" he had found in America. The UN speech came up, with Dziwisz winking at me and saying "it was a great speech" and the Pope musing that he had felt more comfortable at the UN rostrum in 1995 than in 1979; he also said he was quite pleased with the response to the address and its emphases on the rights of persons and nations.

The Pope suggested that I work on document access through Joaquín Navarro-Valls, with Dziwisz agreeing that Joaquín would be the "better intermediator." At the end, the good humor of the entire evening continued as we walked out of the papal apartment through the chapel, the Pope joking at the apartment door about his two secretaries' names and their odd relationship in Polish history: "Stanisław was killed by Bolesław, the son of Mieczysław." I said I didn't think he had anything to worry about, despite his having been the successor of St. Stanisław, and when I said in parting that I thought he looked well, John Paul groaned and shot back, "I look *good*?"

WORSE THAN SOLZHENITSYN

T HE BEST DECISION I MADE IN PREPARING *WITNESS TO HOPE* WAS the first: I wouldn't write anything for a year and a half. I had been writing about John Paul II for more than seventeen years, and rather than just taking off from that platform I thought I should talk to as many people as I could and read as much as I could until the end of 1997; then I'd see what Jamesian figures in the carpet began to emerge. The result of eighteen months of full-immersion research came to more than a thousand pages of interview notes and eight full-size file drawers of materials. Out of that mass of paper, patterns did come into focus even as new questions emerged.

During the July 1996 *Centesimus Annus* seminar in Kraków I extended my range of contacts in Karol Wojtyła's city and deepened the conversations begun while I was working on *The Final Revolution.*

The most striking of the new acquaintances was Monsignor Andrzej Bardecki, then a robust eighty years old, who had been Cardinal Wojtyła's liaison to *Tygodnik Powszechny* and the ecumenical officer of the archdiocese: Wojtyła's link to the Cracovian intelligentsia of all theological persuasions and none. Bardecki told me that Mehmet Ali Agca had asked John Paul II who this "goddess of Fátima" was who had saved the Pope's life; John Paul had assured the crazy Agca that this was Mary, the mother of Jesus, and that she was not coming through the walls of Rebibbia Prison to do unpleasant things to him, as the would-be assassin feared. Agca also believed he was the triggerman in a well-organized plot that would get him away from Rome, according to Bardecki's recollection of the Pope's conversation with the Turk; that suggested that the "lone gunman" or "fundamentalist

Muslim" explanations of what happened on May 13, 1981, were not very persuasive.

Just as intriguing was Bardecki's story of how he had been beaten up by thugs from the Służba Bezpieczeństwa, the Polish secret police, who couldn't get at Wojtyła and brutalized one of his closest associates instead. Why did they fear Wojtyła so much, I asked? Because they thought he had "swindled" them, Msgr. Bardecki replied—and then told me how the communists waited and waited for Wojtyła's name to appear as a nominee for Archbishop of Kraków because they thought he was something of an airhead, a poet and intellectual they could manipulate against the primate, Cardinal Wysziński. Then Bardecki smiled and indulged in a little schadenfreude: all in all, it had been a good example of how "the Holy Spirit can work his will by darkening as well as enlightening minds."

As for Wojtyła's management style as archbishop, Bardecki said he had been a "fantastic" boss in that he trusted his subordinates and let the people he appointed do their jobs without a lot of micromanaging or interference.

Bardecki also explained how Wojtyła and a group of Kraków theologians had tried to help Pope Paul VI craft an encyclical on family planning that was neither the "stupid conservatism" of some Roman theologians nor the German progressivism that would have eviscerated Catholic moral theology—a clue that sent me hunting in the dusty stacks of the Dominican priory library in Kraków for a copy of the document that had been sent to the Pope and later published in an obscure journal, the *Analecta Cracoviensia*. Ever Horan translated the document from the original French; excerpts from it were published in English for the first time in *Witness to Hope* and shed new light on one of the most contentious periods in contemporary Catholic history.

Another new acquaintance that summer was the distinguished nuclear physicist Jerzy Janik, who had known Karol Wojtyła since the young curate's early days at St. Florian's parish in Kraków, and who had been Wojtyła's primary link to the worlds of hard science ever since. John Paul II's biennial humanities summer seminars at Castel Gandolfo were reasonably well known by 1996, but few knew that, on the years that seminar didn't meet, John Paul met with a group of physicists, biologists, and medical doctors organized by Janik so he could keep abreast of developments in their fields. Janik emphasized that Wojtyła was a man of "endless discussion" who not only wanted to know what was going on in physics but who had helped a scientist like Janik see, through Thomas Aquinas and his metaphysics, that there was a "way to speak coherently of everything ranging from this"—he pointed to a vase on his desk—"to God." Yet he was also "an extremely good listener" whose influence on others came from close, careful listening "and then making a few comments that were crucial."

Karol Wojtyła needed a measure of solitude in his life. Yet Professor Janik gave me a first hint that Wojtyła, who had no close living relatives after his father's death in 1941, also cherished his friendships and worked hard to keep them green. Janik and his wife had gone to the cardinal's residence for a Mass marking their twenty-fifth wedding anniversary but were met by Fr. Dziwisz, who told them that the cardinal had the flu and a high fever. The Janiks wished their archiepiscopal friend a speedy recovery and began to go when Dziwisz stopped them and said, "No, no, no, the Mass will not be in the chapel but in his private apartment." So Dziwisz led them to the sitting room next door to the cardinal's bedroom, where the cardinal offered Mass, preaching a homily personally directed to the Janiks, and then said, "I'm sorry but I've got a high fever and I've got to get back to bed."

Jerzy Turowicz, by then a smiling gnome of eighty-five, told me about Karol Wojtyła's relationship with *Tygodnik Powszechny*, which had begun in 1949, and spoke of his old columnist as a man of constant reading who had a small desk and lamp installed in his car so there were no wasted moments on the road. Did I know, Turowicz asked, about Wojtyła's habit of doing his serious writing in the chapel of the archbishop's residence, on a desk set up before the tabernacle? Yes, I replied, and I understood that that habit continued in Rome during his years as pope: the papal chapel was where the serious intellectual work got done. All of this, Turowicz observed, was "interesting from a literary point of view." Most authors write in their studies, surrounded by books, but Wojtyła wrote "from his thinking, his experience, his conversations." He was, in other words, unfootnoted; but that didn't make him less serious.

For all that he cared deeply about friendships, there was also a certain formality or courtliness about Wojtyła, in Turowicz's experience. He always used the formal "you," except with children and perhaps other priests; it was always "Pan Jerzy" or "Pan Dr. Jerzy"—a pattern replicated with me, for in a dozen years I never succeeded in getting John Paul II to call me "George"; it was always "Professor Weigel." Turowicz acknowledged that there had been disagreements between his newspaper and the archbishop but also insisted that "there was no censorship; we may have asked his advice but he never intervened on his own initiative" to alter the content or analysis of the paper—a unique relationship in Poland between bishop and journalists.

Turowicz also made the trenchant observation that, during his last years in Kraków, it was Wojtyła whom the Polish comrades hated and feared more than Cardinal Wyszyński. The old primate hadn't lost his edge, but everyone knew the dance steps in that polonaise. With Wojtyła, the Polish communists never knew what was coming next. Their fears had obviously been reported to Moscow, for an Italian journalist with good Moscow contacts had told Turowicz, on Wojtyła's election, that "the Soviets would prefer Solzhenitsyn as Secretary General of the United Nations than a Pole as pope."

"It Was Always 'Them' and 'Us'"

MY FIRST CONVERSATION WITH JOAQUÍN NAVARRO-VALLS AFTER the project got rolling took place on September 4, 1996.

By 1996, Navarro had spent twelve years as the first lay head of the Holy See Press Office, becoming the most effective papal spokesman ever, in part because everyone knew that the Pope (and Msgr. Dziwisz) had his back and in part because he had learned how to handle what I began to call "the traditional managers of popes." Thus he was full of good advice about how to deal with this, that, or the other curial personality who might not be instinctively enthusiastic about another papal biographer, and an American layman at that.

There was, for example, Cardinal Agostino Casaroli, who was "crucial" but who was not very happy with *The Final Revolution* and my criticism of his *Ostpolitik;* the way to secure his cooperation was to tell him that I had learned a lot from his remarks at the 1995 conference at which he tried to demolish my analysis of the Revolution of 1989 and to stress that understanding his views was crucial to my understanding of the pontificate—then he'd be "very open." As it was true that I'd learned a lot (if not substantively) from Casaroli's December 1995 remarks and that I wanted to get Casaroli's take on the first decade of John Paul II's papacy, I had no hesitation about following this advice.

But there were also subtle warnings. Cardinal Angelo Sodano, Casaroli's successor, had once said (in the Spaniard Navarro's presence) that the *stranieri,* the foreigners, really don't "fit in well" at the Vatican, and I could expect to find that attitude replicated—which it was. This was not a matter of rascality, Joaquín insisted, but the "human framework" of Vatican life. That I should try to work with that rather than against it was a good lesson, first taught me by Msgr. James Harvey, that Navarro reinforced.

Sodano's remark was instructive in another way: it confirmed that the traditional managers of popes were still in shock over the demise of the Italian papacy. Moreover, they had yet to appreciate John Paul II's approach to world politics. Many Vatican diplomats still thought of the Holy See as a third-tier European power, which meant they were still thinking in terms of the old Papal States. This led to the assumption (or pretense) that the Holy See had serious diplomatic leverage (which it didn't). Unburdened by these Italianate fantasies, John Paul II was free to craft a more pastoral and evangelical approach: let's try to change things (like the Cairo world population conference) through an appeal to conscience and, over the long haul, by changing political cultures.

Some of this came into clearer focus six days later, on September 10, when I had dinner with John Paul at Castel Gandolfo and we began to work through a six-page single-spaced memorandum I had prepared over the summer: dozens of questions I proposed to get answered over the next sixteen months, before I started writing. It was three weeks before his appendectomy, but he seemed in good form, having just come in from a long walk in the gardens of the papal villa.

He would mark his golden jubilee as a priest on November 1, so I began by asking him about his vocational struggles as a young man. He told me that he'd learned about the heroic priestly self-sacrifice of Maximilian Kolbe in the Auschwitz starvation bunker "very shortly" after the war; survivors of the concentration camps were among those who most strongly pressed for Kolbe's canonization, he recalled. Contrary to stories floating around that he had once considered leaving the world for a cloister, the Pope said he didn't think he had "a very strong vocation to the Carmelites," but he did stress how interested he was in St. John of the Cross. He was full of praise for Cardinal Sapieha, "a real *pater patriae* [father of the nation] during the occupation: a great moral, religious, and national *authority*" (the papal voice rising on the last word). "It was so important at that time to have a man like that at home." He described the aristocratic Sapieha as a man with whom his seminarians could converse freely, and seemed to enjoy reminding me that he hadn't had "a normal seminary experience; it was *clandestino*." He also spoke of his debt to the lay mystic Jan Tyranowski, who introduced him to the classics of Carmelite spirituality and to the Marian theology of St. Louis-Marie Grignion de Montfort during the war. It was from Tyranowski, the Pope said, that he "learned the principles of the spiritual life, not so much from seminary."

His predecessor as archbishop, Eugeniusz Baziak, was reputed to have been a formidable and cold man, but John Paul described him as "a tragic figure, expelled from his diocese" by the Soviets as part of their postwar clampdown in what had become the Ukrainian Soviet Socialist Republic. "Sapieha," the Pope said, "found it easy to be a prince," meaning that he was at ease with everyone; but Baziak, while "a good man," had "been more difficult to talk with," feeling that he had to make a stern impression during the early 1950s, the worst period of Stalinism—"the most radical oppression, a very difficult period."

This led us to the question of whether his confrontation with the communists had intensified in his last years as archbishop. The Pope replied, with some force, that "it was a *continual* confrontation; they thought they could divide the cardinal of Kraków from the primate." Dziwisz then jumped into the conversation and said, in Italian, that one couldn't think about these things as episodic confrontations triggered by one incident or another—like the struggle to build a church in Nowa Huta, or a speech Wojtyła had given. It was always *them* and *us*, and everybody understood the situation in those terms. Here, the Pope interjected, also in Italian, "Si, erano *loro* e *noi*" (Yes, it was *them* and *us*). John Paul then continued: "The communists tried to be accepted, not just as a political authority but as a moral authority, *as an expression of the Polish nation*" (the papal voice rising again). "The communists tried to pretend that we did not exist." None of this could be understood in Western political terms, by analogy to a government and its opposition, they both said. It was entirely different.

Listening to John Paul and Dziwisz on this point and sensing the passion still there after many years, I got an experiential confirmation of the judgment I had formed long ago about the battle between Catholicism and communism: This was not something adjudicable.

There was no fifty-yard line of coexistence between two utterly opposed views of the human person, human community, and human destiny. Someone was going to win, and somebody had to lose.

We discussed his first social encyclical, *Laborem Exercens*, which "was very important to me personally" because "the first part is based on my personal experience" as a manual laborer during the occupation. When I later measured the distance he said he had walked from his Kraków apartment to the chemical factory where he worked, I discovered that his memory of the length of that trek, some four kilometers, was accurate to within a tenth or two of a kilometer.

He obviously missed the academic life he had managed to continue in a constrained form while archbishop of Kraków. When I asked him whether he still read dissertations, he said, rather wistfully, "I kept reading them at the beginning . . . " (of the pontificate), but couldn't anymore.

THE INDISPENSABLE MAN

CARDINAL AGOSTINO CASAROLI MAY HAVE BEEN "THE MEMORY," AS Joaquín Navarro described him with reference to the first decade of John Paul II's pontificate. And Cardinal Angelo Sodano, Casaroli's successor as Vatican secretary of state, never tired of reminding people that he was "il primo e *più importante* collaboratore del Santo Padre" (the first and *most important* collaborator of the Holy Father)—a self-appellation whose repetition perhaps reflected some anxiety on the point. But as my research progressed, it became unmistakably clear that the indispensable man in the pontificate of John Paul II was the theologian he called to Rome from Bavaria to become Prefect of the Congregation for the Doctrine of the Faith (CDF), Cardinal Joseph Ratzinger.

They were something of an odd couple: a Pole and a German of the same World War II generation; a philosopher and a theologian; a former actor and a man one couldn't imagine on stage; a thinker-sportsman-mystic who became a compelling public personality and a learned but shy scholar who was likely happiest when reading or playing the piano by himself. Yet they worked in harness for over twenty-three years, one succeeding the other as pope. And between them, they gave the Second Vatican Council what it lacked until October 16, 1978—a coherent, comprehensive, and authoritative interpretation that pointed the Church into a third millennium of evangelical mission, which was what John XXIII had hoped for in summoning Vatican II.

In preparing *Witness to Hope*, I met with Cardinal Ratzinger five times over more than seven hours between September 1996 and December 1998. Rather than spreading out the story of Ratzinger's contributions to *Witness to Hope* conversation-by-conversation, gathering them together will better capture the texture of my interaction with the man who became Pope Benedict XVI.

From the very beginning, Ratzinger insisted that John Paul II was a man with an acute sense of the human dilemma in late modernity. It was "the problem of man," Ratzinger said—and then laughed and corrected himself, "the human person"—that drove both Wojtyła's philosophical work and his pontificate. This "passion for man," as the cardinal put it, was at the root of Wojtyła's confrontation with communism and later with secular liberalism: different philosophical anthropologies yielded different ideas of what "history" is and what "redemption" is. And at the bottom line, what was missing from the Marxist and secular liberal views of the human person, history, and redemption was God: God, without whom "man" makes no sense, or can only make sense against himself and against his fellows.

This passion for real men and women and the dilemmas of life in late modernity was at the center of John Paul II's thinking and preaching, his mysticism, his pastoral work, his social doctrine, his approach to world politics, and his intellectual work. Or as Ratzinger once put it in his scholarly way, "Beginning with anthropology and searching for an answer to what is human existence, he comes to God—to the Trinitarian God of love—and returns from this to man, because his Trinitarian vision is not . . . a meditation on what is God in himself, but makes us understand how God is God-in-history. In the deepest mystery of the Trinitarian existence, we are also encountering the concrete possibilities that God, who is himself relation and dialogue, can create history, can be present in history."

This meant that, for John Paul, "Christianity [is] not an idealism, outside of concrete historical reality, but is creating community, creating solidarity. . . . Stalin asked how many divisions has the pope. But he has another power, the power of truth. It is very significant for [John Paul II] that he knew and understood the very different but very real power of truth in history." And over time, Ratzinger suggested, people would come to understand that John Paul II had "made [the world] recognize once again the spiritual dimension in history"—or, to put it another way, the Pope had "made visible the fact that faith in God can be transformative in the world."

Above all, Ratzinger said repeatedly, John Paul II was a radically converted Christian disciple for whom prayer was the reactor core of his life, thought, and action. "His personal dialogue with God is decisive. . . . The deepest source of what he says is that, every day, he is, for an hour, alone with his Lord, and speaking, at least now as pope, about all the problems of the world. But he is also seeking the face of God. . . . In his meditations he is in personal contact with the Lord . . . this dialogue with God is the central element in his spiritual and intellectual life."

On three different occasions, Ratzinger asked John Paul II to let him resign and return to what was left of his intellectual work. Three times, the most consequential pope in hundreds of years asked his indispensable man to stay: saying, in so many words, "I can't—or certainly don't want to—do this without you." And three times, Ratzinger bent his will to John Paul's. Why was this?

In part because John Paul, a man of strong convictions and equally strong will, also knew what he didn't know, recognized in Ratzinger a deeper, broader theological intelligence than his own, and understood that a theologically uninformed pope was likely to get himself and the Church into serious trouble. From Ratzinger's description of their modus operandi, John Paul listened closely to Ratzinger, who was comfortable enough with their relationship to push back when he thought something was theologically or prudentially inadvisable, while recognizing where the buck stopped, which was not with him.

They lunched regularly for years, for, as Ratzinger put it, the Pope liked to hold working lunches that were quasi-seminars. Thus the dining room table in the papal apartment was the place where John Paul thought through the weekly audiences addresses he liked to structure thematically; it was a way, Ratzinger said, for this intellectual-turned-pope to have a "continuous work to do" amid the unavoidable fragmentation of his schedule. Major encyclicals were also hashed out over lunch, as were the two responses to liberation theology that John Paul II commissioned and Ratzinger's congregation produced. So was the apostolic letter, *Ordinatio Sacerdotalis*, on the Church's inability to admit women to the ministerial priesthood.

It was, in a phrase, all conversation all the time—a constant dialogue with serious intellectual collaborators that belied the charge that

John Paul II was an authoritarian imposing a personal (and Polish) view on the Church.

Cardinal Ratzinger knew that he played another role in the pontificate: he was the lightning rod, the man on whom opprobrium would fall when critics thought it imprudent to attack the Pope directly. By the time he came to Rome, though, he was pretty well inured to press criticism, having absorbed his share of it in a Germany where the press treated the tong wars among Catholic theologians as a gift that never stopped giving. What did aggravate Ratzinger, though, was what he regarded as the unfairness, even duplicity, that surrounded the ongoing debate over liberation theology.

He was always the courtly gentleman when we met, another attribute he shared with John Paul II. The only time I heard his voice get steely was when I asked him to comment on the charge that there had been a second CDF instruction on liberation theology because John Paul II was displeased with the first one. When I posed the question, the cardinal looked at me and said, forcefully, "It is not true."

He explained the extensive consultation process that had gone into the first liberation theology instruction, which had to begin from, and deepen, the criticisms of this new theological method that John Paul II made in Mexico in 1979. But at the end of the process of developing the first instruction, and "having clarified what cannot be," it was "clear to us and also to the Holy Father that in a second statement we had to indicate . . . a positive way." That second statement, far from being a "correction," was intended to deepen the Church's reflection on freedom, which, in a luminous sentence I have to believe issued from Ratzinger's own pen, taught that "God wishes to be adored by people who are free."

The other thing that seemed to aggravate and puzzle the cardinal was the recalcitrance of the Catholic left in recognizing that Marxism was an exhausted intellectual project that had done enormous damage in history. "It is incredible" would be his standard response when I asked him to comment on one or another theologian's infatuation with Marxism. As for his own political views, they seemed far from the reactionary caricature that prevailed in the world press. He was, rather, a mainstream Bavarian Christian Democrat, which would put him on the moderate center left of the American political spectrum on certain issues of political economy. Ratzinger was probably a notch or two to the right of John Paul II—another European Christian Democrat, if such labels make any sense—but the cardinal laughed aloud when I told him that one papal biographer described John Paul as the last great democratic socialist.

In these hours of conversation, Cardinal Ratzinger came across as a man of good humor who liked to laugh and was not averse to being kidded but rarely was because of the esteem in which he was held. So I tried to begin our interviews with an amusing story or anecdote, shocking him once with the fact that an American sister with whom his congregation was having some serious problems was once my wife's ninth-grade algebra teacher: which led him to smile and suggest that things would have been simpler if the sister in question had stayed with math rather than venturing into moral theology.

He always smiled or chuckled at his own political incorrectness, but also at the silliness of so much convoluted PC-speak when it came to philosophical and theological terms and concepts. He could also be rather dry. I once suggested that the difference between the Pope's intuition of a new springtime of evangelization and Ratzinger's sense of a European Church becoming smaller and purer had to do with the fact that the Bavarian Church of his childhood had been thoroughly destroyed while the Polish Catholic culture in which Wojtyła grew up was still more or less intact; the cardinal smiled, rather slyly, and said, "Well, we shall see . . . " The scholar was never far from the surface, though, and when I mentioned having seen a picture of young Father Ratzinger in a wide necktie shortly after the Council, he laughed and said, "You see, this illustrates the truth that the Holy Father taught in *Veritatis Splendor*, about the need to go from 'phenomenon to foundation.'"

While I don't think Joseph Ratzinger cared a fig what anyone thought of his political views, the Panzerkardinal caricature of him as a ruthless, vindictive doctrinal enforcer was vicious and unfair, and may have hurt him more than he ever let on. *Odium theologicum* is a nasty vice in which his enemies indulged freely. It took its toll on this quintessentially gentle man and may have had something to do with his inability as pope to dispense with the services of men who betrayed his trust and served him badly.

Spiral Staircase

In mid-December 1996 another member of the John Paul II inner circle became a regular part of my conversations with the Pope and a valuable intermediary with others: Bishop Stanisław Ryłko, a Kraków priest then serving with my old friend and former tennis foe, Cardinal J. Francis Stafford, at the Congregation for the Laity. Ryłko called on the afternoon of December 11, 1996, said that we were having dinner in the papal apartment at 7:30 that evening, and picked me up at the Sant'Anna Gate to the Vatican. We drove through the Belvedere Courtyard of the Apostolic Palace to the small and secluded Cortile Sesto Quinto, where we took what I came to call the "family elevator" up to the papal apartment.

In the months since our last dinner conversation, I had been reading extensively in John Paul's dense philosophical essays and wanted to make sure that I'd cracked the code. After we sat down I took two breadsticks from the table, held them about a foot apart, and said, "I've been reading your philosophical essays and I think I've figured out the method. Most philosophers begin here"—and I indicated one breadstick—"make a series of arguments, and end up here"—the other breadstick. "Your mind doesn't work that way." The Pope started smiling and I continued, having put down one of the *grissini*: "You see a problem or a question and start walking around it, looking at it from different angles. When you get back to where it seems you began, you're in fact one level deeper. So you start walking around it again, only deeper this time. You get back again to that starting point, but now you're two levels deeper, so you start going around the subject again, in a more profound way. . . . It's not a linear journey, it's like walking down a spiral staircase to get where you want to go." At which point the Pope said, with emphasis, "Yes," meaning "You've got it."

During this dinner conversation, Ryłko gave me a manuscript fragment of some twelve double-spaced pages titled *Curriculum Philosophicum,* which may have been left over from *Gift and Mystery* because the subject matter didn't fit into that memoir of the Pope's vocational discernment. It was a boon to me, however, for it summarized in John Paul's own words his philosophical journey, beginning with his struggles to understand metaphysics and epistemology by the dim light of the Solvay chemical factory when he was working the night shift during World War II.

Among other things, *Curriculum Philosophicum* showed me the bridge between Wojtyła's early theological studies and his later philosophical development. For, as he wrote in that fragment, it was his doctoral work in Rome on St. John of the Cross that unexpectedly "prepared . . . the passage from the [Neo-Scholastic] 'theology of the object' to [his explorations in] 'the theology of the subject.'" The text also explained the Pope's mixed reaction to Immanuel Kant: he appreciated the second categorical imperative and its insistence that persons must always be treated as ends and never as means, but Kantian ethics never seemed to him to get a secure foundation in reality: "The construction of the Kantian ethic was completely absorbed in the dimensions of subjectivism." (That part of the fragment reminded me of a funny moment during our December 1995 dinner. Richard Neuhaus had raised the subject of Kant, and the Pope, who read German easily, nonetheless slapped his forehead and, remembering his difficulties grappling with the Sage of Königsberg, exclaimed, "Kant! Mein Gott! Kant!")

Curriculum Philosophicum also put paid to the silly assertion of one papal biographer that he had found a certain sympathy for Marxism in Wojtyła's notes from the social ethics course he taught in Kraków. This was a grave misreading of early Catholic social doctrine's criticisms of unregulated capitalism; in any event, the manuscript said quite clearly that the notes were "in large measure" the work of Father Jan Piwowarczyk.

Then there was the fragment's description of the genesis of Wojtyła's first book on sexual ethics, *Love and Responsibility,* which he wrote had been "born above all from pastoral necessity"—from his work with students in Kraków and at the Catholic University of Lublin, who deserved better answers to their questions about marriage and the family than those on tap in traditional presentations of what the Sixth Commandment meant. The fragment also confessed, a bit sheepishly, that Wojtyła's major philosophical work, *Osoba y Czyn* (Person and Act), had been "largely" written during the sessions of the Second Vatican Council, when not even a skilled listener like Karol Wojtyła could sit contentedly through hours of Latin rhetoric.

This brought our dinner conversation about Wojtyła the philosopher to the vexed question of the English edition of *Osoba y Czyn*, which had been published under the somewhat misleading title *The Acting Person*. The manuscript fragment referred delicately to "ups and downs concerning the text of the translation" prepared by Anna-Teresa Tymieniecka. In our conversation, it was widely agreed that the Tymieniecka "translation" was "*sbagliato*" (mistaken) and that what was published in English was really an interpretation of the book, not so much Wojtyła's thought itself. Yet the Pope, whose indifference to the fate of his philosophical and poetic texts was as striking as his charity, insisted that Tymieniecka should be "given credit" for getting the book—or at any rate her interpretation of it—into English. All of this eventually made for the longest explanatory footnote in *Witness to Hope*.

As the conversation expanded, the Pope described his clandestine resistance activities during the war, which were meant, he said, "to salvage Polish culture while the Nazis were trying to destroy the intellectual class, pulling Poland up by its roots." When I asked how dangerous all of that had been, he said, "Very dangerous" and that "of course" he'd have been shipped off to a concentration camp if his Rhapsodic Theater group had been caught performing the classics of Polish literature—which rather refuted the charge that Wojtyła had a tendency toward "quietism" and the "spiritualization" of all conflict. Dangerous resistance to the Occupation, it was clear, didn't only mean stealing Schmeissers and spraying bullets around.

We also discussed the touchy subject of the clandestine ordinations of priests and bishops in Kraków in the 1970s, which was, strictly speaking, done in defiance of the Vatican *Ostpolitik* of the time.

Dziwisz said that Pope Paul VI "probably" knew what was going on but never intervened. Both the Pope and Dziwisz stressed that these ordinations of Czechs and Slovaks were always done with the written permission of the candidate's superiors, and Ryłko mentioned one security measure they adopted: a torn-card system in which the two halves of the card came to Kraków by different routes (one with the candidate), and their match validated the candidate's claim to be the real thing. All of this, Dziwisz insisted, should be understood not as defiance of Rome but as a work of solidarity with a persecuted neighbor. True enough; but it was also a clear indication that, long before he was elected pope, Karol Wojtyła thought that the deals the Vatican made under the *Ostpolitik* were choking the Church to death, at least in Czechoslovakia.

On a more literary note, the Pope said that he appreciated the recent award of the Nobel Prize in Literature to Polish poet Wisława Szymborska, whose poems he said he had read and liked; but he wished the prize had gone to Zbigniew Herbert, whom he obviously regarded as the superior poet. The problem, he thought, was that Herbert was even more difficult to translate than poetry usually is, and thus his true stature had never been recognized outside the world of Polish-speakers.

As I was leaving, Msgr. Dziwisz gave me two large shopping bags with four boxes of beautiful Polish Christmas ornaments. "You have a wife and three children," he said. "There is nothing for you!" I said I'd just gotten dinner, which was quite enough. I promised to give the gifts to Joan and the children and guarded them like the crown jewels on the flight home.

Tutor, Translator, Librarian, Nun

T HANKS TO BISHOP RYŁKO, I MET AND BEGAN TO WORK WITH AN-
other fascinating character in John Paul II's informal papal family: Sister Emilia Ehrlich, an Ursuline nun who was the Pope's English
tutor, his personal librarian, and the woman with whom I retranslated
some Wojtyła poems for *Witness to Hope.*

We eventually became friends, but it wasn't easy at first. On February 21, 1997, Ryłko drove me to an Ursuline convent on the Via No-
mentana, saying that Sister Emilia would feel easier if he were along as
"chaperone." When we arrived I met a tall, somewhat heavy-set, and
large-boned woman in her early seventies who walked with some difficulty. She looked me straight in the eye and said, in a flat voice, "I am
your reader"—meaning, I think, that she read whatever I sent to John
Paul and then passed it along. I expect she was also my correspondent,
so to speak, and it wouldn't have surprised me to learn that she was
the typist of the *mandatum scribendi.* But even suggesting such a thing
would, I thought, make her even more nervous about speaking and
working with this unknown (albeit "read") American. I finally got her
talking about her own life—which was dramatic in the extreme—and
when I pulled out a notebook she immediately said, "Oh, this looks
dangerous." But Ryłko and I finally convinced her that I was on the
side of the angels, and the conversation began to flow more easily.

She was born in 1924 in Lwów and baptized Constance Krystyna.
Her Polish father, Ludwig Ehrlich, was a distinguished professor of international law. Her mother was a native of Newport, Rhode Island,
which explained Sister Emilia's fluency in English. She was fifteen
and living on her family farm when World War II came crashing into

Lwów. Her mother, a "spirited woman" who hated Germans because of her brothers' experiences with them in World War I, decided that they weren't going to flee, so they stayed on the farm for the next two years.

The area was bitterly contested by the Germans and the Russians. Her father was arrested by the former and tortured, escaped from prison, and hid in the forest. The Nazis expropriated the farm and Constance, her mother, and her brother subsisted on carrots and apples, foods previously used for fodder. Her mother was arrested in December 1941 as an alien: she invited a Gestapo man to carry her valise ("And my bag? . . .") and, according to her daughter, charmed a killer Gestapo Alsatian into submission. Mrs. Ehrlich was eventually released when it became clear that ransom money wasn't forthcoming from America. After further adventures, including a three-week term in the Majdanek concentration camp, Constance was reunited with her mother and brother in Warsaw and lived in an Ursuline convent there. She finished high school in an underground academy in July 1944; the Warsaw Uprising broke out a few weeks later.

After that brave effort was crushed, she and the Ursulines were shipped to Germany and put to work in a thread factory in Heilbronn, a city in northern Baden-Württemberg. There, they worked eleven hours a day on a daily ration of three slices of sausage, a five-centimeter-square of bread, and a minute smudge of margarine, supplemented by apples from a nearby orchard: "The apples saved our lives. We had raw apples for breakfast, apple soup and baked apples for dinner." Appeals to German sisters and the Vatican finally got them released—two days before Allied bombers leveled the factory.

Returning to Kraków, she entered the Ursulines, took the religious name Emilia, did a divinity degree at the Pontifical Faculty of Theology there, tutored Cardinal Wojtyła in English, and was working on a degree in biblical studies in Rome when the two conclaves of 1978 happened. On the night of John Paul II's election she was standing in St. Peter's Square: "Everyone was praying for their cardinal to be elected; I was praying that they wouldn't take ours." When Wojtyła was presented on the central loggia of the basilica as Pope John Paul II, "I got very pale," she remembered. "Isn't he good?" someone nearby asked. "He's much too good," she replied.

Two days later, a functionary at the Pontifical Biblical Institute tracked her down and said, "I don't understand it but they're telephoning and saying that the Pope wants to see you." So she took the notoriously crowded Number 64 bus, a favorite hunting ground of Roman pickpockets, to the Vatican, presented herself at the Porta Sant'Anna, and announced that the Pope wished to see her. "They were quite scandalized. They gave me two Swiss Guards, like I was a prisoner, and walked me for quite a distance, and at last we arrived. I had a color shock. He came in all in white, and I had never seen him that way."

They both stood there for a minute, thinking. Then Sister Emilia began to cry, at which point John Paul said "Let's not go soft" and got down to business. The phone had been ringing off the hook with publishers wanting the rights to John Paul's poetry. He asked her to take care of it and to "see the Secretariat of State." "I didn't know who or where that was," she remembered, but off she went, somewhat like Miss Marple, to do the new pope's bidding. After getting various bits of useless advice from the Secretariat of State about consulting lawyers, it was suggested that she go to the Vatican press, the Libreria Editrice Vaticana, where she was told to put her request in writing and come back in a month or two. It all got sorted out eventually; she finished her degree at the Biblicum and stayed on as "a kind of sub-secretary," doing the back-channel correspondence (like mine) in English and sorting out the Pope's private library of books, journals, and newspapers: "I try to put some order into it" so that the Pope could readily access what he wanted.

Our first interview ended with her informing me that "you're not very photogenic" and that I was handsomer than she'd thought from my pictures. It was a fitting end to a striking conversation with someone who was, like her mother, a spirited woman.

At our second meeting, a month later, she gave me some recently published books in Polish about Wojtyła's poetry and family ministry in Kraków. The latter had a cover photo of the cardinal with a very young Stanisław Dziwisz, full of curly blond hair. "He was very beautiful," Sister Emilia observed, with that curious combination of wryness, insight, and innocence that characterized her conversation. She insisted that I not mention her in my book: "I am just a private person helping the Pope and I do not want to be a second Pascalina"—a reference to Pope Pius XII's powerful housekeeper, Mother Pascalina Lehnert, who was ejected from the Vatican the day Pius XII died and took refuge in the convent at the North American College, bringing the late pontiff's pet parakeets with her. "I have no influence," Sister Emilia insisted. "I just help with the library."

I must have treated her with the diffidence she wanted because we remained friends after *Witness to Hope* was published, and until her death in 2006, I saw her regularly in Kraków (to which she had returned for health reasons). On March 21, 1997, though, I let her ramble through her memories of life with Karol Wojtyła in Kraków, which were punctuated with sharp comments on various personalities from a nun who obviously had a mind of her own—and who would have happily taken a bullet for John Paul II, thinking her life fulfilled by doing so.

She was a linguist of considerable accomplishment and told me that because of Wojtyła's undergraduate studies in Old Church Slavonic, the basis of all Slavic languages, he could read Croatian, Slovenian, Czech, and Slovak. "No pope has ever had this preparation," she insisted. "No pope could speak Slav to the Slavs." Paul VI tried but "had a lot of trouble." Cardinal Casaroli tried but the Poles "tended to snicker at his pronunciation."

Her most telling comment involved the constant winnowing of Wojtyła by Providence:

> There is an odd regularity to his life. Whenever he has a big religious experience, someone dies or is stricken. His mother died while he was preparing for his first Holy Communion. His brother died when he was preparing to be confirmed. His father died while he was considering the seminary. His great friend, Father [Marian] Jaworski, lost an arm just before he became a bishop or cardinal, I can't remember which. Then there was Bishop [Andrzej] Deskur, who had his stroke just before he was elected pope. What would be great moments for anyone else also [involve] tragedies for him. It is almost as if he were being orphaned again and again.

She also remarked on how difficult it was to give Karol Wojtyła anything. The household nuns in Kraków, she said, would get him new coats and other bits of apparel and he'd turn around and give them away. "This got them upset, because they were only trying to take care of him, which was their duty. Fortunately, he can't give white cassocks away, or he would."

As for the man who was always being orphaned, she said that "he was a faithful friend and once you were his friend, you were always his friend." People loved him because "he loved people," kept promises, said what he thought and didn't speak until he had something serious to say: something rare among intellectuals, she shrewdly observed. She also remarked on his exceptional ability to make people in vast crowds think he was addressing them personally. In June 1979, for example, one Silesian coal miner, standing beside another in a throng of over a million in Częstochowa, started to say something and the second miner cut him off: "Damn it, don't talk while the Pope's speaking to me."

The stories and observations were fascinating, but we had to work on Wojtyła's poetry, so at the end of our March 1997 conversation I asked her about that. She said that Bolesław Taborski had done a good job translating Wojtyła's plays into English (and could have added that he did a superb job in writing introductions to them), but that Jerzy Pietrkiewicz's translations of the poems into English missed a lot of their grittiness. He got the job, evidently, because he was the first to apply to the commission the Libreria Editrice Vaticana finally set up to settle the question of foreign rights to Wojtyła's poetry—another indication of curial incompetence in dealing with a new situation. In any event, these comments gave me the opening to ask her if she would help me with new translations, which she agreed to do.

So when I returned on October 1, 1997, Sister Emilia met me at the door with two huge Polish-English dictionaries and the *opera omnia* of Wojtyła's poems in Polish. I brought the Pietrkiewicz translation for comparison, and we set to work. As I was only going to use excerpts from the poems, getting them licked into shape was not too difficult. But we took a long time translating the entirety of what everyone then thought was Wojtyła's last poem, "Stanisław," his valedictory to Kraków. I hoped to publish the new translation of this lengthy and important poem in full in *Witness to Hope*, but space considerations allowed me to use only parts of it.

Sister Emilia helped me see John Paul II "from inside" in many ways. One of the most striking was her entirely natural, unaffected description of the intense loyalty Karol Wojtyła drew from very bright people—and their constant concern that he might be hurt somehow: "He's too good." And the intriguing observation that he had been "orphaned" many times shed new light on a Wojtyła sermon that had been ignored by other biographers: his remarkable homily on October 8, 1978, at the Church of St. Stanisław, the Polish parish in Rome, eight days before his election as pope. There, he reflected on the Risen Christ's three questions to Peter in the twenty-first chapter of John's gospel— "Do you love me?" "Do you love me?" "Do you love me more than the rest of these?"—as a call to complete self-abandonment, "a summons to service and a summons to die" at which "the human heart must tremble." In that sermon, he was referring overtly to the experience of the recently deceased John Paul I when the call had come to him a month earlier. But the more I thought about it through the filter that Sister Emilia suggested, the more it seemed he was thinking out loud about his own possible future.

"Humiliation at the Hands of Evil" and Crypto-Lenin

ROME, JANUARY 1997

I CONTINUED TO WORK THROUGH MY CATALOG OF QUESTIONS WITH John Paul II on my Roman work period in January 1997. But while the Pope began in good form during our dinner on January 16—enjoying some notes that Joan and the children sent to him and asking, in his pastor's way, about a friend's child for whom Joan had asked him to pray—our conversation that night was the least satisfactory thus far.

We talked in a scattered way about several things—his deep desire to go on pilgrimage to the Holy Land; the character of General Wojciech Jaruzelski and his motivations in putting Poland under martial law in December 1981; his relationship with Cardinal František Tomášek and the troubles of the Czechoslovakian Church under communism; the influence of the apostle of divine mercy, Sister Faustina Kowalska (whom he had been "thinking about . . . for a long time"), on his encyclical *Dives in Misericordia*; his authorship of the Vatican II text he frequently cited, *Gaudium et Spes* 24; his sense that the schismatic Archbishop Marcel Lefebvre's real issues with Vatican II were not liturgical but involved the Council's Declaration on Religious Freedom and the aforementioned *Gaudium et Spes*, the Pastoral Constitution on the Church in the Modern World ("His vision of the Church was quite different").

The Pope's most intriguing reflection came when I asked him at the beginning of dinner how he had come to the view that a crisis in the idea of the human person was at the root of so many modern evils. He began to answer at a rather abstract level, but then switched gears and talked about how his wartime experience had shaped his intuition of the source of so much of the world's unhappiness. He hadn't had, he said, that "radical" an experience of World War II: "I wasn't put into prison or concentration camp." But, he continued, "I participated in the great experience of my contemporaries—humiliation at the hands of evil."

It was a striking, poignant comment, said without anger but conveying a lifetime's experience that the world could be a very wicked place indeed—and that wickedness took its toll, not just on bodies but on souls. From then on, it became ever more clear to me that the experience of the war—"humiliation at the hands of evil"—was *the* formative experience of Karol Wojtyła's life, a major factor in his vocational discernment, and the source of his profound commitment to human dignity and human rights.

Yet despite this moment of clarification, the Pope seemed a bit listless, giving very short answers to my questions. After an hour, Msgr. Dziwisz declared, "Basta per oggi!" (Enough for today!) so that was that. Dziwisz saw me out, took me down to the Cortile Sesto Quinto on the family elevator, noted that the Pope had had a very busy day, and then said that, on days like that, "he's finished at eight."

So I thought I would have to content myself, on this trip, with one great line about World War II, a few papal insights delivered in telegraphic form, some useful conversations with Cardinal Ratzinger and Cardinal Cassidy about matters theological and ecumenical, and a long discussion with Rocco Buttiglione about the intellectual genesis of *Centesimus Annus*. Then, on the day before I was to leave, Dziwisz called and said there was "an opportunity to meet with the Holy Father at lunch"—precisely when I ought to have been getting on a plane at Fiumicino. So I quickly rearranged my travel and found an entirely different John Paul II ready to greet me in the papal apartment on January 22. When I said I was afraid he might be getting tired of me, he took me by the arm and said, "No, I was very tired when we had dinner last week and I said, 'Professor Weigel is working so hard he deserves to see me in the daytime'"—and then quoted Augustine to the effect that it's easier to think in daylight. The lunch that followed was excellent and the conversation over ninety minutes was both deep and rollicking, with the Pope, Dziwisz, and Bishop Ryłko all chipping in.

We began by talking about some Polish history, a discussion triggered by my asking John Paul whether his given middle name, Józef, was in honor of Marshal Piłsudski—at which point Dziwisz broke in with a very loud "Franz *Joseph!*" After that moment of Habsburgian nostalgia, we discussed Piłsudski, the architect of modern Polish independence, and his difficult relationship with Archbishop Sapieha (who wouldn't let Piłsudski be buried in Wawel Cathedral, the crypt being extended so that his place is technically outside the cathedral walls). When I mentioned that I'd just reviewed a book of Lenin's correspondence in which the Bolshevik leader wrote that the Battle of Warsaw and Piłsudski's defeat of the Red Army had been a terrible setback for the global communist cause, the Pope noted that the battle took place just after he was born and said he was glad Piłsudski's victory was finally being recognized as decisive, not just for Poland but for the world. Bishop Ryłko mentioned that the only ambassador not to flee Warsaw in those days had been the papal nuncio, Achille Ratti, later Pope Pius XI; John Paul replied that he "was a great pope," emphasizing his three encyclicals against fascism, Nazism, and communism.

This, in turn, led to a lesson in the history of the papal villa at Castel Gandolfo. When the property was recovered in the 1929 Lateran Treaty, Pius XI, who apparently formed a real attachment to Poland during his brief service as Vatican ambassador there, had two scenes painted on the walls of the papal chapel: one depicted the defense of the Jasna Góra Monastery in Częstochowa against the invading Swedes in 1655; the other, complete with maps of troop movements, commemorated the "Miracle on the Vistula," the Battle of Warsaw in 1920. The Częstochowa scene featured the Pauline prior at the time, Augustyn Kordecki, while the more modern incident was constructed around the figure of Father Ignacy Skorupka, a chaplain in Piłsudski's army who was killed in the fighting that saved newly independent Poland in August 1920—and, according to some historians, kept the Red Army from charging straight across Europe to the English Channel. The paintings were covered with fabric by later popes, but John Paul had them uncovered and restored. Ryłko said they had been "waiting for a Polish pope"; John Paul said they were important because they were about "priests defending their people against tyranny."

We then talked about his relationship with the world's bishops since becoming pope. He explained how he had expanded the program for the *ad limina* visit that every bishop makes to Rome every five years, adding to the usual meetings a concelebrated Mass and a lunch together. When I asked whether he got a dossier on each bishop and diocese from the Curia's Congregation for Bishops before he met a bishop one-on-one, he said, with a small chuckle, "Yes . . . even too much."

When the conversation turned to his work with families in Kraków and the ways his family ministry tried to blunt the communist effort to disintegrate the family, John Paul stressed that this was a matter of "the co-responsibility of the laity" for the Church and society, which was why he had integrated lay experts into marriage preparation and family ministry. This turned the conversation to his old friend Jerzy Ciesielski, who had taught him the arts of kayaking and with whose widow, Danuta, he was still in regular contact. There was a beatification cause underway for Ciesielski as a model husband and father, and when I asked how that was going, Dziwisz cut in and said that, yes, Jurek Ciesielski was a fine man, but "the real saint in the family is Danuta" and it was a shame that they couldn't beatify her. For some reason, I blurted out, "Well, the Holy Father can just dispense with the necessity of the candidate having died." There was absolute silence for a moment, and then, to my relief, everyone laughed.

The Pope then urged me to get to know the people in Środowisko, the network of lay friends that began forming around him in the late 1940s and with whom he was still in as much contact as possible. "Środowisko," he observed, is virtually untranslatable, but he preferred "milieu" to the more common translation, "environment," because "milieu" had richer, more humanistic connotations that better captured "a very important chapter in my life."

This got us back to the communist attack on the family, which led to a discussion of the housing in Nowa Huta—deliberately small apartments, meant to discourage large families—and Dziwisz described the whole business as *"un metodo diabolico."* We talked a bit about the struggle for the Ark Church in Nowa Huta, the town deliberately build to exclude God, and after Dziwisz volunteered that the design of the Arka was *"troppo* Corbusier," I proposed that building it was one of the three focal points of his struggle with the regime when he was archbishop, the others being the fight to return the annual Corpus Christi procession to the Main Market Square (from which it had been banned by the Nazis and then the communists) and the fight to restore the theology faculty to the Jagiellonian University. The Pope agreed that those three were the centerpieces of what was all war, all the time, but noted, with some chagrin, that he hadn't been there to see the victory in the fight for the Corpus Christi procession: "I fighted, but the winner was my successor," the communists having finally surrendered after the 1989 elections.

This led into a discussion of that entire struggle being, at bottom, a matter of "place": all these battles, Ryłko said, involved the question of whether the Church would have any place in society. And that in turn led to another aspect of the war between Wojtyła and the Polish communist regime: the battle to build new churches, permits for which were strictly controlled by the state, meaning the Communist Party. Here, the Pope said, he had bent Church law by erecting canonical parishes that didn't already have a church building: "The community was more important" than the building, he said, and once the community had been formed and was functioning, there was leverage on the regime to concede the building permit—*See, the people are here, the people want a church, why are you denying the people what they want and need?*

In this respect, John Paul said, the battle to build a second church in Nowa Huta, in the Mistrzejowice neighborhood, "could have been even more important" than the struggle for the Ark Church, because it illustrated his method of creating social "facts" to which the regime had to respond. A priest who lived in Mistrzejowice came to Cardinal Wojtyła, telling him that the people there needed a church and that he was prepared to go to prison getting them one. Wojtyła backed him to the hilt, replicating the tactic of saying Christmas midnight Mass at the site where the church ought to be built (a key annual moment in the battle for the Ark Church) and keeping the pressure on the government—which finally caved in, so that John Paul could consecrate the church in Mistrzejowice, dedicated to St. Maximilian Kolbe, on his second pilgrimage to Poland in 1983. It was a serious discussion of some serious business, but throughout it the Pope would laugh at this or that, relishing the memory of the fight with the regime.

We then talked about the Polish filmmaker Krzysztof Zanussi, who was making a movie of the Wojtyła play about St. Albert Chmielowski,

Our God's Brother, which would premiere in Poland during the upcoming papal visit in June. The Pope chuckled at the thought of Zanussi's cinematic exploration of his pre-papal life, *From a Far Country*, saying "It is not entirely accurate," which led both Dziwisz and Ryłko to start chaffing me about the importance of accuracy. But then we got back to *From a Far Country*, and Dziwisz, having a hard time keeping a straight face, said, "Oh, yes, there is this scene of *piccolo Carlo, è scandalizzato perché Gesù a bevuto una birra!*" (little Charlie, who was scandalized because Jesus was drinking a beer)—in the film, young Karol blundered into the tent where the actors were relaxing after the first day's performance of the Passion Play in Kalwaria Zebrzydowska. I took the Pope's laughter as confirmation of the story.

On a more substantive point, I got John Paul to answer a question that had puzzled students of his literary work. In *Our God's Brother*, the counterpoint to Albert Chmielowski, the avant-garde artist seeking a vocation to serve the poor, is called "The Stranger": a political theoretician and agitator who also claims to serve the poor but by means of revolutionary violence. The Stranger and Brother Albert debate their respective approaches to seeking justice, neither persuading the other. Readers and critics had wondered whether The Stranger might be a portrait of Lenin. I asked the Pope outright and he said yes, "it is crypto-Lenin." We then discussed the possibility that Lenin and Chmielowski might have met in Zakopane, the town in the Tatras where Lenin was known to have lived for some months. The exiled Bolshevik leader had been arrested there by the Austro-Hungarian police, and I said, "Things would have been easier if they'd just held on to him." No one disagreed.

Dziwisz then declared that "la lezione per oggi è finita," so we prayed grace after meals and the Pope walked me out. He said, wistfully and leaning on his cane, "I used to be a sportsman, you know." I said that I had played some baseball but that I was getting too old for that. The Pope informed me, "You aren't too old for anything," but Ryłko chimed in that, by American standards, I was "already over the hill." Ryłko then gave me a ride back to the North American College and said, on the way, "There is a special feeling between you and the Holy Father."

A Pride of Curialists

WRITING THE STORY OF JOHN PAUL II NECESSARILY INVOLVED DE-scribing his interactions with the Roman Curia, the papal bureaucracy that exists to give effect to the will of the Pope. That's the theory, at least. And it's true that the Curia of John Paul II's era included men whose only purpose was to serve a pope they revered. But there is also no question that the election of the first non-Italian pope in 455 years was a *terremoto*, an earthquake, at the higher altitudes of the Roman Curia.

John Paul was entirely aware of this, and while he was determined to remain himself, he also knew that getting things done meant getting the Vatican bureaucracy to cooperate with him. This he did by appointing men in whom he had confidence and then letting them get on with their jobs without micromanaging. Msgr. Dziwisz was also a broker between Pope and Curia and calmed ruffled feathers at times, while laying down the law in his gentlemanly way when required.

As a general rule, the curial figures who were helpful when I was preparing *The Final Revolution* were cooperative during my papal biography project. There was also residual gratitude in certain curial circles for what I had done in helping prepare the Pope's trip to the United States and the United Nations in October 1995. Most important, there was Msgr. James Harvey: my guide through the labyrinth, my instructor in the m.o. that got me what I wanted, and a close friend with whom I could blow off steam when "the system" was fraying my nerves.

In the recollections below, the curial figures who taught me the most, directly or inadvertently, about John Paul II and the challenges he faced governing the Church are identified by the ecclesiastical title they held when we met between late 1996 and early 1999.

Cardinal Francis Arinze was one of my favorite Roman interlocutors, a man of insight and charm and a first-generation Christian who seemed overwhelmingly grateful for the gift of faith he had been given as a boy. Arinze knew Cardinal Wojtyła from their work together at the Synods of 1969, 1971, and 1977, and told me that, when he first heard of the Pole's election as pope, he immediately said to some Irish priests in Belfast with whom he was staying, "We're going to have a bit of clarity in the Church. Now, we are going to know where we stand, clearly, without being aggressive, but clear."

That word, "clarity," came up frequently in his descriptions of John Paul, as did adjectives like "positive," "optimistic," "courageous," and "dynamic." In Arinze's view, the John Paul II Effect was to make "a Catholic who is a serious Catholic happy that he is living at this time in history." He also understood why John Paul II was such a vocation magnet: "How can young people join a group of permanently confused people who don't know where they're going? The Holy Father is just the opposite. People who see him know that he is happy in his vocation. His general style has encouraged vocations, because young men see that he is happy."

When I asked the cardinal what John Paul's constant attention to the young Churches of Africa had accomplished, he said it had helped Africans "realize that *we* are the Church. . . . We count [and] that feeling of belonging . . . is very important, because in world politics Africa doesn't even rank as second-class but third-class. He's helped people understand that it's not when you become a Christian that counts, it's that all are in the Father's house." Arinze also stressed that John Paul's teaching had been helpful to women in what remained very patriarchal societies. Documents like the apostolic letter *Mulieris Dignitatem* "on the dignity and vocation of women" and the papal "Letter to Women" may not have impressed Western feminists, but "for a continent like Africa" these documents were "good news, and the women of Africa are grateful," because they stressed the absolute equality of men and women in terms of human dignity.

By the time we came into serious conversation, *Cardinal William Baum* had been in the Vatican for almost two decades and was the senior

American there, a quiet but powerful force behind the scenes. The more aristocratically inclined Italians thought him what they deemed a rarity among Americans, a true gentleman. At the same time, Baum had a very good idea of what was right and what was wrong about the Roman Curia.

Both of the 1978 conclaves, he told me, were marked by the sense that something had gone awry since Vatican II: "Many of us did think that the hopes and expectations of the Council had not been realized, that there had been mistakes along the way, that we needed to step back, take stock, and see what we should do to meet this. The problem wasn't with the Council but [with] how we had received and applied it, including in our pastoral practice." Then, without violating his conclave oath of secrecy, Baum helped me appreciate the human dynamics of the second conclave of 1978. The death of John Paul I after only thirty-three days as pope, he said, had been a psychological and spiritual shock to the College of Cardinals; they thought they had done God's will, yet God had taken the new pope quickly: "We saw it as a message from the Lord." Thus the human conditions for doing the unthinkable—going outside Italy for a pope—were set by the shocking death of John Paul I.

As for the world's surprise at their choice on October 16, 1978, Baum confirmed my view that, however unknown Wojtyła was in the echo chamber of the international media, he was very well known to the people who mattered: the papal electors. So for Baum, at least, there was no surprise when Wojtyła won, or when he so quickly put his mark on the papacy. "He 'spoke as one having authority' . . . with great love, but with enormous strength. . . . And knowing him, I wasn't surprised that he had this . . . this *force*."

When I noted that some, grading the pontificate, gave John Paul an A for priest, A for prophet, and C- for king, Cardinal Baum said that he had heard "echoes" of concern that John Paul II wasn't a strong manager and didn't fire people enough, but he contended that the Pope "believes in this other way. He believes in a clear and constant proclamation of the truth." Baum also insisted that no pope in history had taken his brother bishops so seriously: "That's one of the chief characteristics of [the] pontificate—his profound respect for the episcopate and for every bishop. . . . He wants to hear from bishops and he wants the bishops to take responsibility also. It shouldn't always be the Roman pontiff acting." It was a telling comment, even as it suggested that one of the unanticipated downsides to such a strong pope was a sense among those bishops who wanted to avoid controversy that they could pass the buck, knowing that "Rome" (meaning John Paul II) would deal with it. Cardinal Ratzinger expressed the same concern on several occasions.

It was also Cardinal Baum who gave me the line that John Paul II was "the greatest vocations director in history." Baum kept a close eye on the American scene and understood that an entire generation of seminarians was studying for the priesthood because of the influence of John Paul II. William Wakefield Baum had not been a vocation magnet in his days as a diocesan bishop, which coincided with some of the most confused years of the post–Vatican II Church. But he was a man of humility and no little self-knowledge, and he could see and appreciate in John Paul II strengths he knew he lacked, strengths that led to an impact on others he might have wished he had had.

Joaquín Navarro-Valls finally convinced *Cardinal Agostino Casaroli* that he should swallow his unhappiness with my criticism of his *Ostpolitik* and see me, after I had written the cardinal requesting an interview and included in my letter a copy of the *mandatum scribendi*. When we met in the cardinal's apartment in the Palazzina dell'Arciprete on February 14, 1997, Casaroli greeted me warmly, dressed in a plain black house cassock with neither pectoral cross nor ring—and then got the proceedings started in the classic manner of high-ranking Vatican officials of a certain ethnicity and generation. With great diffidence he said he wasn't sure he could be of much help. I said I was confident that was not the case and that I had much to learn from him. He then said that, at eighty-two, his memory wasn't what it used to be about specific events. I replied that I was more interested in background analysis and large themes. These preliminary rituals completed, we sat down in his living room for a fascinating conversation that lasted over an hour and a half. In the course of it, Casaroli demonstrated that his memory was quite sharp and that details of experiences decades in the past were at his fingertips—even as he perhaps unintentionally sharpened my understanding of how John Paul II had brilliantly deployed this veteran diplomat while pursuing a strategy with which Casaroli fundamentally disagreed.

Casaroli first met Karol Wojtyła in 1967 on a three-month-long scouting trip to Poland to gauge the situation: a lengthy visit prompted by the Polish government's complaint to the Vatican that its only "reporter" in Poland was Cardinal Wyszyński. Casaroli's recollections of what he learned in Poland suggested that he and Paul VI initially shared the communists' view that the tough-minded Wyszyński was somehow cooking the books, although Casaroli did admit that he finally concluded that the "Wyszyński picture" and the "real picture" were "substantially the same." It was a remarkable if indirect admission that Casaroli and his collaborators in the Curia had imagined that they understood Polish communists and their ways better than the Church's veteran point man on the scene.

Yet Casaroli also admitted that he came to admire his antagonist in this polite but serious struggle. Cardinal Wyszyński, he said, was "a real prince, although he came from a rather poor family." Moreover, he was "a great man of the Church" with "great political skills," including the essential skill of knowing just where the edge of the precipice was: a point Casaroli illustrated by saying that the Polish primate was "like one of those boys' toys that you wind up"—and here he walked his fingers across the coffee table to its edge—"and then . . . " it stops.

As for the *Ostpolitik*, he repeated the familiar tropes: the *Ostpolitik* was conducted on the principle of *salvare il salvabile* (to save what was salvageable) so that the sacramental life of the Church could continue under communist regimes; it was a quest for a *modus non moriendi* (a way of not dying). Paul VI, he said, was often in "torment" over what he understood was the abandonment of some of the Church's bravest people, the dissidents. But Pope Paul stayed "faithful to the vision" and choked down his instinct to speak out in condemnation of the persecution of men like the Slovak Jesuit Ján Chryzostom Korec. And yes, there were times when Paul VI said, "This is impossible" (i.e., he had to say something) and Casaroli had to "restrain him."

Given that Casaroli knew my views of the *Ostpolitik*, I was impressed by his candor. Yet it seemed to me he had still not come to grips with that policy's abject failure. Rather, with his talk about a "ripening" situation in the late 1970s, he seemed to think that he had successfully prepared the Revolution of 1989. This made even less sense when I began reading communist secret police files demonstrating that the *Ostpolitik* led to a deep penetration of the Vatican by Warsaw Pact intelligence services, even as it accelerated the destruction of the independence of many local Churches behind the iron curtain.

Cardinal Casaroli once said of John Paul II, "I would like to help this pope, but I find him so different." Our conversation suggested that this very intelligent man also had serious problems understanding Karol Wojtyła when he was Archbishop of Kraków. In discussing their interactions in the 1970s, Casaroli remembered being struck by Wojtyła as someone not interested in "concrete political problems." The cardinal also said that he "was impressed that Cardinal Wojtyła had never met the Secretary General of the Party, Gierek, who held the real power." It seemed not to have occurred to Casaroli that Wojtyła's struggle for the Church's "place" in Kraków—like the battle for the church in Nowa Huta—was a matter of addressing "concrete political problems," or that Wojtyła would have regarded an exchange of banalities with Edward Gierek as a complete waste of his time. Casaroli was impressed by Wojtyła's interest in contacts and conversation with intellectuals and other laity; but once again revealing perhaps more than he intended, he described those initiatives as a "restraint" on Wojtyła's ability to be involved in "political conversations."

Cardinal Casaroli's apartment, or at least the parts of it I saw, was revealing. There was a huge oil portrait of Paul VI in the foyer, and photographs and paintings of the cardinal, sometimes with Pope Paul, were evident in the rooms I saw; but there was neither photograph nor painting of John Paul II, who had made Casaroli a cardinal and his secretary of state. There was also something touchingly bourgeois (or perhaps just male celibate) about the breakfront in the living room: it was full of stemware and other pieces of crystal given to the cardinal—and each piece still had the small manufacturer's sticker attached.

My lengthy conversation with Cardinal Casaroli convinced me that John Paul II's choice of him as secretary of state was a stroke of genius. Casaroli was a capable man and that certainly had something to do with his appointment. But John Paul II must have realized that naming the architect and protagonist of the Vatican *Ostpolitik* as his chief collaborator provided him invaluable cover: while he, the Pope, continued to hammer on communist regimes for their human rights violations, there was Casaroli, the first man in the Curia, as living assurance to the communists that there really wasn't anything to this (as Casaroli once put it to the Polish authorities in Kraków after John Paul II had a sharp, table-pounding exchange with General Jaruzelski). It was brilliant strategy on John Paul's part, and its effects were on display throughout the 1980s.

When we parted, Cardinal Casaroli, who seemed to enjoy the exchange, invited me back for a second round. I would have been happy to oblige, for he was full of charm and kindness, but he died in June 1998 before we could meet again.

Cardinal Edward Cassidy, an Australian, was a strikingly open, friendly, and cooperative man, not always appreciated in Rome but very much appreciated by me for his candor and his insight into John Paul II's passion for Christian unity. That enthusiasm eventually gave birth to history's first papal encyclical on the subject, *Ut Unum Sint* (That They May Be One), published in 1995. Long before that, however, the Pope had demonstrated his ecumenical commitment by insisting that every papal trip abroad include an ecumenical meeting or prayer service. This steady papal engagement in ecumenism had already had impressive human results, Cassidy told me: "It's amazing for me to see how many leaders of other churches want to come to Rome, want to meet with the Pope. You don't have to go back many years before these people would never have thought of coming to Rome and meeting the Pope; it was so alien to their own ecclesiology and their understanding of their relationship to the Catholic Church." John Paul's openness, the respect he showed other Christian leaders, his understanding—all of these were "attractive ways in which he exercise[d] the primacy" of the Bishop of Rome.

But all that openness could not open the door that was perhaps highest on John Paul's list of priorities: the door to Russia. Throughout his entire tenure at the Pontifical Council for Promoting Christian

Unity, Cassidy shared John Paul's frustration at the recalcitrance of the Russian Orthodox Church, which had seemed more open in the waning years of communism and the USSR than since the Soviet crack-up and the reemergence from underground of the Greek Catholic Church in Ukraine and other Eastern-rite Catholics Churches in the countries of the former Warsaw Pact. One prime example of this obstinacy was Metropolitan Kirill, Russian Orthodoxy's chief ecumenical officer (and later Patriarch of Moscow), who told Cassidy that the rebirth of the Greek Catholic Church in Ukraine "blocks everything." Cassidy understood that this reflected the Russian refusal to acknowledge that the Russian Orthodox Church had collaborated with the Soviet secret police, the NKVD, in a brutal attempt to liquidate the Ukrainian Greek Catholic Church in 1946: "Sometimes when you've got something to hide, the tendency is to be a bit aggressive. You don't defend it because you can't defend it, so you attack, and you attack us. And that's a very simple thing to attack, the Catholic Church, because of [Russian Orthodoxy's] own history and ecclesiology." Moreover, Cassidy said, the fact that the Russian Church originated in Kyiv, not Moscow, was another factor in Russian intransigence toward Ukrainian independence and the Russian sense that a vibrant Greek Catholicism in the Ukrainian capital posed a threat.

If the historical, ethnic, and geopolitical complexities of ecumenism with the eastern Slavs made Cassidy's work challenging, so did the fact that, in ecumenical efforts with Western Christian communities, the goalposts kept moving. The Anglican–Roman Catholic dialogue, which once seemed so promising, had foundered on the question of the ordination of women, which, as Cassidy rightly understood, was a question of the nature and authority of the Church: the Anglicans looked at the question "as a question of 'who' you can ordain, rather than 'by what authority.' And this is now the real problem"—the question of what is authoritative for the Church. There were once hopes, he said, that the Anglican Communion would think of itself as part of "the 'Catholic Church' in the wide sense, along with the Orthodox and the Roman Catholics," and thus wouldn't take steps that the Catholics and the Orthodox couldn't take. But that hope was now in the rearview mirror. Anglicanism had decided that it was its own authority, as had so many

other mainline Protestant communities that no longer seemed to oper-
ate within stable theological and moral boundaries.

None of these difficulties altered Cardinal Cassidy's good humor
or enthusiasm for the ecumenical task. He did not succeed in arrang-
ing a meeting between John Paul II and Russian Patriarch Aleksii II
(KGB code name: DROZDOV), although he came close at one point
before the Russians dug in their heels. And as we said in one conversation, *that* would have been an interesting session: John Paul II, the
man whom many (including me) believed was at the receiving end of a
bullet ultimately fired by the KGB, and a former KGB officer, meeting
in Vienna.

The career of *Cardinal Roger Etchegaray* illustrated John Paul II's ability to get the best out of people who were on a somewhat different page
theologically. Etchegaray's tenure as Archbishop of Marseilles had not
been a happy one, but John Paul II recognized the Frenchman's talents
as a schmoozer and connector. So he got him out of Marseilles, gave
him the red hat, and turned him into a back-channel papal diplomatic
troubleshooter.

In his apartment in the Palazzo San Calisto, the cardinal spoke
at length and with relish about the almost thirty informal diplomatic
missions he had undertaken for John Paul, traveling to combat zones,
dodging land mines and bullets, and trying to thaw what was frozen
in the Holy See's relationship with difficult countries. These efforts,
he said, were "parallel" or "complementary" to what the Vatican diplomatic service did in trouble spots. The point was to demonstrate,
through "presence," the Pope's concern for stricken people, and to try
and get all the parties to a conflict together. It worked, Etchegaray said,
because John Paul II was *"sopra, non fuori, la politica"*—above, not
outside, politics.

Cardinal Bernardin Gantin, a Beninese, was Prefect of the Congregation for Bishops. Vescovi, as everyone in Rome called it, was responsible for vetting nominations for the episcopate outside mission
territories (which were handled by the Congregation for the Evangelization of Peoples): so it was Gantin who had the task of shaping the

episcopate in the developed world in light of John Paul II's authoritative interpretation of Vatican II.

Like Joseph Ratzinger, he was one of the last of Paul VI's cardinals and was helpful to me in clarifying another of the dynamics of the conclave that elected John Paul II in October 1978. One of the protagonists of that conclave, Franz König of Vienna, saw Karol Wojtyła as a bridge between East and West. Some cardinals knew him as a thoughtful intellectual and a good listener, and others were determined to break the hegemonic Italian grip on the papacy. But according to Gantin's description of him, the Africans—the new Christians—seem to have been impressed above all by two things: the clarity and luminosity of Karol Wojtyła's faith, and his humility.

John Paul rarely looked back on the assassination attempt of May 13, 1981. Cardinal Gantin, for his part, thought about it often, and gave a copy of the famous photograph of the Pope collapsing into Msgr. Dziwisz's arms at the moment he was shot to every new staff member of the Congregation. That image was, for Gantin, an icon: "That photograph has profoundly influenced me. Here is a man who has been shot, and is perhaps collapsing to his death, but with extraordinary serenity and perfect unity with God. He immediately began to say the Hail Mary." John Paul knew, Gantin observed, that "fear is what destroys man," that fear of the future "cripples us." And that is why, the cardinal said, he offered men and women the possibility of receiving God—so that they could live beyond fear.

Archbishop Zenon Grocholewski was part of the tiny Polish contingent in the Vatican when John Paul II arrived in October 1978. A canon lawyer, he was appointed to the second position on the Apostolic Signatura, the Church's appellate court, in 1982, having been one of the seven men who worked with John Paul to complete the revision of the Latin-rite Church's Code of Canon Law, begun by John XXIII. In addition to helping me understand the new Code of Canon Law as an expression of Vatican II's theology of the Church, Archbishop Grocholewski also made the point, a new one to me, that John Paul II was one of the great legislator-popes. In addition to the 1983 Western Code of Canon Law we were discussing, he promulgated in 1990 a new Code of Canon Law for the Eastern Catholic Churches. In 1983 he dramatically changed the paradigm and altered the procedures for considering beatifications and canonizations in the apostolic constitution *Divinus Perfectionis Magister* (The Teacher of Divine Wisdom), and in 1988, he issued an apostolic constitution reorganizing the Roman Curia (*Pastor Bonus* [The Good Shepherd]). Then there was the 1990 apostolic constitution on the reform of Catholic higher education, *Ex Corde Ecclesiae* (From the Heart of the Church). And finally, there was *Universi Dominici Gregis* (The Shepherd of the Lord's Whole Flock), the 1996 apostolic constitution reforming the procedures for a papal election. The world may have thought of him as "John Paul Superstar"; Grocholewski and those of his canonical cast of mind thought of John Paul as an exceptionally prolific legislator.

I had gotten to know *Cardinal Pio Laghi* during his days as apostolic delegate and then nuncio in Washington. He was a wily old thing, something of a northern Italian Catholic liberal at heart, but adept at tacking to the prevailing ecclesiastical winds. He was sent to the United States with clear instructions from John Paul II to bring what might be called "dynamic orthodoxy" to the center of the American episcopate: he was to seek out potential bishops of pastoral skill who were also fully committed to the Church's teaching, capable of explaining it publicly, and good at attracting vocations to the priesthood and religious life.

At our first meeting in his offices at the Congregation for Catholic Education he rushed in late, said he could only give me a half hour, and then proceeded to talk for forty minutes, virtually nonstop, about the Pope, the pontificate, and, of course, himself. It was the old modus operandi I remembered from our Washington encounters, and the only thing to do was sit back and let the tide roll on. He had some interesting things to say about the Pope's role in settling the Beagle Channel dispute between Argentina and Chile shortly after his election, praised the Theology of the Body ("a lasting and original contribution"), and made some pointed comments about the weaknesses in the American hierarchy that led to his Washington appointment and his mandate to try setting a different course.

Our second meeting two months later largely dealt with the Central America controversies of the 1980s. The suggestion bruited by some—that the Pope had been tough on Catholic revolutionaries in Central America as part of a deal with the Reagan administration, which in turn would be tough on Poland's communist regime after the martial law declaration—was rubbish, Laghi insisted. Then he described crisply John Paul's analysis of the Church's troubles in Latin America in the 1980s. There were three interlocking problems, the Pope had said. There was an ideological problem, in that certain forms of liberation theology were off the doctrinal reservation. There was an ecclesiological problem, in that the "popular Church" movement wanted to marry the Church to revolutionary regimes, or, in Laghi's words, "put a rifle in the hands of the crucified Lord." And then there was a persecution problem, with the Castro regime trying to strangle the Church on the island prison while exporting its political doctrine throughout the continent. None of this had anything to do with Poland or Solidarity, obviously.

In this context, Laghi told me a good story about his attempts to explain Latin American theological controversies to President Ronald Reagan. In the mid-1980s, Reagan asked Laghi, "What is this damned 'theology of liberation'?" Laghi, knowing that the president had been at an Italian-American function the night before, said, "The spaghetti is good but the sauce is poisoned"—the spaghetti being the Church's work with the poor and the sauce being a Marxist analysis that led to revolutionary violence in the name of the Gospel. It was a deft response, reflecting Laghi's instinct to find the fifty-yard line in any controversy—although "poisoned" was a bit sharper than one might have expected from a quintessential Vatican diplomat.

The conversation at our third meeting turned to Mother Teresa, who had died the month before, and Laghi made an intriguing observation: she had been to John Paul, Laghi suggested, what Catherine of Siena was to the papacy of the fourteenth century. I wasn't entirely sure the analogy worked—Catherine was known for reading Pope Gregory XI the riot act, which was not exactly Mother Teresa's m.o. with John Paul II—but it was a striking indication of the respect in which the tiny Albanian-born nun was held at the highest altitudes of the Roman Curia.

Archbishop Jorge Mejía, with whom I had done some serious head-butting in 1988, proved to be a friendly source of insight into the pre-papal Karol Wojtyła. The Argentine biblical scholar and the Polish philosopher had lived together in the Belgian College during the immediate postwar years in Rome, and Mejía was full of interesting detail about those days—the poverty of the Belgian College, the ease of getting around on bicycles in a Rome not choked by cars and *motorini.* He also gave me some insight into the atmosphere of the pontifical universities in the late 1940s (and into his own feisty personality). Decades later, John Paul said that he remembered the Argentine for several reasons, including the fact that "you used to raise your hand and interrupt the professors." Cardinal Ratzinger, who was present at this banter, "just looked at me in horror," Mejia recalled, "and said, 'You know, in Germany you had to send a message to the professor to ask a question.'"

As the *Sostituto* of the Secretariat of State, *Archbishop Giovanni Battista Re* was the switchboard through which all papal business flowed. His personality reminded some of an overstimulated child; he charged around Rome in a small Fiat he drove himself; his signature patter— *"Bene, bene, bene, bene, bene . . . "*—was a standing joke in the Curia. But he had a rare reputation for efficiency and the curial machinery worked reasonably well on his watch. I don't think he saw much purpose in my biographical work, for shortly after we met he told Jorge Mejía, "I've seen him once and that's enough."

Still, the forty-five minutes we spent together on December 16, 1996, gave me two insights into John Paul's routine. The first was that the Pope's daily life was punctuated by many moments of prayer: in addition to the hour of private prayer before his daily Mass, he ducked into the chapel of the papal apartment for prayer before and after audiences, before lunch, after lunch, and "throughout the afternoon." The second thing Re noted was that John Paul was frequently doing two or three things at once: "During one trip he's thinking about what should happen on the next trip. During a working lunch he is always talking about the future: the next week, the next month . . . " Multitasking was a characteristic of Karol Wojtyła as Archbishop of Kraków, and while he didn't bring to Rome his Cracovian habit of working on correspondence while attending meetings with his collaborators, he was, it seemed, always thinking several moves down the board.

For a man whose position with the Pope was quite secure, *Cardinal Jan Schotte* was exceptionally reticent about saying anything on the record. So the most useful material I got from the Belgian General Secretary of the Synod of Bishops, when we met for ninety minutes in March 1997, had to do with Karol Wojtyła's work in implementing the Second Vatican Council in Kraków, which Schotte had obviously studied with some care. It was, the cardinal said, the "most intense and holistic" such effort in the world: two years of preparatory prayer, in which six hundred prayer groups organized throughout the diocese met regularly to pray for the help of the Holy Spirit in receiving the Council and its documents; then a two-year study of the conciliar documents, aided by *Sources of Renewal,* the vademecum that Wojtyła wrote on the texts of Vatican II. Only then, after four years of preparation, did the discussion turn to programs for implementing the Council. It was, in effect, a re-catechesis of the entire archdiocese in the form of an archdiocesan Synod. Schotte's description of this remarkable program, plus conversations I had in Kraków during these months, convinced me that one reason John Paul II was a successful pope was that he had been an exceptionally good diocesan bishop.

The cautious Schotte did give me one good story, involving the contentious 1980 special Synod for the Netherlands, where Schotte served as translator. It was a linguistic nightmare: none of the seven Dutch bishops had an international language in common; none of the curial officials present spoke Dutch, and one of them, the Australian Cardinal James Knox, didn't even speak Italian. So Schotte had to translate everything. And at one point, John Paul, who not infrequently used humor to temper tedium, leaned over to the Belgian and whispered, "Sometimes your translations are clearer than what the guy said."

After what I expect was a prod from Msgr. Dziwisz, *Cardinal Angelo Sodano,* the papal secretary of state, agreed to speak with me over lunch on December 13, 1996, in his apartment on the second loggia of the Apostolic Palace—much fancier digs than the papal apartment a floor above. It was Sodano who had said that the *stranieri*, the foreigners, don't really fit in well "here," and that was the approach he took with me, greeting me de haut en bas, as if he were a Nobel laureate virologist and I was a mildly interesting new pathogen. The conversation was, in a word, a monologue: I think I got five sentences in over the course of ninety minutes.

In the course of his lecture, though, Cardinal Sodano helpfully filled in the details of the drama to which Cardinal Laghi had referred: John Paul II's intervention in late 1978 and early 1979 to forestall a war between Chile and Argentina over the border between them in the Beagle Channel—a strait in the Tierra del Fuego archipelago at the bottom of the world. It was the kind of dispute between military dictatorships drunk on machismo that could have blown up into something very nasty. And it was the newly elected John Paul II, Sodano said, who insisted on an offer of mediation by the Holy See—something that hadn't been done since Pope Leo XIII successfully mediated a dispute between Spain and Germany over the Caroline Islands in 1885. Sodano was nuncio in Chile at the time (Pio Laghi was on the other side, as it were, in Argentina), and from both his recollections and Laghi's, it seemed that the Pope's insistence on the two parties coming to agreement, and his sending a veteran Vatican diplomat, Cardinal Antonio Samorè, to knock heads in Buenos Aires and Santiago, made a diplomatic solution to this rather ridiculous fracas possible.

The balance of the lunch was spent on Sodano explaining to me that the Chilean dictator General Augusto Pinochet was a misunderstood and maligned character, while providing a few interesting details about John Paul's 1987 visit to Chile. Pinochet at one point asked the Pope why the Church was making such a fuss about democracy: "One system of government is as good as another," the dictator claimed. John Paul replied that, no, "the people have a right to their liberties, even if they make mistakes in exercising them"—which, Sodano claimed, had a positive effect on Pinochet's subsequent agreement to a referendum on his continued rule (which he lost).

Archbishop Jean-Louis Tauran was the Holy See's "foreign minister" while I was preparing *Witness to Hope*, and in addition to discussing the conceptual premises of Vatican diplomacy, he and I enjoyed exploring the just war tradition and the Catholic theory of international relations during our conversations. The mild-mannered Tauran was the perfectly trained diplomat, never venturing beyond his brief and keeping his personal views on close hold. But on several occasions he came through with telling stories crucial to developing the detailed portrait I intended to paint.

It was Tauran, for example, who confirmed that John Paul II had called President George H. W. Bush the night before the ultimatum to Saddam Hussein requiring him to evacuate Kuwait or face allied military action expired: the Pope said that if diplomacy couldn't resolve a violation of international law that must not stand, he hoped the allies would win, Saddam would be ejected from Kuwait, and there would be as few casualties as possible.

In our discussion of this and other international crises (and in my conversations with the Pope), I came to understand how John Paul conceived his role in these situations. He was not a pacifist; he believed that the just war tradition remained the normative Catholic moral tradition for evaluating a situation like the invasion and annexation of Kuwait or the crack-up of Yugoslavia and the subsequent genocide in Bosnia. He also thought, as did Tauran, that that tradition needed to be stretched to deal with situations that fell under the rubric of "humanitarian intervention," that is, military action to prevent or halt the mass slaughter of innocents. But John Paul II did not see the papal role as that of an international moral referee who would, at a certain point, declare that the just war criteria had been satisfied and thus the lid was off. Rather, John Paul's view was that the pope should press until the last possible moment for reason and diplomacy to work, even as he understood that the just war criterion of "last resort" was not infinitely elastic but a judgment of prudence.

Tauran, a Frenchman, also had some pithy things to say about the moral state of Europe. When we were discussing the continent's birth dearth, he said, with some sharpness, that late-twentieth-century Europe wanted "happiness without constraint"—including the constraints imposed by raising children or caring for elderly parents. But he was also aware of decadence on the other side of the Atlantic, not least because of an appalling interaction he had with Clinton administration Undersecretary of State for Global Affairs Timothy Wirth. Wirth, a fanatical population controller, kept his famous "condom tree" on his desk when meeting with Tauran and gave the Vatican official a banal lecture on sex education (which Wirth seemed to imagine as a subdiscipline of plumbing) as the sovereign cure for "children having children," as he put it.

My greatest debt to Jean-Louis Tauran, however, involved his breaking the bureaucratic logjam I encountered in accessing certain key papal documents I was promised but that Cardinal Sodano and Archbishop Re were not producing: the Pope's letter to Leonid Brezhnev warning against a possible Soviet invasion of Poland in late 1980, the Pope's exchange of letters with Mikhail Gorbachev, and the Pope's letter to Chinese leader Deng Xiaoping suggesting a new conversation between the Holy See and China. I tried to crack the problem for the better part of a year and a half before Msgr. James Harvey came up with a solution.

The kind of archival material I was looking for, Harvey explained, was not in the Secret Archives (and thus under a time-lock); rather, the materials were kept in the Secretariat of State, where they could be easily accessed for reference as needed. So the papers I was looking for were in Tauran's keeping, and as he and I seemed to have hit it off, why not approach him with a very specific set of requests, the *mandatum scribendi*, and a description of the problems I had encountered from Sodano (Tauran's boss) and Re (technically Tauran's peer, but in actuality another boss)? This I did, and Harvey told me on December 12, 1997, that I would have a "productive meeting" with the Frenchman that night.

When he came into the parlor where we met, Tauran said that my request for documents had been "declined" by Sodano and Re for "fear of setting a precedent"—the usual Vatican bureaucratic excuse for refusing to do something the bureaucrats didn't want to do. So Tauran, after consulting with Harvey, had proposed that he be authorized to read me the documents in summary form. Sodano and Re had agreed to this procedure, but I said it wasn't acceptable or sufficient, that I had to see the texts in question, and that if I couldn't take copies away with me he had to translate them with me, in full, on the spot. Tauran agreed to do this (which was likely stretching the boundaries of his deal with Sodano and Re), and we spent the next hour and a half working through John Paul II's letters to Brezhnev and Gorbachev, which he had fetched from his section's archives and brought with him.

In examining the Brezhnev letter, the first thing I noticed was a light pencil notation at the top right-hand corner of the cream-colored official papal stationery: "12/80." I asked what it was. Tauran replied that it was the filing code—December 1980. I was flabbergasted and asked, "Do you mean that everything is simply filed by date and month, no matter what it is?" "Yes," he replied; and that was why it had taken him hours to dig out the letters in question, as they were in boxes with everything else saved from that particular month. At this point I began to understand why the Vatican didn't let researchers dig into the archives of a pontificate until they had been properly culled, organized, and catalogued: something like the Brezhnev letter might be cheek by jowl with a highly delicate matter of conscience that had been referred to the Pope that same month. It was a window into the archaic bureaucratic practice of the Holy See, and walking back to the North American College that night, I remembered that, until President Franklin Roosevelt had sent some staff from the Library of Congress to Rome in the 1930s to help organize the Vatican Library, books there were shelved by size and color.

The letters to Brezhnev and Gorbachev helped make *Witness to Hope* as authoritative as possible, and in discussing the second letter, Tauran let the diplomat's mask down a bit and said that there was a good relationship between John Paul II and Mikhail Gorbachev, who was "much more intelligent than the other ones." (And, I thought, hadn't tried to have John Paul shot.)

It took another year to get the Gorbachev response and the letter to Deng Xiaoping out of Archbishop Tauran, but he finally came through at the very last minute, in December 1998, after I sent a rather stiff letter and told his secretary that time was up, the manuscript of *Witness to Hope* was being finalized, and delivery was imperative. So we met, fourteen hours before my departure from Rome, and I got what I had asked for in the same manner as I had in December 1997.

It was aggravating to have to give Cardinal Sodano any credit for my access to these materials in *Witness to Hope*, because he was nothing but an impediment to my getting what the Pope wanted me to have. The real credit was all to Jean-Louis Tauran's account, with a strong assist from Msgr. Harvey (who was Bishop Harvey by the time this little drama ended). But that was the formulation we agreed to—that I would indicate that the materials were shown to me with Sodano's "authorization"—so I kept my end of the bargain. This untoward fracas taught me invaluable lessons about the traditional managers of popes and their capacity to gum up the works when they put their minds to it. And, as such, it gave me even more insight into John Paul II's skill in getting so much done with such balky bureaucratic machinery around him.

Cardinal Jozef Tomko, a Slovak, was one of the few Slavs in the Roman Curia when John Paul II arrived, a former official of the Congregation for the Doctrine of the Faith and the Congregation for Bishops who became General Secretary of the Synod of Bishops and then prefect of the Curia's missionary dicastery, Propaganda Fide. Tomko gave me two lengthy interviews, in November 1996 and January 1997, which helped me understand John Paul II's way of governing.

The first insight Tomko gave me was into John Paul, decider. He was, the cardinal said, a man who trusted collaborators, who had a "power of synthesis," a striking memory, and an acute perception of the essentials of a situation. Just as importantly, John Paul "is not afraid of making a decision, nor is he wanting to come to a decision if the whole situation is not mature. . . . He is patient, waiting with some situations until the [right] moment comes." And here, I thought, was one advantage of a relatively young pope: elected at fifty-eight, John Paul II could take the long view, not forcing decisions or changes prematurely out of a concern that if he didn't act now he might not have the opportunity later.

At the same time he knew he was both the decider and the agenda-setter. Thus after years of discussion about post–Vatican II Catholicism's lag in missionary fervor, it was John Paul who said that "it was about time" for him to "say something" about the Church's need to rediscover itself as an essentially missionary or evangelical enterprise.

The result was the 1990 encyclical *Redemptoris Missio* and the steady proclamation of a New Evangelization over the last decade and a half of the pontificate.

Tomko spoke with feeling about seeing John Paul II get "this look in his eye when he has an inspiration"— Tomko sensed, somehow, that the channel to God and the divine will was open. One such moment came in 1979 when the Pope asked Tomko, "What are we going to do for Cyril and Methodius?," the apostles of the Slavs, whose invention of the Cyrillic (or Glagolitic) alphabet and translation of the liturgy and the Bible into a standardized form of Old Church Slavonic were key moments in the cultural history of Central and Eastern Europe— and great examples of the inculturation of the Gospel. Tomko was surprised by the question and said, "Perhaps [make them] Doctors of the Church?" Then John Paul "got that look" and said, "Co-patrons of Europe." Ten years before the Berlin Wall came down, John Paul II was already thinking about a Europe breathing once again with both its lungs, East and West.

John Paul the decider and agenda-setter also put heart into his colleagues, Tomko reported. The cardinal had been complaining to the Pope about some serious problems of the Church in Africa and his inability to see any progress in resolving them. John Paul listened carefully and then said, "Look, hope is also a virtue." It was just what Tomko needed to here at that moment. And as he noted, "When you put that together with the title of his book" (*Crossing the Threshold of Hope*) you saw that "this is not a theory" but the reality from which the Pope lived.

Father Roberto Tucci, SJ, the head of Vatican Radio, had been John Paul II's travel agent—the advance man for all papal travels abroad—for fifteen years when I met him in September 1997. The son of an Italian father and an English mother, he was an able organizer, a diplomat of both tact and steel, and a great storyteller. My primary interests were the visits that had caused him headaches, and he told me with some relish about his challenges in preparing the papal trip to Nicaragua in 1983.

I quickly got the impression that Tucci regarded the Sandinistas— the former Marxist guerillas then running Nicaragua—as inept and ill-mannered adolescents, no matter their real age. But he had turned the vanity of teenagers to the Pope's advantage by talking Daniel Ortega and his comrades into allowing a television broadcast of the papal Mass in Managua, which was shown all over Central America. The Sandinistas' attempts to stack the crowd at the outdoor Mass, the silly revolutionary chants they indulged during the Mass from a platform next to the altar, and the Pope shouting "Silencio!" so that his homily could be heard, were shown all over the region and badly embarrassed the regime. What could have been a mess that only a few knew about became the point from which the Marxist tide began to recede in Central America. They were a rather "stupid" bunch, Tucci concluded, "and I could have told them how to be much more effective authoritarians."

When the second papal pilgrimage to Poland was moved back a year, from 1982 to 1983, because of martial law, Tucci had to negotiate the terms of the visit with two of the worst characters in the Polish communist apparat, Czesław Kiszczak, the interior minister, and his deputy, Konrad Straszewski, who had led the department of the Polish secret police set up to "disintegrate" the Catholic Church. The Pope was determined to meet Lech Wałęsa, and Kiszczak was just as determined that he wouldn't—as Tucci told me, Kiszczak wouldn't even pronounce Wałęsa's name, referring to him as "that guy," or the winner of "the so-called Nobel Prize," or "the man with the big family." "Why does the Pope want to meet with a man who doesn't represent anybody in this country?" Kiszczak demanded at one point.

Then there was Chile in 1987. At the closing Mass, some goons, probably connected to the Pinochet regime, started burning tires and a large cloud of acrid smoke began drifting over the altar platform. It was the first and only time, Tucci recalled, that he thought of taking the Pope out of a venue. But the police finally got the situation under control, and Tucci told me that he'd learned a valuable lesson: always have some lemons with you in situations where there might be smoke or tear gas, because if you squeeze lemon juice into a handkerchief you can breathe through it.

Tucci was obviously an able diplomat, because he was the one who had to explain to friendly heads of state or government why they couldn't travel with the Pope when John Paul was in their country: because it would create a precedent that would allow a Jaruzelski or Pinochet to demand similar treatment when John Paul was on their turf. But Tucci could put his foot down when he had to. When we spoke, he said that he'd recently had a sharp conversation with Fidel Castro about John Paul's impending visit to Cuba. Castro was making difficulties on some Church-state issues, and Tucci finally said to him, over the phone, "Look, he's doing you a big favor coming. . . . And he's taking a lot of criticism for it. What are you going to do for him?" Fidel tried to bluff his way out by saying that Cuba had separation of Church and state, at which point Tucci barked at the Jesuit high school graduate, "Don't try that stuff on me or the Holy Father." Fidel, he seemed to think, had taken it under advisement.

"Something Useful for
the Universal Church"

M SGR. DZIWSZ KEPT LONG HOURS AND SEEMED TO ASSUME OTH-
ers did, too, calling me at 11 p.m. on Wednesday night, March
19, 1997, when I was dead asleep, to invite me to lunch with the Pope
the following afternoon. There, we talked at length about the material
I had been reading, analyzing, and trying to summarize for a week: his
Theology of the Body, its origins, and its impact.

It began, John Paul said, with his Środowisko, his young student
friends in Kraków, when he was their chaplain. Even under communism, their question was not, "Does God exist?" It was, "How do we
prepare a good marriage?" A pastor's care for meeting those questions
and concerns was the genesis of *Love and Responsibility*, the archdiocesan institute on marriage and the family he had created, and, ultimately, the Theology of the Body. So he began sketching what would
later be published as *Original Unity of Man and Woman* (the first of
four volumes of that theology) during the balloting that eventually
produced Pope John Paul I.

It was, John Paul II said, an interesting intellectual puzzle, philosophically and theologically, that God created two complementary
creatures, man and woman, who shared one humanity. Pondering that
puzzle with the help of the first chapters of Genesis led to his mature
thought on sexuality, its built-in moral dynamics, and the question
of how the Church could present its understanding of the beauty of
human love to a world that imagined itself "adult" in these matters but
was really just jaded. John Paul II was also aware that *Humanae Vitae*,
Paul VI's encyclical on the morally appropriate means of regulating

fertility, had had a very rough reception, so it seemed time to try a fresh articulation of the Church's marital ethic. Out of that mix of intellectual curiosity and pastoral concern came not only the Theology of the Body but the apostolic exhortation *Familiaris Consortio* (which John Paul clearly liked a lot) and the encyclical *Evangelium Vitae*. The linchpin of the whole structure, though, was the Theology of the Body, and the Pope was happy to hear that it had made an impression on young people who didn't expect to be impressed by a papal reflection on sex and love.

That he kept coming back to the influence of his Cracovian experience on his papacy gave me an opportunity to ask him why so many initiatives in his pontificate had been previewed in Kraków. Dziwisz immediately jumped in and said, "It is the same man," but John Paul had a different kind of answer: "It is confidence in the Holy Spirit, who was calling to the See of Peter a cardinal with this experience, this background. It means that there is something here that is useful for the universal Church."

Bishop Ryłko said that the Pope had a special concern for a world without a real sense of fatherhood, which helped explain the three poems Wojtyła had written on the theme of paternity, including the very difficult metaphysical poem "Radiation of Fatherhood." This led me to ask whether the Pope was still writing poetry, and John Paul answered that "Stanisław" had been his last poem: "I paid my debt to Kraków." He then said, with a smile, "I dedicated it to my successor, who said that he was 'unworthy'"—at which Dziwisz, who also loved Cardinal Macharski, started chuckling: a reminder that poking gentle fun at old friends was very much part of the human dynamic within the inner circle of John Paul II.

Wojtyła's Poland in Depth

WARSAW, KRAKÓW, AND LUBLIN, APRIL 1997

AFTER ALMOST A YEAR OF INTENSE ROMAN RESEARCH, I RE-turned to Poland in the spring of 1997 to Poland to look into the Pope's pre-papal life in greater depth. Having formed a close working relationship with the Dominican priory in Kraków, I wrote the prior, Father Mirosław Pilśniak, asking what might be a good time for an extended research trip. He thought the weather would be fine right after Easter, so he suggested that I come on Low Sunday and said I would be welcome to use a priory guest room as my base for as long as I liked. I took Fr. Mirek at his word and arranged to arrive in Poland on April 6.

It had been freezing cold for weeks; it was snowing when I arrived, and it snowed for the next twenty days, right until I returned to Washington on April 26. At times, the snow was so fierce that I couldn't see the landscape as I traveled by train to Lublin. Moreover, the good prior had believed his own weather forecast, so the boilers in the priory were shut down for repairs on Palm Sunday. The Polish Dominicans of Kraków thus celebrated Holy Week and Easter in a rather arctic Basilica of the Holy Trinity, their half-frozen breath visible to the hearty congregation of university students they attracted. I took to sleeping in the guest room in an overcoat, the inner man warmed by a pre-slumber sampling of one of Kentucky's finest distilled products.

Meteorological circumstances notwithstanding, it was a wonderful three-week research trip, invaluable in painting a portrait of Karol Wojtyła from inside.

If John Paul II had not been so insistent that I meet his old friends from his university chaplaincy days, I probably wouldn't have devoted more than a few pages of *Witness to Hope* to those years of his life. But he had said time and again that I couldn't understand him unless I understood them, so I set out to learn what they could teach me. They had been burned before, by other Americans and other writers, but after some initial reticence was overcome and the doors were opened to their treasure trove of memories, I was so taken by their stories—and by this unique set of relationships that helped form a pope as no other had been previously formed—that I devoted an entire chapter of *Witness to Hope* to Środowisko.

Danuta Ciesielska, the widow of Jerzy Ciesielski, was the titular head of Środowisko and its unofficial historian. But she was quite shy, so my most extended Środowisko conversations were with three couples—Piotr and Teresa Malecki, Stanisław and Danuta Rybicki, Gabriel and Bożena Turowski—and with Teresa Heydel Życzkowska, Stanisław Rodziński, and Karol Tarnowski. The first thing that struck me was that most of these men and women had gone on to professional careers, some of them quite distinguished. And the second thing I noticed was that their stories, while displaying the personal touches that came from intimate friendships involving unique personalities, were completely coherent in the portrait they drew of Karol Wojtyła as priest, bishop, and friend.

The first characteristic they all stressed was what Teresa Malecka called Wojtyła's "permanent openness." Then there was Stanisław Rybicki's recollection, confirmed by all the others, that Wujek, their "uncle" (as he had told them to call him as a sort of Stalinist-era nom de guerre), was a man who had "mastered the art of listening." Those two qualities met in a third: Wujek's insistence on the individual's moral responsibility. They would talk about everything, but he would never impose a view. Even in spiritual direction, his signature phrase had been "*You* must decide."

The result was a zone of freedom in a world of greyness and conformity. In a communist environment that remained stifling even after the worst of the Stalinist repression, they "felt completely free with him," as Teresa Malecka put it. "While he was among us we felt that everything was all right." They also emphasized that all of this—hiking, kayaking, skiing with young people and young couples, parties in their homes for name days and after the baptisms of their children—was

unheard of among other Polish clergy. So was Wojtyła's custom of saying Mass on their summer vacations with an overturned kayak as an
improvised altar.

Stanisław and Danuta Rybicki were among the first of Wojtyła's
"kids" and met for the first time when they were students and a
"young, pious, poorly dressed priest" at St. Florian's parish near the
Kraków Polytechnic was forming a choir to sing Gregorian chant at
Sunday Mass. It was Danuta who told me some of the best stories from
the first years of this unique network of friendships: how they only
gradually broke through the inbred caution of the Stalinist period and
learned each other's surnames; how Wojtyła quoted one of the most
famous lines in Polish literature, "Call me 'Uncle,'" as a humorous
yet serious way to protect both them and himself from the ubiquitous
secret police (organized Catholic youth groups meeting with a priest
was illegal in those days); how they met him in Częstochowa after his
ordination as a bishop and he said, "Don't worry, Wujek will remain
Wujek"; and how he assured them that nothing had changed in their
relationship—"Wujek will remain Wujek"—after his election as pope.

Gabriel Turowski, a physician, went to Rome for three months to
"keep company with a suffering friend" after the assassination attempt
of May 13, 1981, and taught me a lot about that drama—including the
fact that the "second assassin," the cytomegalovirus that threatened
John Paul II's recovery, came from a tainted blood transfusion during
the surgery to repair the carnage done by Agca's bullet. The Turowskis
also added an intriguing detail to the story of Wojtyła's cast of mind before the second conclave of 1978. I knew that Cardinal Wojtyła had been
at their home on September 28, 1978, to celebrate his twentieth anniversary as a bishop with Środowisko. When I asked what he'd been like
that night, they admitted that things hadn't been quite the same. Then
Dr. Turowski said, quietly, "He was saying farewell. He was thanking
people for their friendship. He was behaving differently; there is a mystery here, and when we tried to talk to him about it he was silent."

These extraordinary relationships embodied what ecumenical
theology calls a "mutual exchange of gifts." Karol Wojtyła's friends
knew that they were an "experimental field for his ideas," as one of
them put it, for he had learned from them about the things he hadn't

experienced personally: courtship, marriage, young families, professional careers. Yet, as one said and all agreed, "We don't feel proud that we taught him something; it was a mutual exchange": they knew that they had received as much, and arguably more, than they gave.

Cardinal Franciszek Macharski was his usual gracious self when we met on April 10, 1997, and he gave me a thorough tour of the archbishop's residence at "Franciszkańska Three" (as everyone called it). Karol Wojtyła's small suite—a bedroom with a single bed, a private office, and a small entry foyer—was left exactly as it had been when Wojtyła went to Rome for the second conclave of 1978. It overlooked the Planty, the great greenbelt surrounding the Kraków Old Town, and the Pope used it on his visits to Poland. There was a portrait of St. Charles Borromeo, Wojtyła's patron saint, over the door leading into the private office, and the bed featured a colorful folk art counterpane that was one of the few gifts Wojtyła ever kept.

Macharski also described the office routine when Wojtyła was archbishop: two hours of writing at a desk in the chapel, before the Blessed Sacrament, a few feet from where he was ordained a priest; then two hours of meetings with anyone who wanted to see him; then lunch and a full schedule of afternoon and evening pastoral activities. Wojtyła, the good listener, was typically late for lunch and would tell his associates, when he came charging into the dining room, "The cardinal isn't late; your watches are fast." The numerous portraits and photos of Adam Stefan Sapieha in the residence bespoke the enduring place the man created cardinal by Pius XII in 1946 held in the hearts of his successors as *the* role model.

Monsignor Stanisław Małysiak, a close associate during Wojtyła's episcopate, helped me understand the archbishop's priorities. Wojtyła had inherited a rather simple archdiocesan curia from Archbishop Baziak and opened new offices to broaden the Church's pastoral outreach in the post–Vatican II battle with communism for Poland's future. Thus Wojtyła created a new department of charitable activities to see to the needs of the poor, the addicted, and the sick, and a new department for family life that stressed marriage preparation and trained lay workers for family ministry. Cardinal Wojtyła placed a high priority on youth ministry, but putting programs in place for young people took ingenuity, given the communist ban on organized Catholic youth groups. Altar boys could be taken on hikes and picnics—and catechized along the way. University chaplaincy worked according to the same informal, catechetical multitasking. All of this, Małysiak stressed, was meant to "create a movement," not just structures; Wojtyła never confused meetings, with which post–Vatican II Catholicism was replete, with real pastoral effectiveness.

Msgr. Małysiak said that the cardinal "knew what he wanted" and was "very easy to read"; at the same time, he operated in a rather freewheeling way, open to ideas, happy to hear different views. He was strict in matters of moral principle but also compassionate: once, after telling a young priest firmly that he had to amend his ways, Wojtyła asked the startled young cleric to hear his, the archbishop's, confession.

Bishop Stanisław Smoleński, in very good form at age eighty-two, was Karol Wojtyła's spiritual director and confessor in Sapieha's underground seminary during World War II and later served as one of Wojtyła's auxiliary bishops. A few minutes into our conversation he asked a favor of Father Jarosław Kupczak, OP (who was translating), and me: "Please don't call me 'Your Excellency.' This is Kraków." It was Smoleński who gave me one of the most touching descriptions of Karol Wojtyła when he said that his former penitent was a man who "loved easily"—even though, Smoleński reminded me, he had come to the underground seminary having experienced a lot of sorrow in his life: the deaths of his parents and brother, his friends shot, his experience of hard manual labor.

Wojtyła "loved the style of Sapieha and imitated it—the openness, the spontaneity, the friendliness." He also took from Sapieha, who organized covert aid to prisoners at Auschwitz I and pleaded with Nazi Governor-General of Poland Hans Frank for the lives of Jews, the determination to be the *defensor civitatis*. Wojtyła's other models of what Smoleński called "total sacrifice" were St. John Vianney and *Brat Albert*, St. Albert Chmielowski; St. Maximilian Kolbe was another model, but Vianney and Chmielowski were more important because they were "in the foreground" of Wojtyła's spiritual formation.

And it was Bishop Smoleński who explained to me Cardinal Wojtyła's unique way of addressing problems or pastoral challenges as archbishop. The first question he asked was, "What truth of faith sheds light on this situation?" And the second question was, "Who could help, or who could we get trained, to deal with this?" In other words, it was not about him: it was about Gospel truth and collaborating with people who had been well prepared for their task.

Father Michał Szafarski, a Salesian priest, was one of the youngest members of the Living Rosary groups in which Karol Wojtyła had participated during the war. I met him at the rectory of Wojtyła's old parish, St. Stanisław Kostka in the Dębniki district, to learn more about Jan Tyranowski, the lay mystic and tailor who introduced the future pope to the works of St. John of the Cross, St. Teresa of Ávila, and St. Louis-Marie Grignion de Montfort. Fr. Szafarski showed me a letter he had received the year before from John Paul II, who described Tyranowski as "a very important person in my life [whose] example . . . showed me the beauty of eternal life, which is connected to the gift of vocation to the service of Christ." The Pope's memories were similar to those of Tyranowski's spiritual director, Father Alexander Drozd, who, Szafarski told me, had described Tyranowski as a "spiritual alpinist" who was "going to heights I could never reach. . . . Grace radiated from his face, his eyes, his person, demanding reverence."

Fr. Szafarski, who was serving on an archdiocesan commission preparing Jan Tyranowski's beatification cause, walked me through Tyranowski's spiritual diary, in which he recorded his daily points for meditation in a fine, almost calligraphic handwriting that seemed to be that of an artist, not a tailor. There was obviously a precision and discipline to his method of prayer and meditation, and it was intriguing to imagine this "unexpected apostle" (as Wojtyła described him after Tyranowski's death in 1947) instructing the future pope in the arts of contemplative prayer as Nazi bullhorns blasted out news of the latest triumphs of the invincible Wehrmacht.

Then there was Fr. Józef Tischner, whom I had first met while working on *The Final Revolution*. This hearty soul had real insights into Wojtyła's philosophical mind, emphasizing that he was a man of "synthesis," a "connecter" of ideas: thus love *and* responsibility; Aristotelian-Thomistic realism *and* phenomenology; person *and* act. Tischner also stressed Wojtyła's humanism, his effort to "meet someone wisely" by being open to what others had to say. Or, as Tischner put it in an intriguing comparison with another contemporary philosopher: "[Paul] Ricoeur remembers a text, even if he forgets who wrote it; the Holy Father is the opposite"—he remembered the person.

Tischner loved to tell jokes and in one of our conversations asked me to solve an "ancient problem in Polish moral philosophy: if Poland is invaded again by Germans and Russians, at whom is Polish army to shoot first?" I said I hadn't a clue. "Shoot first at Germans," Tischner said, "on ancient moral principle, business before pleasure." But it was John Paul II's sense of humor that Tischner regaled me about on April 23, 1997. Tischner had invited the German theologian Johann Baptist Metz, the intellectual father of liberation theology, to one of John Paul's summer humanities seminars at Castel Gandolfo, and when the group photo was being organized, people were shuffling around, not wanting to seem to be pushing themselves closer to John Paul, who was left standing a bit alone—and who then called out to Metz, "You, Metz, a little closer to the Pope!" At which point everyone, including Metz (who did what he was told), cracked up.

But there was, of course, more to joke-telling in Tischner's evaluation of John Paul II, which he summed up in one lucid phrase: "his ideas turned into institutions."

The Catholic University of Lublin (KUL, in its Polish initials) was the only Catholic institution of higher learning between the iron curtain and the Pacific hinterlands of the Soviet Union—or as Stefan Swieżawski, one of Karol Wojtyła's colleagues in the KUL philosophy department, put it, "the only place between Berlin and Vladivostok where philosophy was free." KUL was Wojtyła's academic base from 1954 until his election to the papacy, and I had to get to know its people and their history in order to understand him "from inside." But before I went to Lublin for two very busy days in April 1997, I spoke with Professor Swieżawski and his wife in Warsaw, where they were living in retirement.

They were a sprightly couple: Maria, who had asked the young Father Wojtyła to be the catechist of her children, was Cardinal Sapieha's great-niece; Stefan, as he insisted I call him, had just turned ninety and built a biographical and conceptual bridge between Wojtyła's wartime experience and KUL in the 1950s. The catastrophe of the war, he said, had raised "fundamental questions," to the point that even metaphysics classes were oversubscribed, with students sitting on seats, in the window sills, on the floor—"everywhere." This was the atmosphere—an intense interest in questions of first principles—into which Swieżawski, who served on the committee approving Wojtyła's habilitation thesis, invited the young priest to come as a junior lecturer in philosophical ethics. He also recalled how he introduced Wojtyła to the works of the French philosophers Étienne Gilson and Jacques Maritain, which took Wojtyła beyond the intellectual milieu in which he was immersed at the Angelicum during his doctoral studies. But his most extraordinary story had to do not with Lublin but with a Thomistic Congress held at the Abbey of Fossanova in 1974 to mark the seven hundredth anniversary of Thomas Aquinas's death.

Wojtyła gave an academic paper and celebrated one of the Congress Masses, during which he preached on the "two Thomases," Aquinas and the doubting apostle. During the homily, the thought came, unbidden, to Swieżawski: "He will be pope." After Mass, he told his wife and said he thought he had an obligation to tell Wojtyła; she was having none of it, saying that if her husband insisted on telling their friend "this stupidity," he was on his own. So Swieżawski went off, found his old friend and colleague in the sacristy of the abbey church, stood in front of him, and said, simply, "You will be pope." Wojtyła looked at him, said nothing, and walked away.

Wojtyła's philosophical project came into sharper focus in my conversation with his chief philosophical disciple, Fr. Tadeusz Styczeń. An energetic talker and a Salvatorian priest, he had done his master's, his doctorate, and his habilitation degrees under Wojtyła's direction, and then served as his assistant when Wojtyła's pastoral responsibilities as auxiliary bishop and later archbishop in Kraków drastically limited the time he could spend at KUL. While our conversation ranged all over the philosophical landscape, several points stood out. The first was that Wojtyła, the unfootnoted philosopher, liked to do philosophy "from the standpoint of Adam: astonished with the world, while recognizing that what is wonderful in this world is yet incommensurable with the human person, who is the only one who can 'wonder.'"

Second, the "Lublin Project" in which Wojtyła, Styczeń, and their students (some of whom later became colleagues) were engaged was nothing less than an attempt to change the course of Western philosophy since the eighteenth century: to overcome David Hume's is/ought fallacy and put moral philosophy back on a secure intellectual footing, so that ethics would not drift off into subjectivism and then relativism. But they would do this not from abstract principles but by thinking through a philosophical anthropology that would get them to the truth of things built into the human condition, then working up from there to ethics. It was a formidable goal, never really achieved; yet its very scope said something about the boldness of the minds involved in it.

Styczeń also pointed out that this commitment to truth as something that can possess us was at the root of Wojtyła's fearlessness. It was the dissident Marxist Milovan Djilas, Styczeń told me, who said that John Paul II was the only man he knew who was without fear, and it seemed to Styczeń, and to me, that the Pope's fearlessness came from his security in the truth. Which in turn shed some light on the old Solidarity slogan, "For Poland to be free, 2 + 2 must always = 4." At first blush, it seemed a slap at communism's ubiquitous lies, but on further reflection, it was a recognition that one is only free when living "in the truth."

If Tadeusz Styczeń was Wojtyła's philosophical son (and the man close enough to him to say, of the draft of *Person and Act,* "perhaps it could be translated from Polish into Polish to make it easier for the reader to understand—including me!") Father Andrzej Szostek, a Marian priest, was John Paul's philosophical grandson, whose doctoral dissertation was the last he ever read (and did so as pope). Szostek pointed me to the centrality of what Wojtyła would call the "Law of the Gift" in his philosophical ethics: the truth, built into the human person, that we come to fulfillment through the gift of ourselves, rather than the assertion of ourselves.

Sister Zofia Zdybicka, an Ursuline nun then the Dean of Philosophy at KUL and another Wojtyła protégé, thought it providential that, amid the contemporary West's current cultural crisis, a pope whose entire intellectual project had to do with rebuilding humanism had been called to Rome. Yet another Wojtyła doctoral student turned professor, Jerzy Gałkowski, told me of the overflow crowds that packed

Wojtyła's undergraduate KUL lectures, which reflected Wojtyła's ability to relate his teaching to real-life issues. His graduate-level lectures were different in that he was clearly thinking something through in them—including the utilitarianism of Jeremy Bentham, as if anticipating the next challenge to Christian humanism after Marxism imploded. Professor Gałkowski also told me a wonderful story about him and his wife being married by the cardinal archbishop in a small chapel in the woods at seven o'clock in the morning: "Adventures weren't unusual with Karol Wojtyła."

And then there was Stefan Sawicki, who helped me locate Wojtyła's poetry in the history of Polish literature. Sawicki had enough critical distance on his old colleague to say that he wasn't a poet of the first rank like Czesław Miłosz, Zbigniew Herbert, or Miron Białoszewski. But Wojtyła was a serious poet, and modern Polish poetry "would be incomplete without him," for he formed a bridge between the country's tradition of mystical poetry and the contemporary literary scene. Sawicki also recalled that it was Wojtyła who urged him to read what Sawicki called "dark literature," such as Camus's *The Plague* and Graham Greene's *The Power and the Glory*: another insight into the range of Wojtyła's imagination and its fascination with the human condition in all of its aspects.

Danuta Michałowska, a teenager when she joined the Rhapsodic Theater during World War II, later became a successful actress and drama teacher. Back in Kraków, I was struck by the precision with which she pronounced her words while giving me tea and a glimpse into a world of young people resisting totalitarianism through that theatrical troupe, under the tutelage of another exceptional personality, Mieczysław Kotlarczyk.

Miss Michałowska grew up in Kraków and didn't know Kotlarczyk before he came to live with Karol Wojtyła during the war. But in the pressure cooker of the occupation, she got to know his story. Kotlarczyk's father, she said, had been a "fanatic for theater" who would wake his family up at night to share a new dramatic idea that had just occurred to him. It was a single-mindedness he passed along to his son, who was "a man of one idea—the theater" but also a deeply converted Christian believer who thought of theatrical work as a "way of perfection." He was, Miss Michałowska said, "a radical man, stubborn and fanatical," compared to whom "Savonarola was nothing." Yet it was precisely that stubbornness that was needed to create an avant-garde theatrical group as "a conspiracy," wielding the weapons of poetry and drama to frustrate the Nazis' efforts to "demoralize Polish culture."

As a keen student of Polish literature, Danuta Michałowska saw her fellow Rhapsodist, now the pope, through the lens of some of the Polish authors she knew so well, especially Juliusz Słowacki, whose plays and poems combined Christian themes with Eastern religions, German romanticism, and Hegelian philosophical idealism in an intoxicating brew. She suggested that his epic poem, *King-Spirit,* anticipated John Paul II and his impact on the world when Słowacki wrote of a spiritual leader who "will give love as others give weapons" and thereby bend the course of history through peaceful revolution.

Danuta Michałowska struck me as a woman of a deep spiritual sensibility who'd had something of a hard life but wasn't embittered by it. The story of her one-woman play, *I Without Name*—a meditation on Augustine's anonymous concubine and the mother of his son, which she had performed for John Paul II in the Vatican—was one of my favorites among the many tales I heard while preparing *Witness to Hope.* She kindly autographed and gave me one of the last remaining copies of a book memorializing the Rhapsodic Theater that she assembled for the troupe's fiftieth anniversary. At the end of our conversation, she told me she hadn't been enthusiastic about meeting me, since she had "met so many people who write nonsense about him" (meaning John Paul), but now she understood that I was "serious." I thanked her and said that my predecessors in the papal biographers' union were my cross in this project.

To catalog Tadeusz Mazowiecki as a journalist may seem to do scant justice to Poland's first noncommunist prime minister since World War II. Still, Mazowiecki made his living by his pen for decades, and what he did in editing Solidarity's weekly magazine, *Tygodnik Solidarność,* was not dissimilar to what James Madison, John Jay, and Alexander Hamilton did in writing *The Federalist Papers*: using the tools of journalism to give depth of thought to a popular democratic movement. In April 1997, I was eager to clarify with him what I suspected were erroneous depictions of the Pope's role during martial law, which he was very helpful in doing.

Mazowiecki was imprisoned like the rest of the Solidarity leadership and communicated with the Pope during those hard days by smuggled letters, the couriers being his son and Cardinal Macharski. There was no question in anyone's mind that the Church would protect Solidarity and its people, he said, because by the time martial law was declared, Solidarity had enrolled a vast number of Poles, so to protect the Polish people was to protect Solidarity. The concern was that the Church, in the name of peace, would interpose itself with the regime as society's representative, thus inadvertently undercutting Solidarity, which, having been declared illegal, was officially defunct. The Solidarity leadership knew from Radio Free Europe that they had the Pope's support, but it was important to get a statement from the Pope that there would be no abstracting the idea of "solidarity" from the mass movement the regime was trying to crush. And that meant the legal restoration of Solidarity the trade union and national renewal movement: "There were some things that could not be given back."

Mazowiecki told John Paul all this in a smuggled-out letter. And when the Pope wrote back in a letter smuggled into the jail where Mazowiecki was being held, Mazowiecki was relieved: "We understood each other." The Pope, knowing that other, unfriendly eyes, might eventually see his note, wrote, "I've read your letter and I've been thinking very carefully about the situation. I have read your letter three or four times."

In other words, they agreed. The Pope would keep the idea of solidarity as a social virtue alive, press the regime for the legal restoration of Solidarity, and thus make clear to churchmen tempted to substitute themselves for the Solidarity leadership that that was not the kind of publicly engaged Church he had in mind.

Mazowiecki also had an interesting response to my question about what most powerfully struck him, an active layman, about John Paul II. He said that Cardinal Wojtyła had always been thought of as a good bishop and a serious intellectual, but as very much a Polish bishop and a Polish intellectual; the surprise was how easily he made "the transfer to the world stage." Or, as he put it, "What strikes me most in the Pope's personality is that his personality was 'fulfilled' when he became pope."

Marek Skwarnicki was another multitasking journalist, a *Tygodnik Powszechny* staffer, published poet, and novelist. His descriptions of Karol Wojtyła just prior to Conclave II in 1978 influenced my depiction of those days in *Witness to Hope*. But he was just as helpful in giving me insights into Wojtyła the literary man. For Skwarnicki, Wojtyła wrote in order to work through questions and issues, like the question of the legitimacy of revolutionary violence in circumstances of serious oppression, which he explored in *Our God's Brother* and which Skwarnicki saw as a preview of John Paul II's later critique of liberation theology and its dalliance with armed resistance to injustice. As Danuta Michałowska explained to me how Wojtyła's literary work was influenced by Juliusz Słowacki, Skwarnicki was my tutor in the influence of Cyprian Kamil Norwid, perhaps the most untranslatable of Polish poets, on Wojtyła, especially on his ideas about the creativity of work.

Unlike Mazowiecki and Skwarnicki, Halina Bortnowska, another *Tygodnik Powszechny* writer, had drifted away from the John Paul II circle by the time I met her in April 1997. She was a peppery personality who didn't have much use for the current Church leadership in Poland and suggested to me that things in Poland had never been quite as "integrated" as people thought they were—one example being the fracture of the Solidarity coalition a few years after 1989. She had been Wojtyła's student at KUL, thought him a "better lecturer than a writer," and remembered him as an excellent seminar leader, reading and commenting on a text and getting students to dig into what they were reading.

She understood the gap between the world in which Wojtyła had written *Love and Responsibility* (whose second edition she had edited) and the postcommunist world of the late twentieth century: "It was a different culture of emotions then, living was more restrained, with more control." But this thinker and writer who, in the conventional categories, had moved steadily to the left over her life still believed that the argument for chaste, ecstatic love in *Love and Responsibility* held up: "If it doesn't stand up today, people are the poorer for it."

INSIDE THE HOLY SEE–
ISRAEL NEGOTIATIONS

AUSTIN, MAY 1997

T WO WEEKS AFTER I RETURNED FROM POLAND, I WENT TO AUSTIN, Texas, to get inside one of the great controversies in the pontificate of John Paul II: the establishment of full diplomatic relations between the Holy See and Israel, an initiative widely applauded throughout the world but one that caused serious heartburn in parts of the Roman Curia. My interlocutor was the kind of person who could only have played a significant role in a pontificate like John Paul's, in which a pope was willing to go outside the box to achieve his goals.

When we met, Father David-Maria Jaeger, a Franciscan, was the only native-born Israeli of Jewish background to have been ordained a Catholic priest since the state of Israel was founded in 1948. His conversion to Catholicism had been an intellectual one, but he was baptized in an Anglican church at eighteen because he couldn't find a Catholic priest willing to baptize a *sabra*, a native-born Israeli. So he accepted baptism from the Anglicans and then presented himself at the Latin Patriarchate of Jerusalem, the local Roman Catholic headquarters, and announced, "All right, you can now receive me as a Protestant convert."

Jaeger entered the Franciscans of the Custody of the Holy Land at twenty-six and was sent to Rome for studies. He was dispensed from the prescribed baccalaureate course and awarded the baccalaureate degree in sacred theology after being examined by a specially appointed pontifical commission, which recognized that he had already taught himself more theology than he was likely to learn in the classroom. He later completed a doctorate in canon law with a dissertation on the role of the popes in defending Holy Land Christians.

David Jaeger may have been the only man in the world with the requisite skills the Holy See needed for the stickiest parts of its negotiations with the state of Israel over a Fundamental Agreement between the two parties. He was a native Hebrew-speaker who knew Israeli law as well as Church law. He had extensive on-site experience with the problems that needed to be resolved to regularize the Church's legal position in Israel. He was a tough negotiator. He was a priest who could be trusted with the Church's interests.

I took away from our two days of conversation in Austin (where Jaeger was working for the local diocese) almost thirty single-spaced, typewritten notes. Throughout, he insisted that full credit for getting the Fundamental Agreement done be given to Archbishop Andrea Cordero Lanza di Montezemolo, who had led the Vatican negotiating team, and Monsignor Luigi Gatti, the Secretariat of State's expert on the Middle East. But Fr. Jaeger also made it clear that the key man in pushing this forward was John Paul II: "No one else would have had the courage to do it." It was also clear that, at several key moments, Jaeger's back-channel work with Israeli diplomats cleared out logjams created by ignorance, bureaucratic sluggishness, and political nervousness on both sides.

The story of this epic achievement turned out to be the longest single section in *Witness to Hope*. It was a story worth telling at length because it illustrated John Paul II's vision, tenacity, and patience in pursuing something that he knew would bend the history of Catholic-Jewish relations in the direction he was convinced the Lord of history wanted. At the same time, it nicely illustrated the human passions, fears, and prejudices that made what might have seemed a simple matter a complex business indeed.

Back in Sync in Poland

WHEN WE WERE FIRST DISCUSSING THE LOGISTICS OF MY PROJECT, Joaquín Navarro-Valls told me never to travel with the press party on a papal trip. "We're in a tunnel," he said, and it was better to be with the people experiencing the visit to get a feel for these events. It was good advice that proved itself in the summer of 1997.

The 1997 papal pilgrimage to Poland went far better than its 1991 predecessor, in part because the country's mood had changed and in perhaps greater part because my friend Fr. Maciej Zięba helped shape the themes of the visit and the Pope's texts. Their collaboration meant that the Pope was in far better sync with the situation than had been the case six years before and could speak accordingly, to the enthusiastic response of his audiences.

I got some follow-up interviewing done during the maelstrom of the papal visit, but my fondest memories of those days revolve around two bits of fun, sandwiched around something astonishing.

On my April visit, I had left behind in Fr. Zięba's office a magnum of W. L. Weller Special Reserve, to which I attached a Post-it note: "NOT TO BE OPENED UNTIL JUNE 4, 1997." With unhappy memories of a dry Warsaw during the 1991 papal visit, I didn't want to get caught in an officially decreed desert again. My prudence had good journalistic results, for on Saturday, June 7, I got a call from Celestine Bohlen, the *New York Times* bureau chief in Rome and a friend. Celestine had just arrived in Kraków and wanted to get together; she also asked, "Where can you get a drink in this place?" I invited her to meet me at Fr. Zięba's office that evening for a little Kentucky succor, after which we would have dinner with several Dominicans who could fill her in on the local scene. We had a delightful time; the gallant Dominican moral theologian Wojciech Giertych escorted Celestine back to her hotel after our dinner (all the more convivial because my Dominican friends convinced the proprietors of the restaurant that the intention of the law would be honored if they served us wine in teapots); and Celestine wrote a terrific story about the next day's canonization of the fourteenth-century Polish queen Jadwiga.

That canonization was the astonishment. Fr. Zięba had secured seats for us near the platform from which John Paul II would celebrate the canonization Mass on the Błonia Krakowskie, the vast Kraków Commons—Europe's only in-city meadow, created in the Middle Ages and preserved as a meadow ever since. With all vehicular traffic in the city banned until after the Mass, we left the Dominican priory at 7 a.m. to walk—along with over a million others—to the venue. The Mass was wonderful, a unique experience of 1.2 million people falling completely silent at the same time, when the Pope preached and during the consecration of the Eucharist. Perhaps even more amazing was the sight of those vast throngs, dressed in formal religious garb or regional folk costumes, walking through Kraków to the Błonia. In my entire Catholic life, which was not without colorful scenes, I'd never seen anything more vibrant and vivid than what I saw during that hour-long morning walk across the city, amid what seemed a Slavic foretaste of the Wedding Fast of the Lamb in Revelation 21.

That evening, Krzysztof Zanussi's film of *Our God's Brother*, Karol Wojtyła's play featuring "Crypto-Lenin" in contest with St. Albert Chmielowski, premiered at the Słowacki Theater in the Kraków Old Town: a grand old building modeled on the Paris opera house, from which the author of what was about to be shown had been banned during the German occupation, like all other Poles. For some reason I had been given a premium seat in the orchestra and found myself in the midst of the papal party. Immediately to my right was Archbishop Giovanni Battista Re, who seemed to remember me and asked what I was doing in town. "Working," I replied, and then tried to interest him, without much success, in some of what I had learned before the papal pilgrimage reached Kraków. Forty-five minutes later, I felt a head on my right shoulder. It was the high-energy *Sostituto*, fast asleep. I left Archbishop Re in peace, thinking my forbearance might later help me get the documents to which he was blocking my access. Alas, that tactic didn't work.

Camels for Daughters?

I RETURNED TO KRAKÓW IN JULY 1997 FOR THE ANNUAL *CENTESIMUS Annus* seminar, and when I wasn't teaching I continued my interviews with the local Wojtyła experts, making two new acquaintances who helped me get inside my subject.

One evening, I drove over to Wadowice with Msgr. Tim Dolan, in town visiting the seminar, to talk with the pastor of Karol Wojtyła's parish church, Father Kazimierz Suder. In addition to giving me a copy of the parish registry page on which the significant events of Wojtyła's life, from baptism to papal election, were inscribed, Fr. Suder told me some interesting tales of young Karol Wojtyła and the local priests who had influenced him, not least in shaping his profound respect for Jews and Judaism. Then I met with Maria Ćwikła, the younger sister of Rhapsodic Theater impresario Miecyzsław Kotlarczyk, who lived briefly with Wojtyła and the Kotlarczyks during the war. Having known the house at Tyniecka 10, she sketched for me the layout of the "catacombs," the basement apartment in which Wojtyła and his father lived and in which the latter died in 1941: a helpful recollection, as the apartment was not open to the public in 1997. Her memories of the rehearsals and recitals that constantly took place in the "catacombs" gave me a sense of the atmosphere of fearlessness that surrounded Karol Wojtyła even then.

The following month I went to Paris and stayed with my old friend Jean Duchesne and his family for World Youth Day 1997. I had met Jean, who did a lot of work with Cardinal Jean-Marie Lustiger of Paris, the year after my Wilson Center sabbatical: Lustiger was in Washington, Jim Billington set up a meeting for him in the Smithsonian Castle, and I was invited for coffee and conversation. Duchesne and I hit it off immediately and stayed in touch over the years on various projects.

His large apartment in the Auteuil neighborhood was part of a complex owned by his wife's family, which included the flats in which the families of two of Jean's old friends, the distinguished philosophers Rémi Brague and Jean-Luc Marion, also lived. The three men were part of Cardinal Lustiger's cultural surround, so it was all conversation, all the time, in an environment that combined serious Catholic faith with cutting-edge intellectual life and a lot of fun, each of these scholarly gentlemen being a devotee of the cartoon character Tintin, whose adventures they insisted I read.

My daughters Gwyneth and Monica were part of the Washington pilgrimage group to World Youth Day, so after the papal opening ceremony on the Champs de Mars, we met at a designated leg of the Eiffel Tower and went to a restaurant near the Duchesnes' apartment for dinner. We must have run into Rémi Brague that evening; a few days later, this world-renowned scholar of (among many other things) Islamic philosophy and law asked me over lunch, "How many camels do you wish for your daughters?"

The papal Mass closing World Youth Day 1997 was held at the Longchamp Racecourse, into which a half million souls packed themselves. Later that afternoon, Jean Duchesne and I drove to his family's country house in the Norman village of Nonancourt to relax after a very busy week. We turned on the evening news, and there was our friend, the cardinal, speaking with an obviously stunned anchorman, who couldn't believe that so many young people were passionate about the Church. Lustiger was in a robust, even combative mood. You shouldn't read these young people through your own experience, he told the anchorman. You abandoned the faith of your fathers and think of that as something mature and superior. These young people have discovered Jesus Christ and want to explore all that that means. They don't think that being Christian and being intelligent, engaged, and compassionate are mutually exclusive. Don't put them down for that.

At which point, we opened another bottle of champagne.

Polonia on the Potomac

M Y RESEARCH ON THE POLAND THAT SHAPED KAROL WOJTYŁA— and his role in helping liberate his native land—wasn't conducted solely along the banks of the Vistula. It also took place along the Potomac littoral, in conversation with two native-born Poles who had led dramatic lives, were longtime residents of Washington, DC, and taught me important things about John Paul II and the darker recesses of world politics.

Zbigniew Brzezinski's first response to my request to get together for my biography project set the tone for our future discussions: he said that he was glad I was doing the book because others hadn't gotten the story right—by which he meant the attempts by several authors to suggest some sort of collusion between John Paul II and the United States government in the collapse of European communism. John Paul, he insisted, had a "long-range and more detached view" than the conspiracy theorists imagined.

Zbig had first met the future pope in 1976 when Cardinal Wojtyła lectured at a Harvard summer school, where Brzezinski found him a man of "calm strength" and "intelligence." They shared the view that communism was not just evil but corrupt and inefficient, and thus doomed to fall eventually. And both were convinced, as Zbig put it, that communism's disintegration could be "accelerated" by a cultural resistance: one that, by emphasizing human dignity, would provide an alternative to the brutal, but also hopeless, project of creating New Soviet Man.

Unpacking this, we got into a discussion of Agostino Casaroli and his *Ostpolitik*. Casaroli, as Zbig understood him, thought that a "normalization" of Church-state relations behind the iron curtain would set a foundation for some measure of social pluralism and religious freedom. John Paul II had a different view. For him, Brzezinski said, "'normalization' was a part of . . . should I call it 'destabilization'? Well, perhaps not. A tool for transformation." Casaroli, like the German Social Democratic leader Willy Brandt, believed in a politics of "convergence" between East and West during which the geopolitical status quo—a divided Europe—would not change but would be made more "palatable." John Paul II, by contrast, thought that making the status quo more palatable by creating zones of freedom in communist-dominated countries was a tool for undermining things-as-they-were.

My most striking conversation with Zbig was about the Solidarity crisis of December 1980, when the Soviet Union was poised to invade Poland and strangle the nascent "independent, self-governing trade union" in its cradle. It was an intriguing tale of cooperation between the outgoing Carter administration and the about-to-be-inaugurated Reagan administration, in which various levers of hard and soft power were deployed to cause Brezhnev's Kremlin to think again and then back off. In the course of this discussion, Brzezinski repeated the famous story of his calling John Paul at the height of the crisis, briefing him, asking for the Pope's private number in case of emergency—and then hearing John Paul whisper to Stanisław Dziwisz, "Do I have a private phone number?"

Brzezinski did not wear piety on his sleeve, but he never thought of himself as anything other than a Catholic, and a Polish Catholic at that. Moreover, his intellectual work recognized the role that religious and moral conviction play in world politics in a way that challenged the secularist bias often found in international political analysis. Thus I wasn't surprised to learn that Zbig, who had great respect for John Paul as a shrewd political analyst and operator, was most touched by the depth of the Pope's spiritual life. After Brzezinski left government, he was in Rome and attended a papal audience. John Paul, spotting him, pulled him aside and asked quietly, "Can you stay for lunch?" Dziwisz got him up to the papal apartment on the family elevator, and as the former national security adviser was walking to the dining room he passed the chapel and saw the Pope kneeling there, his head bowed to the floor in prayer. "It wasn't a trance or an ecstasy," he said, "but a sense of a man in profound conversation with God."

The most extraordinary figure in the Washington Polonia was a man far less well known to the general public but a legend in the anticommunist community, which in those days included both liberals and conservatives: Jan Nowak.

Born in 1914, Zdzisław Antoni Jeziorański was doing doctoral studies in economics when World War II broke out. After escaping a German POW compound, he joined the Polish underground in Warsaw and was given the nom de guerre he retained for the rest of his life: Jan Nowak, the Polish equivalent of "John Smith." He smuggled crucial information for the Polish government-in-exile out of occupied Poland on hair-raising missions to Sweden and London, where he briefed Winston Churchill. He got back to Warsaw in July 1944, just in time for the Warsaw Uprising, during which he married Jadwiga Wolska—whom Washington would later get to know, during the fifty-five years of their marriage, by her code name, "Greta." When the Uprising collapsed under a torrent of Wehrmacht artillery shells and Luftwaffe bombs, Jan and Greta escaped through the sewers with precious film records of the gallant attempt by the Polish Home Army to take back Poland's national capital, made their way to London via Germany, Switzerland, and France—and didn't return to Poland for more than four decades.

Jan ran the Polish service of Radio Free Europe for years; on meeting him, John Paul II told Jan that he recognized his voice as that of the man he had listened to (illegally) while shaving in the morning. Jan also worked with the National Security Council during both the Carter and Reagan administrations and was widely respected across the partisan divides of political Washington as a man of integrity, courage, discretion, and sound judgment. When we began discussing my biographical project in May 1998, he began exactly where Zbig Brzezinski had begun in February 1997: with a critique of other papal biographies, whose major mistake had been to "make John Paul II into a political pope." John Paul had no "program" for the overthrow of communism, Jan insisted; he thought of himself as a pastor, and in pursuing that vocation he made an important contribution to the communist crack-up.

Jan also shed light on one of the most intriguing characters in the drama of Poland's self-liberation, Colonel Ryszard Kukliński, a Polish army officer so revolted by the Warsaw Pact invasion of Czechoslovakia in 1968 that he became an American intelligence asset in 1972. Thanks to Kukliński, American officials knew the details of the Soviet invasion plan for December 1980 (including their plans to execute the Solidarity leadership after summary courts-martial) and were able to respond in the ways Brzezinski had described. In Jan's view, Zbig and the heroic Polish colonel "saved Poland from invasion—I am sure of it."

Jan told me that John Paul II was thoroughly briefed on Kukliński and his clandestine role because President Reagan had ordered that the Pope be told "everything," both information and sources. Kukliński was finally exfiltrated from Poland with his family in 1981 after his cover was blown; both his sons died in strange circumstances while the family was living in the Washington area. When the question of Kukliński's return to Poland after the fall of communism became controversial, some claiming that he had violated his officer's oath, John Paul II quietly put the word around that Ryszard Kukliński should be welcomed back to Poland as a national hero. (Zbigniew Brzezinski, for his part, described Kukliński as "the first Polish officer in NATO.")

Jan was also full of insight into the martial law imposition in December 1981, which he thought entirely the doing of Wojciech Jaruzelski. Everything the Soviets did after the thwarted invasion of December 1980, he argued, was "bluff." They wanted Jaruzelski and the Poles to do the dirty work; Jaruzelski, for his part, wanted a small Soviet military contingent to come into Poland right after martial law to provide him with cover ("See, I had to do it or they would have invaded . . . "); the Soviets, knowing the game, refused. Jaruzelski, Jan insisted, lied in the 1990s about what he did in December 1981 and why, but he was not a traitor in that he didn't liquidate the Solidarity leadership, as both the Soviets and Polish communist hard-liners would have done.

As for Karol Wojtyła's role in sowing the seeds that eventually grew into the Solidarity movement, Jan suggested that it was primarily a matter of changing the Church: that when Wojtyła changed the focus of Catholic anticommunist polemic from defending the rights of believers to defending everyone (including dissident Marxists), the possibility emerged of creating a Solidarity-like coalition across the usual ideological and class divides.

Jan confirmed my hunch that the appointment of Józef Glemp as Cardinal Stefan Wyszyński's successor was done at Wyszynski's urging, and suggested that the relationship between Warsaw and the papal apartment was not nearly as warm and cordial as it had been when the old primate was alive. And, like just about everyone else, Jan believed that the trail backwards from the assassination attempt of May 13, 1981, eventually led to Moscow, the Lubyanka, the KGB, and Yuri Andropov.

Literary Architecture

O N MY RETURN FROM PARIS IN AUGUST 1997 I CALLED MY FRIEND Father Jay Scott Newman at Divine Redeemer Catholic Church in Hanahan, South Carolina, near Charleston: might I stay with him for a week while I decided how to structure *Witness to Hope*? The amount of material I had gathered was threatening to become overwhelming, so it seemed the right time, and Fr. Newman's rectory the right place, to erect a framework on which the book could be built. Ever the gracious Southern gentleman, Fr. Newman replied that his guest room was at my disposal for as long as I liked.

The biggest structural problem in designing *Witness to Hope* was to figure out how to insert discussions of Karol Wojtyła's thought and John Paul II's magisterium into the narrative without bogging down the story. When I finished wrestling with this problem at Fr. Newman's, I had an outline of some 125 pages, into which I inserted references—to books, articles, or interview notes—so that when it came to writing, I wasn't juggling masses of paper trying to find what I was looking for.

Books in progress are like children: a book has a kind of mind of its own, and it will push back against an author. No matter how well planned, at some point or another the book is going to want to go *that* way and the author is going to say, "No, we're going *this* way." There was one such tug of war when it came to writing *Witness to Hope*, involving where to insert a discussion of Wojtyła's philosophical work. Other than that, the long outline I completed during that week in South Carolina stood me in good stead over the next year of intense writing.

Mother Teresa of Calcutta died a week before I got to Hanahan, and the Princess of Wales died five days after the foundress of the Missionaries of Charity. As Fr. Newman and I watched the evening news, we couldn't help but notice the sharp contrast between how the world was reacting to the deaths of these two widely admired women, icons of different facets of the late twentieth century. Mother Teresa's death was generally handled as it should have been, even by secular people skeptical about consecrated religious life: here was a saint, whether you believed in sanctity in the Catholic Church's terms (heroic virtue made possible by grace) or the world's terms (manifest decency and compassion). The contrast with the British reaction to Diana's death was shattering. As I said to Fr. Newman when we were watching one TV news report of the semihysterical crowds outside Buckingham Palace, it wasn't a pretty picture to see "an entire country having a nervous breakdown." What on earth was going on? The subject would shortly recur at the papal board.

"Who Eez Bob DEE-lahn?"

ROME, SEPTEMBER 1997

On Saturday evening, September 27, 1997, John Paul II went by helicopter to Bologna to close an Italian national Eucharistic Congress. Some imaginative soul in the Italian bishops' conference had decided that Bob Dylan should be the setup act for the Pope. It seemed strange but perhaps interesting, so I planted myself in front of the television in the North American College faculty lounge and waited.

And there he was, Dylan himself, floppy hat, guitar, and harmonica, coming on stage. I can't remember how many songs he did—three or four—but he did them in that inimitable voice and then closed with "Blowin' in the Wind." Dylan left; John Paul came on stage and, discarding his prepared text, gave a wonderful impromptu talk about the Holy Spirit blowing in the wind of the last decade of the twentieth century and preparing the Church for the Great Jubilee of 2000. The man, I said to myself later that night, has *game*.

The following Tuesday, I was up in the papal apartment for lunch and work. The Pope said grace, sat down, fixed me with that look across the table, and began the proceedings by asking, "Who eez Bob DEE-lahn?" To the everlasting aggravation of my daughter Monica, a great Dylan fan, I replied, "Holy Father, think of him as someone whose songs always sound better when someone else sings them." Then we got into more serious matters.

We talked at some length about Mother Teresa. John Paul said that her death had "left us all a little orphaned" and that, as Albert Chmielowski had been God's brother, Mother Teresa had been the "sister of God." I mentioned that Joan had been baptized in the same church in Calcutta where the diminutive nun had been laid out, and

John Paul reminisced a bit about visiting her first Calcutta shelter. A few days later, the prime minister of India had said to the Pope, "You must come and visit India again," at which point Msgr. Dziwisz, who, as usual, had gotten more puckish as the meal went on, said, "Perché no?" (Why not?) Which, as intended, elicited a roll of the papal eyes, a gentle self-smack on the papal forehead, and a muttered, "Dio mio!" Bishop Ryłko said, with the Pope nodding agreement, that Mother Teresa had been a "person-message" for our time and that she had embodied many of the great themes of the pontificate: pro-life, pro-family, concern for the poor, concern for women, human rights. Dziwisz, back in a more serious vein, said that John Paul and Mother Teresa had a kind of mutual or reciprocal understanding "*senza parole*" (without words), while the Pope recalled that every time they met, "she always said the same thing: 'I have started a house in Russia, I have started a house in China,'" etc., etc. Her materially impoverished life was in sharp contrast to that of the Princess of Wales, although John Paul, ever the pastor, remarked thoughtfully on how Mother Teresa seemed to be a positive influence on Diana, who clearly admired the foundress of the Missionaries of Charity.

We talked briefly about the upcoming award of the title Doctor of the Church to St. Thérèse of Lisieux, which the Pope thought "fit well" with the recent World Youth Day in Paris, of which she had been one of the co-patrons; earlier in the conversation he said that the very idea of World Youth Days "had its origins in my Środowisko." Then he switched gears and said that he had been "talking directly with Cardinal Ratzinger" about the long-delayed beatification cause of John Henry Newman, for whom he said he had a "great respect." I asked him what in Newman drew his admiration and he replied that Newman had "opened new horizons" for the Church's intellectual life.

We talked about my recent conversations with Środowisko, and I mentioned that Piotr Malecki, whom the Pope remembered as "my first altar boy when I went to the parish of St. Florian," had referred to himself as the "enfant terrible" of the group. John Paul chuckled and said, "I think not so *terrible*." When I told him that Danuta Rybicka said that she heard her husband's voice, as it were, at several moments in Wojtyła's play *The Jeweler's Shop*, John Paul admitted it was true, that he took situations "that only those present at the time could recognize" and wove them into his drama. My mention of Maria Kotlarcyk Ćwikła led the Pope into a reminiscence about the Rhapsodic Theater. He spoke of all those in the original group and, when he came to Danuta Michałowska, said, "She is a great artist," then confirmed that Miss Michałowska had performed her play *I Without Name* in the parlor where I had been before lunch.

The Pope asked whether I had yet spoken with Jerzy Turowicz and Marek Skwarnicki and when I replied that I had, several times, he said that these two colleagues at *Tygodnik Powszechny* were "the only two who understood" his poetry. I asked, "And Sister Emilia?" Dziwisz broke in again "Si, anche Emilia" (Yes, Emilia too). The Pope, chuckling at Dziwisz, said, "She has been very helpful to me," and I said that Dziwisz was the real enfant terrible in the papal surround, which led to more chaffing in various directions. I left with John Paul saying that he hoped to see me soon, "at the next interrogation."

"Are You *Proud* to Be an American?"

A Synod for America was meeting in Rome in late November 1997, which seemed a good opportunity to discuss the Pope and the pontificate with bishops from throughout the Western Hemisphere. I got a lot of useful interviewing done in the interstices of the Synod and spoke with several key Italian political figures about John Paul II, but only after solving an urgent personal problem.

John Paul nominated my close friend Father Richard Neuhaus as a Synod member; Richard and I were staying in small guest rooms on the top floor of the North American College, and as I should have expected, Richard was quickly getting bored. He was accustomed to the fast pace of his professional and pastoral life in New York; he was used to being the center of the action and conversation in any world in which he found himself; and here he was, the absolutely last name on the roster of Synod members, compelled to sit through hours of tedious ecclesiastical rhetoric, muffled—and to what purpose?

So by the third or fourth night of the Synod, with Richard keeping me up to all hours while complaining about what a waste of time the whole exercise was, our decades-long friendship was becoming seriously strained. Then the light bulb came on and I interrupted one of his disquisitions on the futility of it all with a suggestion: "Why don't you write a book about all this?" He immediately perked up and started scribbling some notes, which was my signal to escape. The book, *Appointment in Rome*, aggravated Cardinal Jan Schotte, the Synod General Secretary, by its criticism of Synod process, and Schotte wrote Richard to share his pain. The very same day Schotte's minatory letter arrived in New York, Richard got a letter from the Pope about the book; John Paul II had loved it, and Richard enjoyed enclosing a copy of the Pope's congratulatory letter in his response to Cardinal Schotte.

During the last week of the Synod I took an overnight train to Vienna to talk with its archbishop emeritus, Cardinal Franz König, and the incumbent archbishop, Christoph Schönborn, OP, who was instrumental in preparing the *Catechism of the Catholic Church* under the direction of Cardinal Ratzinger.

Cardinal König was one of the Great Electors at the second conclave of 1978, and perhaps the key man in advancing the candidacy of Karol Wojtyła when the chief Italian candidates, Cardinals Giuseppe Siri and Giovanni Benelli, deadlocked. The cardinal was a spry ninety-two when we met in his apartment on the top floor of a retirement home run by the Daughters of Charity. He had gotten to know Karol Wojtyła during Vatican II, he said, and in those days, the Viennese cardinal had found him "intelligent," "modest," and "interesting for three reasons": he spoke German well and was committed to Polish-German reconciliation; he presented his ideas clearly ("This is a clever boy"); he was from behind the iron curtain and yet thought his part of Europe was as much "Europe" as the West.

König's esteem for Wojtyła must have grown, for a day or two before Conclave II in 1978 opened, König said to his old friend, Cardinal Stefan Wyszyński, "Who is your candidate?" The Polish primate replied, "I don't know, I don't really know anyone, I don't have a candidate." To which König replied, "Well, perhaps Poland could present a candidate?" Wyszyński snorted, "You think I should go to Rome? That would be a triumph for the communists . . . " Then, when the Austrian replied, "No, not you, but there is a second . . . " Wyszyński dismissed the idea out of hand: "No, he's too young, he's unknown, he could never be pope."

After Wojtyła was elected, König walked out for the presentation of the new pontiff with Cardinal Pericle Felici, the senior cardinal deacon who would announce the new pope from the central loggia of St. Peter's. "How do you spell the name?" the Italian cardinal asked König. After König had spelled it out for him, the veteran curialist muttered, "What a terrible spelling."

Cardinal König had other interesting things to say about the conclaves of 1978. He had, for example, received letters from Italians toward the end of Pope Paul's pontificate, asking him to help elect a non-Italian "because we are in such a mess here in Italy and would like to have a non-Italian pope." But the Italian cardinals at Conclave I in 1978 brushed aside the notion of a non-Italian pontiff, saying "Look, we know this situation better; we've done this for centuries; we know how to do it." The cardinal laughed at this last recollection and noted that John Paul II's "impression on the international level [had been] enormous"—and that he was listened to much more in the US than in Western Europe.

We got into a polite tussle over Paul VI's encyclical on marital chastity, *Humanae Vitae*, the cardinal saying that its teaching ought to be understood as a matter of "guidelines" from which "personal conscience" would make decisions: Did I agree? I said that the encyclical, coming in 1968, couldn't have happened at a worse time; the cardinal agreed. I then said that John Paul II's Theology of the Body had given the teaching a more humanistic foundation than *Humanae Vitae* had provided; and the cardinal agreed with that. Then I said that, had *Humanae Vitae* been complemented by something like a recent Vatican instruction for confessors, which urged sensitivity and compassion in dealing with the challenges of chaste conjugal life, the encyclical might have had a better reception; and König agreed with that, too. Finally, I said that John Paul II had "gotten the Church over St. Augustine in matters of human sexuality," such that the Church's teaching about human love could be "heard" now in cultural circumstances in which a lot of people had been hurt by the sexual revolution; and the cardinal said, at least in respect of overcoming Augustine, "There is no doubt about that." What struck me in all this, though, was that this very senior churchman, who was at the center of global Catholic affairs from the Vatican II through the mid-1980s, seemed genuinely surprised by my suggestions, as if he'd never heard such a presentation before.

After another interesting exchange about German theology and its possibly harmful impact on pastoral life, which the cardinal was "ashamed to [say] is not . . . good," König took me downstairs and hailed me a cab. We never met again, but I've thought many times of something he said at the end of our two-hour conversation: "If the question of God means nothing to people, if the question of Jesus Christ disappears, this is a great decline . . . this is terrible."

Archbishop Schönborn was a bit late for our meeting, so while I was waiting I studied the portraits of his predecessors in a parlor and noticed that one of them was a Doctor of the Church, St. Peter Canisius. When the Dominican Schönborn came in to greet me, I said I hadn't know there was a *Doctor Ecclesiae* among the bishops of Vienna and "maybe there will now be a second"; he quickly replied that the Jesuit Canisius "was only apostolic administrator for a little while."

Perhaps the most interesting part of our conversation on the *Catechism* was his description of how it challenged the contemporary cultural situation. Modern intellectual life says that we have no real link to historical sources and our origins; the *Catechism* says that "the origins are present in a living way, because the fountain, Christ, is present" in the Church. Contemporary culture says that plurality is absolute; the *Catechism* speaks "in a very convinced way" about the unity of faith through time and space—"the Church speaks with one mouth, from one heart." Late modernity is convinced that there is "your truth" and "my truth" but nothing properly called "the truth"; the *Catechism* says that "truth is necessary food for the human soul," that "we die without truth." And the culture tells us that intellectual life is ineluctably incoherent—that the various bits and pieces of the human experience can't be fitted together—while the *Catechism* "solemnly and joyfully confesses the coherence of faith." The archbishop also found it interesting that only the Catholic Church thought it important to say, on the threshold of the third millennium of Christian history, "Here is what we believe, here is how we worship, here is how we think we should live," and in a comprehensive, coherent way. Thus a project that had begun in 1985 in an attempt to stop the bleeding in postconciliar catechetics turned out to be a unique, millennial confession of faith and a robust challenge to the shibboleths of a late modernity heading toward the intellectual quicksand of postmodernity.

Archbishop Schönborn thought that the grave difficulties of Catholicism in the German-speaking world had a lot to do with his fellow academics. The German-speaking professoriate seemed determined to stand outside the Church and judge its doctrine from an "external [intellectual] standpoint." But, Schönborn said, "this is not Christian. We are called, we have received a vocation, but we have not received a universal understanding." Christ is not Archimedes: "Belonging to Christ, we understand—but it is his understanding we 'put on,' not ours." The "deep difficulty of the German-speaking world is to surrender, intellectually and emotionally, and to bow the knee of the intellect before revelation." The archbishop then said, a little sheepishly, "Maybe this is too Freudian," to which I could only reply, "Well, we *are* in Vienna."

The day I got back to Rome from the Austrian capital, Msgr. Dziwisz called with an invitation to lunch the following day. After I'd arrived and absorbed some good-natured chaff from the papal secretary, John Paul came in at 1:40. After we shook hands he poked me with his cane, saying, "The Synod for America is over—are you *proud* to be an American?" Laughing, the five of us—John Paul, Dziwisz, Bishop Ryłko, the newly promoted Monsignor Mokrzycki, and me—walked into the dining room for *risotto con funghi porcini* and veal cutlets, followed by a sesame seed tart that the Pope, true to form, ate to the very last crumb.

John Paul asked how my project was going and I told him that the "architecture"—the outline—was done and I would get down to writing after Christmas. As we discussed my conversations in Vienna, I got the impression that the Pope was quite concerned about the Catholic situation in the German-speaking world. Then we got back to working through the memorandum of questions with which we'd begun more than a year ago.

There was the question of Padre Pio and the story that, when young Father Wojtyła had gone to confession to him, the Franciscan stigmatic and thaumaturge had told him that he would become pope. I asked the Pope whether he had ever met Padre Pio, and he said, "Yes, I met him when I was a student here in Rome, in 1947. I found him a very simple man. I went to confession to him. He was a very simple confessor: clear and brief. But my greatest impression of him was at Mass. He had the stigmata, you know, and he physically suffered at Mass." Nothing was said about any predictions, and the Pope's description of Padre Pio the confessor as "clear and brief" seemed to tell against the legends.

I had wanted to get some things straightened out about John Paul's interactions with longtime Soviet foreign minister Andrei Gromyko, as several of my predecessor biographers had written things that didn't seem quite right. So I asked John Paul point-blank whether he had raised the question of religious freedom in the USSR with Gromyko at their first meeting, and if so, what was Gromyko's response. There was no hesitation: "Of course, I raised it the first time—and every time. I saw him three times, and each time I spoke about religious freedom and the liberty of the Church. The first time he said that he was a deputy from Byelorussia and knew how full the churches were there"—meaning that this consummate liar was, in effect, asking the Pope what he was making such a fuss about. "The last time I saw Mr. Gromyko he was very worried about the American Strategic Defense Initiative; he was looking for the Church's help against the United States." Which, of course, he didn't get. I then recounted the old saw about why the dour Gromyko never smiled: he had been told by Stalin in 1933 that smiling was counterrevolutionary and was still waiting for the order to be rescinded.

Gorbachev, he said, was "of a new generation. . . . He thought that perestroika could save the Soviet Union. . . . He wanted to save communism 'with a human face'"—a metamorphosis and goal that the author of *Centesimus Annus*, with its sharp analysis of the anthropological root of communism's failure, obviously thought doomed because it was a contradiction in terms.

I then switched to the beatifications and canonizations that were a hallmark of the pontificate: why? After speaking of John Henry Newman as someone "who merits being a Doctor of the Church," he said he was simply following the teaching of the Second Vatican Council on "the universal vocation to sanctity." As for the beatifications of the martyrs of the Spanish Civil War and the Cristero Rebellion in Mexico, which Paul VI had put on hold so as not to ruffle political feathers, John Paul was crisp and to the point: "I am convinced that this century needs a new martyrology. There are so many martyrs because of the Nazis, the communists . . . " Dziwisz added, "And Mexico," and I said that the martyrdom of Father Miguel Pro, SJ, during the Cristero revolt may have been the first in Christian history of which we have a photo of the martyr at the moment of death, as Fr. Pro, dressed in his civilian "disguise," exclaimed "Viva Cristo Rey!" (Long live Christ the King!) as the firing squad's bullets hit him. The Pope seemed to find the notion intriguing.

This led to a discussion of Edith Stein, whom the Pope would canonize the following year as a martyr. She was, John Paul said, "a paradigmatic figure": in her period of doubt, she embodied the twentieth-century crisis of faith; her work with Husserl was part of the turn to new philosophical methods; she was an early feminist; and she was a modern martyr. As we talked about her, it seemed that the Pope was determined to make the Church understand that we were living through the greatest period of martyrdom in Christian history, which ought to have a positive effect on the living Church rediscovering its vocation to mission. Bishop Ryłko suggested that I pray to Edith Stein to get the book done.

We talked a bit about his work with old Cardinal Tomášek in Prague and his admiration for Václav Havel, and then turned farther east. I noted that the Pope had made a generous offer to Orthodoxy in the 1995 encyclical *Ut Unum Sint* (That They May Be One): that Eastern Christians not in full communion with Rome help him think through an exercise in papal primacy that could serve them, too. Yet there had been consistent problems since, especially with Russian Orthodoxy. "They're not so easy to work with," the Pope replied—and then suggested that I get in touch with Mrs. Irina Alberti, his personal envoy to Russia and Russians. I promised I would and the Pope kept pressing the point: "That's a very big chapter—Russia, Orthodoxy." I asked him whether he had read Vladimir Soloviev and he said that he had, confirming my sense that Karol Wojtyła and Soloviev had a lot in common: spiritually, intellectually, and in their sense that the future of a world threatened by militant secularisms depended on the reestablishment of full communion between Catholicism and Orthodoxy.

An inquiry about Aleksandr Solzhenitsyn, whom the Pope said he'd met "once or twice," started a free-for-all between Dziwisz and Ryłko about the relative merits of Solzhenitsyn's novels, with both finally agreeing that *Cancer Ward* was the best of them. I suggested that *One Day in the Life of Ivan Denisovich* ought to be read by every high school student in the world and the 264th Bishop of Rome agreed.

Two days later, Msgr. Dziwisz gave me a behind-the-scenes tour of the papal apartment. John Paul, who cared nothing for his physical surroundings, had changed "very little" since moving into the apartment, Dziwisz said. The Pope's formal office had only one photograph, of Cardinal Sapieha. There was an image of Our Lady of Guadalupe on his desk, presumably because of the recent Synod for America; the desk itself faced a large icon of the Black Madonna. The Pope's bedroom was similarly spare, and the only photo in it was a small, simply framed portrait of his parents, taken shortly after their wedding. The small table on which that photo was displayed also had several large photo books of nature scenes; Dziwisz said John Paul like to look through books like these, I expect because they fired his poet's imagination. On the back wall was a map of the Diocese of Rome, indicating all its parishes; the ones the Pope had visited were marked with a pin.

I was then taken up to the solarium on the roof of the Apostolic Palace, built by Paul VI and constructed in such a way that tourists in the square below can't see anyone walking up there on a sunny day. John Paul had added a modern set of Stations of the Cross, which he prayed every Friday and every day during Lent, when weather permitted. The view was quite fantastic and on a clear day the Pope could look out to the Castelli Romani and see Castel Gandolfo.

THE ISLAND PRISON

O N JANUARY 2, 1998, I WENT TO MASS AT MY PARISH, HAD A QUICK breakfast, sat down at the desk my wife had designed for easy access to my working materials, said a brief prayer—and began writing.

I'd been much impressed with the narrative drive of Edmund Morris's book *The Rise of Theodore Roosevelt* and wanted my biography to begin with the kind of gripping prologue Morris had written. So I began with a story from the long dark night of occupation in Kraków, briefly summarized the drama of Karol Wojtyła's life and what could seem the paradoxes in it, and then laid down the book's basic assertion: John Paul II, a radically converted Christian disciple, could only be understood from inside the convictions that were the source of his personality, his thought, and his action.

It was good to be actually writing after a year and a half of research. Two and a half weeks later, however, I abandoned my desk for eight days in Cuba with John Paul II.

Getting there was not entirely easy. I had an anti-Castro paper trail behind me and there were some problems with my visa until it was quietly explained to the Cuban authorities that blocking the Pope's biographer from entering the country would not set a good tone for the papal pilgrimage. With that resolved, I flew to Havana from New York with the group accompanying Cardinal John O'Connor, which included such other friends as Mario Paredes, the Chilean-born director of the Northeast Hispanic Catholic Center; Fr. Richard Neuhaus; and my former vice president at the Ethics and Public Policy Center, Robert Royal. We got to the Cuban capital in the early evening of January 20, where there was one instructive moment. Mario Paredes waited until the rest of our group had gotten through immigration so that he could handle any problems that might arise. Then he went through, carrying a large case. The Cuban official couldn't recognize what was in it from the X-ray, so he asked Mario to open the case. Inside was a large gold chalice that Cardinal O'Connor intended to leave in Cuba as a gift for the Church there. The Cuban official, thinking it a trophy, asked what soccer team it had been awarded to.

The next morning, Neuhaus, Paredes, Royal, and I walked through Old Havana, which showed the telltale signs of communist economic catastrophe: government office windows held together by duct tape; streets and sidewalks crumbling; pharmacy shelves bereft of even aspirin. There was an array of American cars from the late 1950s, which inventive Cubans kept running by cannibalizing parts from other cars that had fallen to pieces. But if you subtracted the old DeSotos and Dodges and added some bottles of aspirin to the pharmacy shelves, it wasn't entirely unlike some of the rougher patches of Warsaw in 1991. What was appalling about Havana was the ubiquity of crude, cartoonish propaganda, displayed on innumerable billboards and posters, most of which mocked the awful *Yanquis*. The ne plus ultra of this juvenile idiocy was the Museum of the Revolution; its most obscene object was the burlap bag in which Che Guevara had been carried through the Bolivian jungle after his execution, displayed in obvious imitation of the Shroud of Turin.

The Pope arrived that afternoon and went to Santa Clara the following day; the detail from that Mass for families came later in the evening from another old friend, Luis Lugo, who had been born in the city and once played baseball on the field where the Pope celebrated Mass. While Luis was revisiting his childhood haunts, Fr. Neuhaus, Father Robert Sirico, Mario Paredes, and I went to lunch at La Terraza de Cojimar, a Hemingway hangout near the cove where Papa's old man set off for the sea. A creaky black-and-white TV in the restaurant was showing the conclusion of the papal Mass in Santa Clara when we arrived. The proprietor heard the four of us speaking English, came over, and asked whether we were in Cuba for the papal visit. We said that we were and he began weeping. He had tried to hold his family together as Catholics for almost forty years of communism; to hear the Pope preaching in Cuba about the importance of the family made it all seem worthwhile, and he just had to tell people he thought would understand.

Later that afternoon, I went to the Miramar neighborhood where my parents spent their honeymoon in 1949 and found the house in which they stayed, which in those days belonged to the family of a cousin of my mother's who had married a Cuban; the family later lost everything in the Revolution and came to Baltimore. When I showed my Cuban-American cousins a photo of the building after I returned to the US, they barely recognized it for the decay.

At 5 a.m. the next morning, I left for the airport to fly with Cardinal O'Connor and two dozen or so others to Camagüey, in central Cuba, where the Pope was celebrating the visit's designated Mass for young people. A generous benefactor from Buffalo had arranged for the cardinal to use what was called a "Cuban executive jet." It was no Gulfstream, however, but a Russian junker known as a Yak-40. The door into the passenger compartment didn't close flush with the fuselage; the bulkheads were made of linoleum; the seats were wretched, even by airline standards; half my seat belt came off in my hand when I tried to fasten it. But it got us to Camagüey, where Mass would be held at a sports complex fronting onto a vast open field a fifteen-minute bus ride from the airport.

There was a jury-rigged sacristy near the large raised platform on which the Pope would celebrate Mass, and I found myself carried in there with the cardinals, bishops, and priests in our group. It was a hot day with a high sun, so I had the honor of anointing the head of my archbishop and friend, Cardinal James Hickey, with suntan lotion before he joined the procession of clergy forming up before Mass. I was hanging out with Jerry Costello, Cardinal O'Connor's guardian, who was taking personal time off from the New York Police Department, and I suggested to Jerry that we work our way to the front of the Mass platform (which featured concrete bas-reliefs of El Jefe in his trademark fatigue hat) so we could watch both the Pope and the crowd during Mass.

The roar when the Pope arrived was deafening, with some of the youngsters chanting, "Juan Pablo, amigo, take Fidel back with you!"

The Mass and papal homily were moving and all seemed to be going well—until I got separated from Jerry Costello in the chaotic scrum after Mass and couldn't get back to the makeshift sacristy, where I was to meet the rest of the O'Connor party to be bused back to the airport for our return flight to Havana. After forty-five minutes I was getting nervous, so I decided to start walking back down the dusty and barely paved road toward the airport, figuring that someone would notice I was missing and turn the bus around to fetch me. I had gotten about a mile down the road when up over a small rise and heading towards me came the Popemobile, with John Paul and Msgr. Dziwisz in the back. They drove right past, pointing at me and laughing. Several weeks later, in Rome, I said, "Thanks for the ride in Camagüey."

My absence from the bus was eventually noticed and I made it back to Havana on the Yak-40, only to get up at 4:30 the next morning for a flight with Cardinal O'Connor and his guests across the entire island prison to Santiago de Cuba in Oriente Province: the romantic heart of the Castro cult. There, for the first time in almost forty years, the small statue of Our Lady of Charity of El Cobre, Cuba's national icon, would be publicly venerated. It was a three-hour-plus flight, and when we got to the outdoor venue for the Mass, the Caribbean sun was even hotter than it had been the day before in Camagüey.

The Mass venue was hard by a memorial to the Castro revolution composed of gargantuan steel beams thrust into the ground at weird angles, reminding me of the "asparagus" that Erwin Rommel planted all over Omaha Beach to obstruct the D-Day landings. Mario Paredes and I decided to watch the Mass from a building a hundred yards or so away from the papal altar; the half-finished structure had a veranda and some shade. There we heard the courageous Archbishop of Santiago, Pedro Meurice Estiù, welcome John Paul with an address that severely criticized the Castro regime's assault on religious freedom. Raúl Castro was sitting in the front row of the congregation, arms crossed and scowling; later that evening, I heard, the electricity in Archbishop Meurice's residence mysteriously cut out and the house was electricity-free for several days. After Mass, the statue of Our Lady of Charity was processed around the site on the back of a pickup truck, to the enthusiastic response of a huge crowd.

Then more trouble began.

When the O'Connor party arrived at the airport, we were told that our flight back to Havana would be delayed for hours because the Cuban government had decreed that no planes could be allowed in Cuban airspace while the papal plane was in the air. This was an obvious lie, as we could see planes taking off and landing while we stewed in the un–air conditioned airport. What had happened? It wouldn't have surprised me if the regime, seriously put off by Arch-bishop Meurice's denunciation of Fidel but unable to retaliate against the Pope, decided to stick it to the Americans by holding us in Santi-ago for a good long time. The former US Navy admiral John Joseph O'Connor was not amused, and as the hours wore on it was not hard to envision steam emanating from his ears.

When they finally decided to let us go, I walked out of the fetid air-port with Cardinal Hickey. We were chatting about nothing in partic-ular when a Cuban security official stepped in front of our party and said, "Gentlemen, would you please stand against that wall there for a moment?" As we lined up, Hickey, not previously known for rapierlike wit, stage-whispered to me, "Could I please have a written statement that I'm about to be shot *in odium fidei* [in hatred of the faith]? It'll simplify the beatification process."

One more story from those days should be told here. On the night of the Mass in Camagüey, I was sitting in the hotel bar with some American colleagues, rehashing the day and sharing intelligence about the politics of the visit and the bailout of most American journalists, stampeding back to Washington to cover what they expected would be the resignation of President Clinton because of the Lewinsky affair. The hotel was one of those five-star monsters built for conscience-light tourists who didn't mind vacationing in an apartheid society far more rigidly segregated between rich foreigners and poor locals than Jo-hannesburg ever was between whites and blacks. Clumsily disguised "bellboys"—Cuban internal security goons—were everywhere, mak-ing sure that the proper apartheid distance was being maintained and that we weren't slipping dollars to the waiters (which we did anyway).

Then, in walked an American cardinal with a gang of youngsters he had just met at a local church trailing behind him. The cardinal invited them into the bar for a Coke and, as they were a choir, asked them to sing. Their beautiful, clear voices got everyone's attention and I asked the cardinal what was going on. "I met them in their church," he answered, "and asked them to come here and sing about the real revolution—the revolution of Jesus Christ."

The cardinal wasn't through yet. As the ferrets watched, speechless, he took these twenty kids up the escalators to one of the hotel's posh restaurants and stood them to a dinner the likes of which none of them had ever seen before, walking up and down the buffet and explaining to these impoverished youngsters in fluent Spanish what each dish was. After they had eaten the cardinal encouraged them to sing again and sat nearby so that the security types wouldn't interfere. Everything in the restaurant simply stopped, as guests, staff, and goons were serenaded for perhaps twenty minutes by songs about the love of Christ.

In the middle of this impromptu concert I went over to where the cardinal was sitting and whispered, "I doubt that this is accurate theologically, but I think you've performed a kind of exorcism here tonight." He smiled and we shook hands, knowing that we were living a very special moment

The cardinal was Bernard Francis Law of Boston. What he did that night—working a small miracle of evangelical love—is another part of his legacy that deserves to be remembered.

"What Are You Doing Here? You Are Not from Milwaukee . . ."

In July 1997, Msgr. James Harvey was named Assessor for Or-dinary Affairs in the Secretariat of State—the first American to hold the third-ranking position at the top tier of the Vatican bureau-cratic pyramid and a kind of chief of staff to the papal chief of staff, the *Sostituto*. Harvey was not to stay assessor for long, though. In Feb-ruary 1998 John Paul II decided to rearrange the senior papal staff to get some order into the preparations for the Great Jubilee of 2000, and in that reshuffle, Harvey was named Prefect of the Papal Household, to manage the Pope's entire public schedule along with a new *Prefetto Aggiunto*, or "adjunct prefect," Stanisław Dziwisz. Both Harvey and Dziwisz were named bishops, as was Piero Marini, the Master of Pon-tifical Liturgical Ceremonies.

Their ordinations were set for March 19, and while I was writing furiously and making good progress, I wasn't going to miss the epis-copal consecration of one of my closest friends. So I made a quick trip to Rome, squeezing in some follow-up interviewing before and after the ordination. What I hadn't anticipated was that the three ordinands would each choose one person to be a lector at the ordination Mass and that Harvey would choose me. At the rehearsal the day before, a rather supercilious and quite short junior master of ceremonies asked me whether I would "read in English or American." I looked down and gave him what my children used to call "the look," which ended that line of inquiry. At the end of the walk-through, he asked me whether I would sing the *Verbum Domini* (The Word of the Lord) at the end of the reading or whether a Sistine Choir cantor should intone it. Old choirboy that I was, I said I'd take care of it—and then spent fifteen minutes practicing on the roof of the North American College that evening.

Before Mass began, I went over to the choir and said to the director, twice, and in Italian, "I'll sing the *Verbum Domini*." When the moment came for my reading from 2 Samuel, I was brought up to the portable ambo then used in St. Peter's by Monsignor William Millea, a Connecticut priest and one of the other assistant emcees. Coming in front of the Pope, who was seated before the altar, we made a deep bow. When I looked up, there was John Paul II waving at me—and the same thought probably ran through several thousand Italian minds: "Chi è quel laico?" (Who's that layman?). The reading went fine. But I hadn't gotten a half second into intoning the *Verbum Domini* when the wretched Sistine Choir cantor cut in—and I just kept going. Bill Millea, escorting me back to my seat, muttered, "Nice stereo."

The next day the Pope was meeting guests of the three new bishops and Bishop Harvey invited me to join his family and friends from Milwaukee. I tried to decline, saying that I saw the Pope frequently and his friends ought not have an interloper when they had their chance, but he insisted. The audience was in the Sala Clementina and I put myself at the end of the queue. When I finally got to the Pope, John Paul looked at me, put on a mock-stern expression, and said, "What are you doing here? You are not from Milwaukee. You should be home writing." He then laughed and I said, "Be not afraid: I've got four chapters done."

"Joan or Gwyneth?"

ROME, APRIL 1998

M Y OLDER DAUGHTER, GWYNETH, WAS DOING HER UNIVERSITY OF Dallas Rome semester in the spring of 1998, and as she and I were both going to be there for Holy Week and Easter week, it seemed a good time to bring the rest of the family over. On the morning of April 7, I was having breakfast in the North American College faculty dining room before leaving with the librarian, Sister Rebecca Abel, OSB, to pick up Joan, Monica, and Stephen at Fiumicino. Then the phone rang and Msgr. Tim Dolan went to the small alcove between the dining room and the faculty lounge—the famous Red Room—to take the call. Dolan is the only person I've ever known who can make me laugh at breakfast, but on this particular morning, he administered a shock rather than a joke to jolt me into full consciousness. "That was Marini's office," he said when he got back to the table. "They need an English-speaking woman to read at the Pope's Easter Sunday Mass. So who's it going to be—Joan or Gwyneth?" I said I thought Gwyneth might have other opportunities, so let's make it Joan.

She was a bit surprised to get the news later that day, but Joan handled the assignment with aplomb—no easy business, as the Mass was outdoors on the Sagrato, the platform in front of St. Peter's, which was a lot harder venue in which to read than the basilica itself. It began raining lightly toward the end of Mass and the five of us huddled under raincoats and umbrellas as the lengthy queue of cardinals, bishops, monsignori, and lower clergy lined up to process back into the basilica. Bishop Dziwisz, ever alert, spotted me and gave me a wave, meaning "Follow us." So the tail end of the procession that day was *la famiglia* Weigel, slightly bedraggled from the rain and a bit late because we had to rescue Monica from a plainclothes Vatican policeman who didn't understand that she was with us.

Inside St. Peter's, the Pope had unvested in the chapel of the *Pietà,* which became a makeshift sacristy during outdoor papal Masses. After greeting and thanking the altar servers and others, he came up to the five of us, still clad in rain gear. Everyone got a papal hug and kiss, with no chaffing this time about "What are you doing here?"

That Holy Week and Easter week were full of unforgettable moments in addition to that very familial session with John Paul: eleven-year-old Stephen falling asleep onto a restaurant tabletop; Msgr. Dolan completing the fastest celebration of the Easter Vigil in the history of the Roman Rite, with cigars and bourbon to follow; Christopher Nalty, then a New Orleans seminarian, inadvertently putting a post-Lenten champagne cork through a window of the pediatric hospital beside the North American College; Bishop Harvey giving the five Weigels the Sistine Chapel to ourselves for an hour, including a visit to the "Room of Tears," where newly elected popes first don papal garments. But there was also work to be done, and while the family did some touring, I spent more than four hours with another member of his informal papal family whom John Paul II insisted I meet.

"He Is a Source of Light"

IRINA ILOVAYSKAYA ALBERTI WAS THE DAUGHTER OF RUSSIAN émigré parents who fled the country after the Bolshevik Revolution. She was raised in Yugoslavia, where she met her future husband, an Italian diplomat; separated during World War II, they married in Rome in 1946. Her husband died in 1975, at which point Aleksandr Solzhenitsyn asked her to come to Cavendish, Vermont, as a personal and family assistant. With her own children grown, she accepted the offer and spent four years with the Solzhenitsyns in the Green Mountain State.

On October 16, 1978, she was doing some shopping for the family in a drugstore owned by Polish-Americans when the news came over the radio of Karol Wotyła's election as pope—"It was a madhouse" of celebration, she recalled. When she got back to the Solzhenitsyn farm, they turned on the news to verify the story, and when it was clear that Wojtyła was in fact pope, the Nobel laureate threw his arms out and said, "It's a miracle! It's the first positive event since World War I and it's going to change the face of the world!" Why did the great author think that, I asked Mrs. Alberti? Because, she answered, while he didn't know Wojtyła, Solzhenitsyn knew what the election *meant*: resistance to communism would now be rooted in religion and culture, which were the strongest forces in the world.

After she moved back to Europe, a Polish friend arranged for Irina Alberti to be in the first row of a papal general audience in 1983 or thereabouts. She and John Paul spoke briefly, and the Pope was "very friendly and interested." Mrs. Alberti said she felt "a great emotion" at this Pole's love for Russia, for "Poles hate Russians and they're right" to

do so. Yet here was a man who was interested in her ancestral homeland, "not only in a scholarly way but in a human and spiritual way."

The next encounter came when another Nobel laureate, Andrei
Sakharov, was on hunger strike in Gorky, trying to force the Soviet authorities to let his wife, Elena Bonner, leave the country for heart surgery.
Elena Bonner and Irina Alberti were old friends, and when Bonner's
children came to Rome as part of the international agitation on their
mother's behalf, Mrs. Alberti flew to Rome from Paris, where she was
then living, and got them in to see John Paul. Despite fretting in the Secretariat of State about a public "confrontation" with the Soviets, the Pope
immediately agreed to see the Bonner children, spoke with them for ten
minutes with Mrs. Alberti translating, and promised to keep working
on the case. As the papal managers whisked John Paul away, he turned
back to Irina Alberti and said, "Come and see me the next time you're in
Rome." "How?" she asked. "Talk to my secretary," the Pope replied.

That seemed a bit unusual, but her French confessor said she
should just call the Vatican and ask for Msgr. Dziwisz. A meeting at
Castel Gandolfo was arranged for the summer of 1985; there, they had
a long conversation about conditions in the USSR, about the new Gorbachev government, and about the situation of Christian communities
in the Soviet Union. At the end of the meeting, John Paul invited her to
get in touch when she next returned to Rome.

When Elena Bonner was finally allowed to leave the USSR for
medical treatment, Irina Alberti arranged for her to meet the Pope in
an "absolutely secret and private" meeting. One condition for Bonner's
getting a passport was that she wouldn't meet with public figures, and
Sakharov, back in the USSR, was a hostage to her good behavior. So
Mrs. Alberti and Mrs. Bonner sandbagged the world media into following the Bonner children while the two women snuck into the Vatican. Elena Bonner spent two hours with John Paul in an extensive
discussion of life in the USSR. The Pope listened carefully while showing Bonner a lot of personal kindness. When this very tough dissident
came out of the meeting she was sobbing: "He's the most incredible
man I've ever met. He's all light. He is a source of light."

There was another two-hour meeting, some time later, with both
Sakharov and Bonner; assistants kept trying to interrupt and pull the

Pope away, but he insisted on staying with his two guests. Sakharov was then being wooed by Mikhail Gorbachev to stand for election to the Supreme Soviet and didn't like the idea; he thought Gorbachev was still a communist who believed in reform communism, and Sakharov didn't. The whole matter was weighing heavily on him, and Elena Bonner said, "This may be the only place in the world where you can ask the question that's been tormenting you." So Sakharov explained his dilemma and asked John Paul, "By getting into this game, am I directing it onto a better course, or will I be compromised?" It was, Mrs. Alberti said, a form of going to confession—something new for Andrei Sakharov. The Pope thought awhile and replied, "You have a strong and clear conscience. You can be sure you won't make mistakes. . . . I think you can be of use." And the greatest of Soviet dissidents took the Pope's advice and "got into the game."

Sakharov, Mrs. Alberti said, was "a theist unsure of his relationship to God." When the great physicist and human rights champion died, the Pope sent a "beautiful telegram" to Elena Bonner over the objections of the Secretariat of State—Sakharov was a private person, he wasn't a Catholic, it will make things more difficult, etc., etc. John Paul just went ahead and sent it. Mrs. Bonner was invited to a Mass in the Pope's private chapel after her husband's death and once again came out crying and saying to Irina Alberti, "He is a source of light."

The Pope's burning desire to reach out to Russia and the Russians manifested itself in his intense interest in the celebrations being planned for the millennium of the baptism of Rus' in 1988. He was "never judgmental," Mrs. Alberti said, about what she called "the greatest mistake in history," the Russian Church's adhesion to Constantinople after the latter's split with Rome in 1054; rather, he knew the immense spiritual power of Orthodoxy. But he also knew the Soviet government was "playing games" with the 1988 millennium, proposing one or two big public events for elites with no media coverage—and thus no effect on the general population. By proclaiming all over the world that the Catholic Church was going to celebrate this great moment in Christian and Russian history, John Paul effectively took that option off the table for the Soviets. And thus the great irony: the Pope whom Russian Orthodox Patriarch Pimen (a KGB lackey) said was "unwelcome" in

Moscow in June 1988 was the one who compelled the regime to acknowledge the baptism of Rus' as a great historical moment.

Mrs. Alberti also remarked that many curial officials were surprised by the Russian Orthodox leadership's negativity toward the possibility of a papal visit to Moscow for the 1988 millennium, thinking they had a good relationship with Russian Orthodoxy. But as Mrs. Alberti noted, all these curial Russophiles ever did was "give in to [Russian] demands," so there was no incentive for the Orthodoxy to be anything but difficult.

Irina Alberti was not sanguine about the near-term future of Russian Orthodoxy. Its leadership did not share John Paul's view that the pursuit of Christian unity is a Christian's duty before God. The Pope, for his part, understood the ROC leadership's tendency to think of everything in terms of power; but it was a completely asymmetrical relationship, she said, because they "simply don't get" what the Pope said about the religious obligation of ecumenism in *Ut Unum Sint*.

When we met, Mrs. Alberti was going to Russia every month for ten days or so; if she learned "anything interesting," she let John Paul know. She obviously knew the Pope's mind well and told me that, while there were differences between Karol Wojtyła and Aleksandr Solzhenitsyn—for John Paul, World War I meant the beginning of free Poland, while for Solzhenitsyn it meant the end of free Russia—they shared a Slavic view of spiritual power in history: God is Lord of history, which means that spiritual and moral values are historically decisive. She spoke knowledgeably about the Pope's regard for Vladimir Soloviev and told me that John Paul had read deeply, in French or Polish translations, in the works of exiled or émigré Russian Orthodox thinkers, including Nikolai Berdyaev, Sergei Bulgakov, Semyon Frank, Pavel Florensky, and Georges Florovsky. These men, some of them converts from Marxism to Christianity, had helped him understand "what is Russia" and "what it could give the world," which was "more than the evil of communism."

Irina Alberti was already concerned about a renascent Russian "messianism," in which an Orthodox/nationalist ideology would serve as the replacement ideology for communism. But this was of no interest to the mass of Russian people; it was a political phenomenon, she thought, an ideological justification for reestablishing a Russian-dominated empire. (She told me this, I now remind myself, when Vladimir Putin was Deputy Mayor of St. Petersburg, an unknown figure outside certain intelligence circles.)

She had "no doubts" that the KGB concocted the assassination attempt of May 13, 1981, and convinced the Soviet politburo to buy into it. Thus there was no Henry II / Thomas Becket scenario, with Leonid Brezhnev saying, in effect, "Will no one rid me of this troublesome priest?" The instigator was Yuri Andropov, the Bulgarians were the instrument for running Mehmet Ali Agca, and strong political pressures might have caused the Italian government to cut short its investigation. As for John Paul, who obviously thought Satan had a hand in the affair, what did he think? "I think he *knows*," she said—not in the sense that he had evidence that could stand up in a court, but that he *knew* who Satan's likely agents were.

She was also quite clear-eyed about the Russian politics of Vatican statecraft and ecumenism, locating the trouble, not only in the diplomatically genteel Secretariat of State but in the Pontifical Council for Promoting Christian Unity, where the French bishop Pierre Duprey had set the Russophile default positions decades ago. He was "an appeaser" in communist times and "he is an appeaser now," she told me, insisting that this pusillanimity (or whatever it was) had done serious harm to Russian Orthodoxy.

She was not uncritical about the Pope she revered and with whom she shared a Slavic-mystical sense of the dynamics of politics and history. She didn't share John Paul's view of Gorbachev as "providential," saying that the Pope couldn't get completely "outside" his Polishness politically, even though he had done so culturally and spiritually. Thus John Paul thought of Gorbachev as the man who allowed Poland its freedom in 1989, while she believed Gorbachev had no choice. But that analytic difference was minor compared to the depth of understanding between this remarkable woman and the Pope she served as an informal secret agent.

I was completely taken with Irina Alberti, a woman of high intelligence, deep faith, shrewdness, and historical insight who had obviously gotten the signal from John Paul and Msgr. Dziwisz to tell me everything. I was also aware that Mrs. Alberti raised hackles in various Vatican offices, but I gave full marks to John Paul II for ignoring the clerical jealousy while keeping her close as a trusted source of information on Russian affairs.

"You Are Getting Grey"

T HE FINAL PUSH TO COMPLETE *WITNESS TO HOPE* TOOK ME TO
both Poland and Rome twice in the last half of 1998. There were
loose ends to tie up and further questions to get answered. As things
turned out, what later seemed to me some of the most interesting
things in the book were the product of these four working trips.

My friendship with Piotr and Teresa Malecki had deepened over
the course of several Środowisko interviews, and while I was in Kraków
in July for the 1998 *Centesimus Annus* seminar, they invited me to their
flat for dinner. They told a few more Wujek stories from their rich
trove of memories, and the Maleckis agreed to set up a Środowisko
meeting for me in November to discuss the relationship of the women
in the group to Wojtyła's *Love and Responsibility*. That convivial dinner brought a new character into the Wojtyła drama: the great Polish composer Henryk Mikolaj Górecki, whose Third Symphony—the
"Symphony of Sorrowful Songs"—had become a surprise bestseller in
the West.

Teresa was Vice Dean of the Kraków Academy of Music and had
met Górecki after the Third Symphony, which seemed to sum up the
Polish experience of late modernity, made him a national musical
hero. To mark the nine hundredth anniversary of the martyrdom of
St. Stanisław, at which the archdiocese would conclude the Synod he
called to implement Vatican II, Cardinal Karol Wojtyła commissioned
Górecki to write a piece of his choosing. Then Wojtyła was elected
pope, and Górecki called the Maleckis that night. He was "completely
crazy," Teresa remembered, saying that he had intended to write a piece
for St. Stanisław, but now he had to write a piece for the Holy Father, so

he had to come to Kraków from his base in Katowice, meet the people, sense the atmosphere, etc., etc. Teresa got him invited to an upcoming academic conference at the Academy of Music and Górecki went around the city "absorbing atmosphere." The Maleckis later invited him to their apartment to hear stories of the papal inaugural Mass in Rome from Piotr's sister and her husband. Piotr also loaned Górecki the Latin-Polish daily missal that Father Karol Wojtyła had given him years ago, so that the composer could find texts for his composition: Górecki chose several psalm fragments, taking the title of the work from Psalm 34.8: *Beatus vir (qui sperat in eo)* (Blessed is the man [who trusts in Him]).

Górecki kept working on the composition until the very end, getting up at all hours of the night in the Maleckis' apartment to try harmonies on the piano. Then he had to rehearse the piece with the Kraków Philharmonic during the Cracovian portion of the Nine Days of June 1979; the woodwinds interrupted the rehearsals by rushing to the windows to play "Sto Lat" (May you live a hundred years) to John Paul whenever the Popemobile drove by. *Beatus Vir* was finally premiered in the Basilica of St. Francis, where Karol Wojtyła had prayed the Stations of Cross regularly, on June 9, 1979. Górecki conducted, and after the performance, with tears running down his cheeks, he walked to the back of the church to greet John Paul. Three days after the papal visit, he returned to Katowice, where communist repression was harsher than in Kraków—and was continually hassled by the regime until the changes in 1989.

The Maleckis had spent some time in Castel Gandolfo the previous summer; every morning they could hear the Pope, a floor above, pounding about with his cane. He asked them at breakfast one day whether he was disturbing them, and they said no, they were getting up for Mass anyway, but "why do you get up so early, Wujek?" Because, he said, "I like to watch the sun rise" over Lake Albano.

And there it was, wholly unexpectedly: the perfect last sentence for *Witness to Hope.*

After two weeks of vacation with my family and Fr. Neuhaus at his cottage on the Ottawa River, during which Richard gave me some very helpful editorial advice about my ever-growing manuscript, I was back at the desk in mid-August and stayed there through September, leaving for Rome on October 2. I had been adopted by the Class of 1999 at the North American College and wanted to attend their diaconate ordination on October 8—three days before the canonization of Edith Stein, where John Paul preached one of his greatest homilies. I continued my interviewing, filling in various gaps, and attended the Mass for the twentieth anniversary of John Paul II's pontificate (which coincided with his fortieth anniversary as a bishop) on October 18. Two further meetings with Fr. Tadeusz Styczeń, in Rome for the anniversaries, clarified a few loose ends about the Pope's Lublin period and philosophical projects.

Msgr. Dziwisz called on Friday morning, October 23, and asked me to come to the papal apartment for dinner at 7:40 that evening. I was taken up on the family elevator and, after a few minutes of chat with Msgr. Mokrzycki in one of the apartment parlors, John Paul II came in, looking tired but in good spirits, and when I congratulated him on his double anniversary, he mused wistfully, "Twenty years the pope . . . forty years as bishop . . . " When we sat down at the table, I told him that I had written something a little short of two thousand double-spaced pages since January, to which he replied, eyebrows raised, "Due mille? Mein Gott! Mein Gott!" I said that it was all his doing, as he'd been rather busy for seventy-eight years; he then looked across the table and informed me, "You are getting grey."

After suggesting that he might have had something to do with that, I asked him about the reform of conclave procedures that he'd introduced two years before in the apostolic constitution *Universi Dominici Gregis* (The Shepherd of the Lord's Whole Flock). He said he'd consulted several canon lawyers about it, and those conversations convinced him to make the changes he did: proscribing election by inspiration (a cardinal proclaims that he believes God has chosen X as pope and a two-thirds majority vocally agree—the method of election in the novel *The Shoes of the Fisherman*) and election by delegation (two-thirds of the cardinals agree on a committee and agree to abide by its choice), and, perhaps most controversially, permitting election by a simple majority after dozens of ballots had failed to produce a two-thirds majority. The latter provision, I suggested, would help prevent an intransigent minority from blocking the election of a clear favorite who fell just short of two-thirds, and the Pope seemed to agree. Dziwisz interjected that a conclave couldn't be understood on the analogy of democratic politics, and the Pope vocally agreed. As for election by inspiration and delegation, those seemed to John Paul a diminution of the moral responsibility of each cardinal-elector, and as he had long taught the human capacity for moral responsibility, I imagine he thought eliminating those options was compatible with the approach to moral decision-making he had developed in *Veritatis Splendor,* his encyclical on the reform of moral theology, and in his Theology of the Body.

The Pope asked about the reaction to his most recent encyclical, *Fides et Ratio,* in the United States. When I said that his friends had framed their presentation of it in terms of its continuity with the very beginning of the pontificate—the twentieth anniversary of "Be not afraid!" had been marked with "Be not afraid of the truth"—John Paul agreed that *Fides et Ratio* was "in a line of continuity with *Redemptor Hominis,*" his first encyclical (and the first ever) on Christian humanism, which he had begun writing "right after I was elected." That remark strengthened my conviction that *Redemptor Hominis* was deliberately crafted as the "program notes" for the entire pontificate.

Back in Poland, I had a conversation with Bohdan Cywiński, a former Solidarity leader turned professor, to clarify some points about John Paul II's role during the martial law period in Poland. Fr. Maciej Zięba, an old comrade of Cywiński's from the heyday of Solidarity, arranged a meeting at the Dominican priory in Warsaw's Old Town on November 14.

As I suspected, another papal biographer who had tried to portray the pope as a new Gandhi vastly overplayed John Paul's role as the alleged mastermind of the "Solidarity underground," with St. Martin's Church in Warsaw acting as a clandestine supply depot for contraband snuck into Poland from the Vatican. Cywiński had been in Rome when martial law was declared and met with the Pope several times in the week immediately following the clampdown, trying to analyze the situation with what little information they had. But the question of an underground railroad, or anything else about "what to do," didn't come up, Cywiński said; the Pope had been "shocked" by martial law, communication with Poland was cut off, and their entire discussion was an exchange of driblets of sparse information, plus some talk about what Cywiński, the senior Solidarity leader outside the country, should do—stay in Rome or return to Poland?

During the martial law period, the Pope was not involved with clandestine relief shipments to Poland, which primarily involved food, clothing, medicine, and ink and spare parts for copiers—some of which did go through St. Martin's. As for the idea that there was some secret, Vatican-run financial conspiracy behind this, that was "nonsense," Cywińksi said; Solidarity *wanted* the world to know it had financial support from the West. Cywiński's summary: "One thing is positive and certain—the Pope had nothing to do with this. If he had, it would have happened through me, and I made sure he wasn't dragged into it."

Bohdan Cywiński was full of interesting comments on personalities and events: Cardinal Wyszyński had been "a little slow to grasp what was going on" with Solidarity; Solidarity itself had underestimated Polish communism's staying power; the 1983 papal visit during martial law was a big risk for the Pope (who might have been manipulated by the regime), but he played his part spectacularly well, "restored hope," and denied General Jaruzelski even a modest victory; Cardinal Józef Glemp, Wyszyński's dour successor, was a shrewder tactician than was generally appreciated; Poland was still burdened by the fact that it was "first" in 1989, when no one knew that Gorbachev had no cards left to play and fear of a possible Soviet intervention led to a power-sharing agreement between Solidarity and the communists. All of which raised interesting questions about the Church and strategies of "dialogue" with dictators; but with a book to finish, there was no time to pursue those questions further.

In Kraków that month, I finally met the other surviving member of the original Rhapsodic Theater, Halina Kwiatkowska, who as a schoolgirl in Wadowice had bested Karol Wojtyła in a poetry-reading contest. Her husband was seriously ill but she kindly received me in her apartment on November 8, and we talked of the war and what the Rhapsodists tried to do to resist the decapitation of Polish culture.

Interestingly enough, she used the same word to describe Mieczysław Kotlarczyk's devotion to his dramatic ideas—"fanatic"—as Danuta Michałowska the year before. The young Kotlarczyk, she told me, was a "striking-looking man, almost Greek: sharp, penetrating eyes; an expressive mouth and hands; very black hair." Curiously, "he didn't have a colorful voice." Yet he could make them hear afresh things they all knew by heart, like the first sections of the national epic poem *Pan Tadeusz*, because he articulated them in an "absolutely distinctive" way.

Karol Wojtyła, she said, would play a role "from inside the character," with each repetition becoming "more ascetic and deeper," and in this sense he was "very mature" as an actor—the opposite of those who strove for "external effects." When I brought up that high school poetry-reading contest, she laughed and said the Pope still chaffed her about it, waving a finger and saying "You beat me!"

When I speculated that their culture-based resistance to the occupation might have been the seed from which John Paul's "culture-first" strategy of resisting evil and forcing historical change had grown, and that Kotlarczyk's theater of the "living word" reflected the Christian notion that the Word, incarnate, drives history, she "fully" agreed and told me that there were echoes of both themes in letters from Wojtyła to Kotlarczyk in 1939–40.

As for Wojtyła's decision to become a clandestine seminarian and his friends' reaction to that, she said it was a "complicated business, because everyone thought he would be an actor, but we also knew his piety and devotion"—so they "understood it."

She was an impressive personality, and despite being obviously drained by her husband's condition, there were moments when I could see flashes of the highly successful actress she had been—in her expression and articulation, and in the way she spoke with her hands.

On Teresa Malecka's advice, I had written four of the women who had been among the earliest members of Środowisko, asking that we meet on my last research trip to Poland to talk about their relationship to Wojtyła's book *Love and Responsibility*. Teresa warned me that Poles didn't talk easily of these matters, so when we met in the Maleckis' apartment on the night of November 9, I began by saying that I wanted to dispel the myth of John Paul II, misogynist, and to challenge the feminist critique that the Pope didn't understand or empathize with women. None of these women had encountered the harder forms of Western feminism, but they were all well read, most were professionals, and their unanimous reaction to the suggestion that Wujek was somehow anti-woman was astonishment: Teresa Heydel Życzkowska said, "I can't understand it," and Teresa Malecka, who had probably had the most contact with Western feminism, said, "It's completely crazy."

There didn't seem much point in pursuing that discussion further. But as I began to try and steer the conversation toward *Love and Responsibility*, Teresa Życzkowska altered the course of the evening by opening a leather satchel containing dozens of letters and notes she had received from Wojtyła over the years. She then plucked out several of these, and we spent the next ninety minutes or so deciphering Wojtyła's spidery handwriting and translating these remarkable notes, with Paweł Malecki, the youngest of Piotr and Teresa's three sons, doing the heavy translational lifting.

After some further translation-polishing by Rodger Potocki and his wife, Magda, I was able to insert all three of these previously unknown letters at appropriate points in the almost-completed manuscript of *Witness to Hope*. They illustrated the warmth, openness, and candor of Karol Wojtyła, spiritual director and friend, in a unique way. In one of the letters, from 1956, Wojtyła was reflecting on marriage and said that those who thought Wujek wanted to see all his young friends married were wrong. What was important was love: "Everyone lives above all for love. The ability to love authentically, not great intellectual capacity, constitutes the deepest part of a personality. . . . Authentic love leads us outside ourselves in affirming others, devoting oneself to the cause of man, to people, and above all, to God. Marriage makes sense, above all, if it gives one the opportunity for such love."

When Paweł Malecki finished reading out the translation, each of the woman present said this was exactly how Wujek would have talked with a man. There was no difference in how he talked with women. Love, he thought, was a human problem, not a "man or woman problem."

The letters that didn't quite fit the book were nevertheless revealing. They weren't ethereal: Wojtyła the correspondent always remained in touch with the quotidian, asking for someone's children, sharing a couple's happiness at finally getting an apartment amid the chronic housing shortage in communist-era Poland. Thus his counsel, which he didn't hesitate to share with these close friends, was always "informed by reality," as Teresa Malecka put it.

He was constantly on the alert for ways to show kindnesses. Danuta Rybicka wrote him after her first childbirth, complaining that she was still confined to bed. He wrote back in a letter "so in touch with my feelings that my own father couldn't have written it" more intimately. When Teresa Malecka's mother was ill, the first instinct of the cardinal archbishop of Kraków was to say, "I'll come to the house and say Mass"; it was Christmastime, and his gesture of friendship enabled the family to have something of a real Christmas celebration, with tea and cakes following the Mass.

I was deeply touched by Teresa Życzkowska's willingness to share her letters and notes, which even her close Środowisko friends hadn't seen before. The topics—her emotional life, finding a husband and then learning to live a good marriage, coping with children—were not the easiest to discuss. There were moments when we were reading the letters that the emotion started coming to the surface, even after forty years. That she was willing to do this with someone she had only met once before, in order to straighten out a misimpression of Wujek that this smart and feisty woman thought completely ridiculous, said a lot about her—and about him.

In Rome on December 15, Joaquín Navarro-Valls called to say we were dining with the Pope that evening. I brought along the Christmas greetings that Monica's and Stephen's classes had written; one of Stephen's classmates also made a two-foot-tall Styrofoam model pope, which I was to deliver to the real Pope. All of these were laid out on a table in the parlor where Navarro and I waited for John Paul, who came in, enjoyed the cards, raised an amused eyebrow at the Styrofoam pope, and walked us into the dining room.

We talked again about the possibility of his having a Carmelite vocation, and I was surprised to see that, when the Pope started talking about his debt to Jan Tyranowski, both Dziwisz and Navarro seemed to find this news. When John Paul said that Archbishop Sapieha had told him during the war, when he inquired about the Carmelites, "First you must finish what you started," Dziwisz muttered, semi–sotto voce, "A *good* bishop . . . "

Lutheran theologian George Lindbeck had sent me a story from *Hasidic Tales of the Holocaust* that claimed that young Father Wojtyła declined to baptize a small Jewish orphan until it could be determined whether the youngster had living relatives who wanted to adopt the child and give it a Jewish upbringing. "It's a legend," the Pope replied, and one he'd evidently heard before. "I simply don't remember doing it." There was no suggestion that his having done such a thing would have been out of character; it would have been entirely in character. "But I cannot remember such an incident."

There was still a bit of detritus to clean up from earlier biographical projects, so I pressed the Pope about an alleged March 1981 meeting with the Soviet ambassador to Italy, during a very tense period with Solidarity in Poland. Previous biographers had made a fuss over this; it sounded fishy to me; the Pope had said in a previous conversation that he didn't remember any such meeting; and I wanted to nail the point down. Dziwisz left the table, came back a few minutes later with a large leather-bound desk diary, carefully went through every entry for March 1981, and said, "There was no such meeting." I replied that there must have been some disinformation at work, into which my predecessor biographers had been trapped, and everyone agreed.

Then I said to Dziwisz, "What is *that*?" He said, "Oh, I have one of these for every year of the pontificate." So a question I first posed in September 1996, over dinner at Castel Gandolfo, was answered. I had told the Pope then that I would like to see any memoranda of conversations he had dictated after meeting with Gromyko and other such people. "I don't do those," he replied. What he did do, evidently, was get together with Dziwisz every night, and the two of them went over every meeting of the day, on or off the official calendar, noting in those diaries themes discussed and important points; the diaries were kept for future reference in the papal apartment. Why? Because, I surmised, they knew the Vatican had been seriously penetrated by Soviet-bloc intelligence services, and they didn't want any paper on sensitive matters to be filed in the Secretariat of State, where it might be accessible to hands with malign intentions.

Laden with Christmas presents, I left the papal apartment after a big hug from John Paul II, pondering the fact that this mystically inclined poet who believed that everyone lived for love also had a firm grip on the realities of human weakness, including the weaknesses, and worse, in his own bureaucratic surround.

IMPEACHMENT INTERVENES

B Y 1998, I HAD BEEN DRAFTING SPEECHES FOR CONGRESSMAN Henry Hyde for fourteen years. I couldn't possibly have imagined when we met that one day I would be writing texts for Henry that would help set the moral framework for an impeachment inquiry against the President of the United States in the Judiciary Committee of the House of Representatives, or later in the House's debate over articles of impeachment, or still later in the president's trial before the Senate. Still less could I have imagined doing all of that while writing and editing the biography of John Paul II. But that is what happened between the summer of 1998 and February 1999.

It was more than a bit hectic. On the days before Henry needed something, I would work in the morning and the early afternoon on John Paul II, either writing or editing; then I would spend, say, 5–7 p.m. on impeachment affairs; then after dinner I'd do a bit more work on the Pope.

Henry Hyde was a model of fairness throughout the House Judiciary Committee inquiry, the House debate, and the Senate trial, as a stalwart defender of President Clinton, Representative Barney Frank, later acknowledged. Henry's own falls from grace, decades in the past, were dredged up by reporters, aided and abetted (I am convinced) by unscrupulous Clintonistas—all of whom, like too many in the media, imagined that this entire business was a matter of extracurricular sex. Henry was badly hurt by these revelations and called me late one night, saying he was thinking of resigning. I replied that no two people I ever met had been more married than he and Jeanne (who had died in 1992) and that he owed it both to her forgiveness and his duty to press ahead.

Which he did, in the conviction that President Bill Clinton had put the Congress and the country in an impossible position: for how could the nation have as its supreme law-enforcement official a man guilty of crimes—perjury and obstruction of justice—for which more than a hundred other men and women were serving time in federal prisons?

When the House managers solemnly carried the articles of impeachment across the Capitol to the Senate on the night of December 19, 1998, Henry Hyde saw in Senate Majority Leader Trent Lott's eyes that (as he told me later that night) "we're not going to make it; Trent won't fight." I replied that, if we were going to lose, then we should create a public record with which history would have to reckon. So rather than let the trial of the president descend into farce, Henry tried heroically to keep the country focused on the nobility of the rule of law.

The Senate, voting largely along partisan lines, acquitted the president on February 12, 1999. But students of American history will read Henry Hyde on the impeachment and trial of President Bill Clinton for decades after Clinton's memoir and its bitter criticisms of Hyde is pulped. Throughout this entire episode, for all that it was a distraction from my biographical labors, I couldn't help feeling that what I was doing with Henry was a matter of vindicating John Paul II's faith in the United States as the model of a law-governed democracy.

LAST LAP

DIANE REVERAND AT HARPERCOLLINS SECURED THE HELP OF A talented freelance editor, Carolyn Fireside, to edit the two-thousand-plus-page manuscript that would become a book in which, Diane said, "the [page] number 1,000 will not appear!" It was a good editorial collaboration, and Carolyn was particularly helpful in whittling down papal documents and addresses to tolerable and readable length. Diane and Carolyn sent me edited copy on the fly; I reedited by hand and rekeyed the reedits on my study desktop computer before sending things back to New York. The routine we established went well, despite getting off to a bad start, thanks to a fierce ice-and-snow storm in Washington in early 1999. There was no electricity in the house, and the children bailed to the homes of electrified friends. Joan and I held the fort in North Bethesda, and for days I sat in my study, clad in a Navy peacoat and wearing gloves with the fingers chopped off, editing by hand until power was restored.

I had another bit of fun at this stage of the project. On my Roman research trips I was often hosted by NAC seminarian Christopher Nalty and his friends at a student kitchen in the college known as "The Carnivor" (spelled just like that). They insisted that our evenings of *rigatoni all'amatriciana*, rib-eye steaks, and Tuscan wines had to be memorialized in *Witness to Hope*. I agreed but told them that they'd have to search for the reference. Having determined that there was no Polish equivalent of the English word *carnivore,* Rodger and Magda Potocki came up with the neologism *mięsożerny,* meaning, more or less, "meat-eater." So my thanks to "Krzysztof Mięsożerny and his colleagues" were duly inscribed in the book's acknowledgments.

"Krzysztof" Nalty and his friends were stumped until another member of the Carnivor set, Roger Landry, brought the book to a NAC student who knew Polish, asking him to look at all the Polish names in the acknowledgments. He found what my NAC friends were looking for and said, in his somewhat halting English, "This is not Polish name. It is not really very good word. It means 'meat-eater'!"

One of Diane Reverand's other gifts to the project was to assign the book to a superb copy editor, Sue Llewellyn, with whom I quickly developed a friendly and cooperative relationship. There are lots of problems with making a book of more than five hundred thousand words as error-free as possible, and as I said time and again to the patient Sue, "The standard is perfection." We didn't meet that lofty goal, but the finished product was as close to flawless as we could make it. There was one hair-raising moment at the galley proof stage when a computer glitch led to almost an entire chapter of endnotes—almost a hundred of them—being misnumbered. But after a panicky moment or two I figured out what had gone wrong and we fixed the problem.

One other potential faux pas sticks in my mind. I had chosen the cover photo for the book, and when the proofs of the cover came, I thought it looked terrific. Then I looked again, picked up the phone, and called my pastor, Monsignor Donald Essex: "Have you got a cassock in the rectory that I can look at quickly?" He must have thought I was coming unglued but said I was welcome to come and inspect one of his choir cassocks, which I did fifteen minutes later. And happily so, for what was nagging me about the cover came clear: the buttons were on the wrong side of the Pope's white cassock, because the cover designers had inadvertently reversed the photographic image. Thanking Msgr. Essex, I quickly drove home, called New York, and things got straightened out.

I was invited to address the Young Presidents' Organization in Rome in June 1999; Monica was in the city attending a University of Dallas "Shakespeare in Italy" program for high school students; so it seemed a good moment for Joan and me to have a brief holiday there before what promised to be a very busy fall. On June 22, I wrote Bishop Dziwisz, explaining the publication plans for the book—the United States in October; France, Italy, and Spain in November; Poland in the spring of 2000; other language editions to follow. I also mentioned that Joan and I were in the city, and an invitation to dinner on Sunday, June 27, followed.

It was a glorious Roman early-summer evening, and Joan and I were walking slowly up the Via della Conciliazione toward St. Peter's Square when a small blue car pulled over next to us and a voice said in shaky English, "Get in." It was Msgr. Mokrzycki, who said, "There are a lot of people visiting the Holy Father right now. Stanislao thought there might be some confusion getting you in, and he sent me to find you. I thought you might be walking this way." After taking us up on the family elevator, Mokrzycki put us in the usual parlor and told us to make ourselves at home, as he had to get back to the Sala Clementina, where the Pope was being serenaded by a Polish choir. So there we were, with the papal apartment to ourselves.

Joan had been in the chapel once for Mass but it had been very crowded, so I suggested that we walk down there so she could see it again. The windows of the chapel open into the Sala Clementina on the floor below, so we could hear the choir singing as we sat in the papal chapel by ourselves. It was beautiful—indeed, it was almost unreal—and I said "Let's not forget this; it may not happen again."

John Paul was in very good form after spending an hour with the choir and the dinner conversation ranged all over the landscape. Dziwisz grilled me about the Church's situation in the United States; there was some talk of Joan's parents having known Mother Teresa in Calcutta; we spoke of the upcoming Great Jubilee of 2000. I explained a bit more about publication plans and said to the Pope, "So you can't do anything historic for the next three months." He shrugged—and declined to agree.

The evening was a fitting cap to what had begun three and a half years before at a dinner of consequence. Now there was nothing to do but wait for *Witness to Hope*, my effort to present John Paul II "from inside," to be published.

JUBILEE PILGRIM'S PROGRESS

Pope John Paul II was in a festive mood at lunch on Tuesday, January 4, 2000. He always loved the Christmas season and Christmas 1999 had been something special: at Midnight Mass on December 24/25, he'd opened the Holy Door of the Vatican basilica, St. Peter's, to begin the Great Jubilee of 2000—the "key" to his pontificate, as he often put it.

Outside the windows of the papal apartment a Goodyear blimp sailed lazily back and forth across the Roman sky, circling a Piazza San Pietro full of tourists and pilgrims. John Paul seemed to find this aerial Americana both amusing and an omen for the year ahead. Twice during lunch, he pointed out the window as the blimp floated past and said to his guests, "You see? *Buon'anno!*"

It was indeed a good year, the last before the world changed on September 11, 2001. It was also a peripatetic one for me as I spent the better part of the Great Jubilee on the road, speaking about *Witness to Hope* as it appeared in one language edition after another. Between September 1999 and December 2000, I traveled to more than forty American and two Canadian cities (some of them multiple times), as well as to Rome (five times), Paris, Madrid, Mexico City, Lisbon, Pamplona, Sydney, Melbourne, Warsaw, Gdańsk, Poznań,

Wrocław, and, of course, Kraków. I was also in Jerusalem for John Paul's epic Holy Land pilgrimage in March 2000, working with NBC News. By the end of the jubilee, *Witness to Hope* had appeared in English, Czech, French, Italian, Polish, Portuguese, Slovak, and Spanish; Russian, German, Slovenian, Romanian, and Ukrainian editions would follow over the next decade.

Richard Neuhaus's intuition that my life would be dramatically changed by that dinner of consequence in December 1995 proved true: I became a kind of "witness to the witness," explaining John Paul II's life and thought in venues ranging from wholly friendly to deeply hostile. In doing so, I continued to learn new things about the world Church and the reception of John Paul's historic papacy. Yet as my lectures and interviews looked back on what Karol Wojtyła had accomplished in a remarkable eight decades, I was also looking ahead, for I never thought of *Witness to Hope* as the end of the journey. Rather, it was the first installment of a story I intended to complete. So as I was speaking about that book, I was gathering materials and conducting interviews that would help me finish the John Paul II story when the time came.

And, of course, my conversations with John Paul himself continued. In the years after the Great Jubilee of 2000, our joint pilgrims' progress would enter several dark valleys. Here, I want to describe my experience of John Paul in the jubilee and the reception of *Witness to Hope,* which in some respects was as instructive about the state of the Church and the world as the journey preparing it had been.

A Long Embrace

O N September 3, 1999, a box with my author's copies of *Witness to Hope* arrived at my home. I had to steady myself before opening it; my hands were trembling. When I got the box open I was exultant, and while finding a few typos (that were my fault) I was deeply grateful to Sue Llewellyn and the others on Diane Reverand's team for a beautiful piece of bookmaking. Handel's *Dettingen Te Deum* was cued up on the CD player in my study and accompanied me as I read around in the book; that seemed right, as Sue, Diane, Cathy Hemming, and the other good people at HarperCollins were not the only parties to whom I owed thanks for the culmination of over three years of work.

I left for Rome on September 18; I wanted to give the book to John Paul II before it was officially released in the United States, and Msgr. Dolan at the North American College had arranged for a public lecture in which I could present the book to a Roman audience. Dolan then went one better and offered to host a lunch for curial officials and other locals who had been helpful in my work, which was held in the college's Red Room on the afternoon of September 23. There were *aperitivi,* and when the guests came to their places at table, each found an autographed copy of *Witness to Hope* waiting for him.

It was fun to see some of the more senior of these churchmen picking up the book, examining it, but not daring to look at the index for fear of seeming self-interested. Msgr. Dolan proposed a first toast, to the Holy Father, and we had an antipasto. Then Dolan asked me to propose a second toast. I said I wanted to offer a toast of thanks to all present for their help—and in doing so, to note the self-discipline of the members of the Roman Curia, for no one had yet snuck a look at the index. The toast was quickly drunk and no sooner were the glasses on the table than everyone was perusing the index and the comments were shooting to and fro—"I have four citations." "Well, I have six."

Bishop Ryłko seemed extremely happy with the book and must have called Castel Gandolfo on his return from that luncheon, for at 7:30 that evening he called to say that we were to have dinner at the papal villa the following night.

With three books in my briefcase, I walked from the college down to Trastevere and the Palazzo San Calisto, where Ryłko had his office, on the evening of September 24. We left on the dot of 6 p.m., but the Roman traffic was even more purgatorial than usual. We were due at 7:40, and at 7:42 we careened through the back entrance to Castel Gandolfo, near the papal farm with its lovely cows. As we wove our way toward the papal villa, a Vatican policeman stopped us so a car could pass. It was the Pope, returning from his evening swim in the pool he had built after Conclave II in 1978 (telling the critics who were carping about the cost that he had to get exercise and in any event the pool was cheaper than another conclave). So we were on Wojtyła Standard Time, and all was in order.

There was another guest that evening, Father Stanisław Nagy, a Polish theologian and old friend of John Paul II; alas, I had only three books, all pre-autographed—one for the subject, one for Dziwisz, and one for Msgr. Mokrzycki. Fr. Nagy couldn't have been more understanding, and as we walked into the dining room I showed Mokrzycki his copy, saying that he could use it for his English textbook and that Sister Emilia would be pleased.

John Paul said grace, we all sat down, and then the thought occurred: what do you say to a subject on handing him his biography? "This is your life" didn't seem right. So I took the book out of my briefcase, walked around the table, and handed it to John Paul while saying something completely anodyne like, "Well, here it is." He simply looked at it and said, "My God . . . my God . . . "

Dziwisz described our meal with enthusiasm as a "good *country* dinner" and informed me that the eggs came from the papal chickens, of which there were four hundred, who lived in harmony with twenty-six cows. As we ate, the papal secretary turned on the portable TV set in the dining room so we could watch the verdict in the trial of Giulio Andreotti, the old Christian Democratic warhorse with whom the resurgent Italian left was settling scores. The motivations in the prosecution were well understood in what was the only discussion of Italian politics I ever heard at the papal board.

After that little drama played itself out, the Pope and his two secretaries started riffling through the book, beginning with the photographs—there was considerable chaffing of young Dziwisz with thick curly hair—and looking up names in the index. I walked back around the table and showed John Paul how the book was organized: the chronology and the thematic vignette that opened each chapter; the analysis of his magisterium and the key documents of the pontificate. Fr. Nagy professed amazement that this could be done in a little over three years, and I said that I had had a lot of help.

As we were eating some wonderful local peaches for *dolce,* the Pope asked if I knew that he had mentioned *kremowki,* his favorite dessert, when he was in Wadowice a few months earlier. I assured him that, thanks to his efforts, the entire world knew about *kremowki.*

Nagy wanted to know about the different reactions to the Pope in the United States and in Europe; I mentioned that I had seen the encyclical *Evangelium Vitae* on sale at a supermarket checkout counter, which I doubt would have happened in Europe. Dziwisz wanted to know if the book explored the Pope's poetry; I said that it did, and that Marek Skwarnicki and Anna Karoń-Ostrowska (who had done her doctorate on Wojtyła's poem "Radiation of Fatherhood") had been very helpful in explaining it to me thematically. John Paul smiled broadly at the names—he had a special affection for Anna—and then Dziwisz went off on one of his riffs about my ability to pronounce Polish names (which I always found a little odd, in that pronunciation strikes me as the easiest part of Polish, the real challenges being the Slavic-based vocabulary and the complex grammar).

When the peaches were done, Dziwisz brought in official documents for John Paul to sign—mostly parchments to heads of state acknowledging his acceptance of their ambassadors' letters of credence. The Pope signed with a large Montblanc Meisterstück; as one document after another was laid before him, a weary John Paul looked over the table with a raised eyebrow, smiled at me, shrugged, and said, "Povero Papa!" (Poor Pope!)

After the documents were finished, we said grace after meals, and as we began to leave the dining room, the Pope drew me into a big hug . . . and just, well, held on, for what seemed like two minutes, pressing my head firmly into the side of his face. When he finally let me go, Dziwisz murmured, "C'era un grande lavoro" (This was a great effort), to which Ryłko added, "Un lavoro d'amore" (A labor of love). The Pope, for his part, didn't seem to want our meeting to end. He turned back after he had started to leave the room, gave me another long hug, asked to be remembered to Joan and the children, and then said, "Now the next time you come we must have a real talk."

John Paul went off to the chapel while Dziwisz and Ryłko walked me through the modest offices near the dining room. There, Dziwisz showed me some funny photos of the Pope receiving U2's Bono earlier that day, playfully grabbing the singer's trademark sunglasses and putting them on. "I have the negatives," the ever-vigilant secretary noted. We then went to the chapel, with its frescoes of Polish scenes, which Dziwisz and Ryłko knew I wanted to see again. The Pope was finishing his postdinner prayer; I heard one small groan. While we were kneeling there, I noticed something new: a stunning Russian crowned icon resting beneath the altar, just where John Paul, kneeling at his prie-dieu, would see it. After the Pope left, Dziwisz picked up the icon so that I could examine it closely. It had been given to the Pope, he said, "so that he can take it to Moscow." That priceless icon—the famous *Kazanskaya,* one of the great models of Marian iconography in Russian Orthodox art—would appear at a different papal table three and a half months later.

On our way to Bishop Ryłko's car, Bishop Dziwisz gave me another Polish bear hug and pronounced himself "completely happy" with what had happened over the past three and half years. It was an easier drive back to Rome than on the way out. Ryłko spoke with some amazement of the Andreotti trial, wondering how Italy could run so long "with all this chaos": a good question, to which I don't think either of us ever found an answer.

On the Road

THE UNITED STATES, CANADA, AND EUROPE,
OCTOBER 1999–JANUARY 2000

REVIOUS EXPERIENCE HAD TAUGHT ME THAT ENGAGING THE argument surrounding a book was almost as important as writing it. But nothing had prepared me for the whirlwind in which I now found myself. Between late September and Christmas 1999 alone, I gave 46 lectures on *Witness to Hope*, usually accompanied by book signings, and 117 print, radio, and TV interviews. As I said to Bishop Dziwisz in a letter of November 21, "This is the 'New Evangelization' in a very concentrated form." My Catholic audiences were, in the main, interested in seeing their pope "from inside," while the tendency in media interviews, in both North America and Europe, was to focus on John Paul II's public impact, although I tried to link the Pope's role in world politics to his evangelical and moral leadership.

I prepared two standard talks for presenting John Paul and the book to lecture-and-signing audiences: one, drawn from the book's epilogue, summarized the chief accomplishments of the pontificate thus far; the other focused on what I called the "souls" of John Paul II—his Polish soul, his Carmelite soul, his Marian soul, and so forth. The latter presentation seemed to intrigue people more, as it got "inside" the Pope in a fresh way and, despite his obvious uniqueness, made him more accessible.

The Paris press conference for the presentation of *Witness to Hope* was scheduled for 10 a.m. on October 29 and I had arrived in the City of Light four hours earlier; so I did the presser, as well as five interviews and a lecture, on adrenaline. The striking thing about the press conference was the questions raised about John Paul's Theology of the

Body, which gave me the opportunity to say a few things about the self-induced demographic winter into which Europe was descending. There was something wrong, I suggested, when an entire continent, richer, healthier, and more secure than ever before, was refusing to produce the human future in its most elemental sense—the next generation. John Paul II's analysis of the contraceptive mentality and its effect on culture was worth considering, I said, not least in a country that prided itself on its talent in the arts of *amour*.

The next afternoon I flew to Rome, where I met my agent, Loretta Barrett, her sister Irene, and my publisher, Diane Reverand, for dinner at my favorite Roman trattoria, Armando's, just off the Borgo Pio near the Vatican. Armando, his brother Berardo, and Armando's daughter Orietta had become friends over the years, and I wanted to give them a copy of *Witness to Hope* as a small token of thanks for many kindnesses.

At noon on November 2, the Barretts, Diane Reverand, Leonardo Mondadori and his daughter, and I met for a half hour with John Paul II. After I introduced the others to the Pope, John Paul turned to me with a big smile and said, "I am on page two hundred forty!" There was some talk of families and mutual acquaintances, and then Diane presented the Pope with a handsome leather-bound edition of *Witness to Hope*. Leonardo gave him a copy of the Italian edition, and we talked a bit about future language editions. On the way out, Bishop Dziwisz pulled me aside and asked me how things were going. "So far, so good," I said, and while there were doubtless attacks to come, I was pleased with the enthusiasm with which so many people had received *Witness to Hope* and by their evident esteem and affection for its subject. I got the usual bear hug and the standard Stanislavian admonition: "Coraggio!" (Courage!)

The weeks following my November 4 return to Washington were a blur: two trips to the West Coast for book lectures, signings, and interviews, sandwiched around a quick return to the East Coast for my parents' golden wedding anniversary. I spent Thanksgiving 1999 in Madrid; there was no turkey but rather dinner with the king and queen's son-in-law, who represented the royal family after the queen, who wanted to attend the book presentation, was told by the royal handlers that it would set a bad precedent—proof positive that all court bureaucracies, civil or ecclesiastical, are much the same. The Spanish presentation was well handled by the book's Spanish editor, Deborah Blackman; interest in *Biografía de Juan Pablo II: Testigo de Esperanza* was further stimulated by Joaquín Navarro-Valls's coming to Madrid for the event.

Joan, Gwyneth, Monica, Stephen, and I flew to Rome on December 22 to begin the Great Jubilee of 2000 with John Paul as he opened the Holy Door of St. Peter's before Christmas Midnight Mass. The pyrotechnic cope the Pope wore for the occasion got everyone's attention, but the surprises of that Christmastide were not over. On the evening of St. Stephen's Day we were having dinner with friends when one of them said, out of nowhere, "Have you seen what the Cuban embassy to the Vatican is faxing around town?" I had to reply in the negative, as I wasn't on the Cubans' fax distribution list. So my friend left the table and brought back a copy of the fax, which he proceeded to translate with some glee.

One of Fidel Castro's people in Madrid had gotten the Spanish edition of *Witness to Hope* and had gone immediately to the section of the book on the 1998 papal pilgrimage to Cuba, which he sent back to Havana. Fidel took great offense at what I had written, and in a multi-hour harangue to foreign journalists, El Jefe devoted several minutes to denouncing the book and its *Yanqui* author in colorful language. The Cuban embassy to the Holy See was faxing a protest around to everyone on its list, with the presidential denunciation appended. I was, of course, delighted, and one of my Cuban relatives back in Baltimore had a grand time translating the denunciation in full.

On December 29, the family and I redeployed to Castelgandolfo, the town. Earlier that year, it occurred to me that it might be fun to begin the Great Jubilee in Rome with some of the graduates of the *Centesimus Annus* seminar. I expected that perhaps two dozen would attend; in the event, well over a hundred did, so we took over the University of Dallas Rome campus in Due Santi, just below the town of Castelgandolfo. The seminar graduates stayed there and our reunion events were held in the campus auditorium, while the faculty was housed up the hill at the Hotel Bucci, overlooking Lake Albano.

It all worked very well: until New Year's Eve, that is. Monsignor David Malloy, who worked for Bishop Harvey in the Prefecture of the Papal Household, had procured tickets to the annual New Year's Eve *Te Deum* in St. Peter's for everyone in our group, so we took three buses into Rome and parked them at the North American College. I told everyone that they were on their own after the *Te Deum* but should be back at the college, ready to return to Due Santi, at 1 a.m. That would give people time to see the Pope bring in the calendrical new year, celebrate a bit, and get back up the Janiculum to the buses.

After the *Te Deum*—during which one of our company's children, held out into the basilica's aisle, received a papal smooch that made the papers—and a leisurely dinner at Armando's, my family and a few faculty colleagues ventured out into the New Year's Eve maelstrom and made our way to St. Peter's Square for the countdown to 2000—and who knew what, the end of the world perhaps, as computers went awry.

The countdown ended, the Pope wished everyone a good new year from the window of the papal apartment, and our group worked its way in threes and fours back up to NAC and the buses. But while the Y2K bug turned out to be another example of media-driven hysteria, Something Very Bad was in store for some of us.

One of our drivers had enjoyed his dinner too well (or so we surmised) and was AWOL. But with a bit of squeezing, we managed to fit everyone into the remaining two buses, whose drivers were on hand. In the biblical manner, though, one was wise and the other foolish. The wise driver took a back route through Trastevere, away from the now-riotous city center, and arrived at the University of Dallas campus at a reasonable hour, about 2:30 a.m. or so. The foolish driver took the standard route—or tried to—and got us utterly gridlocked in a carnival of craziness: Romans were abandoning their cars in the streets, there was no traffic control, and we went through Rome at something less than a snail's pace.

We said the rosary. We practiced the Polish Christmas carol the seminar graduates would sing to John Paul II a few days later. We tried "Ninety-Nine Bottles of Beer on the Wall." We said another rosary. The bus was completely packed; I was sitting in the doorway, and someone finally dubbed us the "Bus of Martyrs." We got to Due Santi and Castelgandolfo at 5 a.m. I immediately canceled the 9 a.m. lecture scheduled for that morning and had two fingers' worth of scotch, nobly saved for me by Fr. Richard Neuhaus and our friend and colleague Jody Bottum: the first and only time in my life I had a drink before the sun was over the yardarm.

Before the reunion gathered in Rome, I wrote Bishop Dziwisz, asking him for the favor of a ten-minute meeting with John Paul for our group. Ten minutes only, I swore: we'll gather in the Sala Clementina, the seminar graduates will sing a Polish Christmas carol, the Pope will give his blessing—that's all. On that basis Dziwisz agreed, and the audience was set for January 3 at noon.

My Polish colleagues and I prepared sheets with the Christmas carol *Wśród Nocnej Ciszy* (The Silence of the Night) in phonetically rendered Polish and all seemed ready. Everyone got into the Vatican without difficulty and we arranged ourselves in the Sala Clementina as a kind of chorus facing the Pope's chair. A few minutes after noon, in came John Paul II and Bishop Dziwisz, accompanied by a Swiss Guard or two. Fr. Maciej Zięba and I greeted the Pope, the group sang the carol—not too badly, with the pontiff singing along—and then John Paul said, "I want to meet them all." Thinking of my promise of "ten minutes, period," I didn't dare look at Dziwisz but stationed myself to one side of John Paul; Fr. Zięba stood at his other side, and we introduced about 150 people to the beaming Pope, who had a blessing and a rosary for everyone. Dziwisz, far from being out of sorts, saw what a good time John Paul was having and asked Zięba, "Can the faculty come to lunch tomorrow?"

When the last person had been introduced and the last rosary bestowed, there was a group photo, later to appear in *L'Osservatore Romano*—and on his way out, John Paul said to me, "I'm on page four hundred [and something]!"

At 1:15 p.m. on January 4, Mike and Karen Novak, Fr. Neuhaus, Fr. Zięba, Joan, and I rendezvoused at the Bronze Doors and were taken up to the papal apartment for lunch; Bishop Ryłko joined us. The apartment was overflowing with Christmas decorations, including a huge crèche that filled one end of the main hallway. In the dining room, Dziwisz sat me next to him at one end of the table, so that he and I could talk sotto voce about how *Witness to Hope* was being received; when I mentioned a cranky review by Archbishop Rembert Weakland, Dziwisz said not to worry, "il suo tempo è passato" (his time is over). As *dolce* was being finished, the papal secretary turned to me and quietly asked, "Do you think the ladies would like to see the icon?" I said that I thought everyone would, so off he went to the chapel and returned with the *Kazanskaya*. "Explain what it is," he whispered. "If I did, everyone would get too nervous," I replied. So without explanation, we simply passed the priceless icon of Our Lady of Kazan down the table, one set of hands to another, as if we were examining a Christmas present or an ornate box of chocolates. John Paul repeated what he had said at Castel Gandolfo in September: he had told Russian Orthodox Patriarch Aleksii II that he wanted to return this jewel of Russian Orthodox art and devotion to Moscow, in person. (The old KGB man Aleksii wasn't having any of that, alas.) Later, when I explained the icon, its provenance, and its significance to my friends, they were stunned, both by the history and by the fact that we had passed it down the table so casually.

At the end of the meal, Bishop Dziwisz distributed the usual gifts, with Neuhaus and Zięba getting pectoral crosses left over from the recent Synod for Europe; handing the crosses, made for bishops, to the two priests, Dziwisz wisecracked, "You will have to wait for the chains."

WISDOM PERSONIFIED

T HE JUBILEE PACE SLOWED A BIT AFTER MY RETURN FROM ROME. In mid-March, I went to Mexico City for a presentation of the Spanish edition of *Witness to Hope* arranged by Mario Paredes: my first opportunity to be amazed by the beauty of the miraculous tilma of Juan Diego and its image of Our Lady of Guadalupe. The book presentations in the Mexican capital went well and I was happy to get to know the able archbishop of the city, Norberto Rivera Carrera, a bold John Paul II appointment: a man of Indian heritage who had broken the racial and class patterns of previous Mexican primates. The one slightly odd note was struck during the press conference, which produced the strangest question about John Paul I had yet encountered. The brief dialogue went as follows: Q. "What does he eat?" A. "Food."

In December 1998, Joe Alicastro, a senior producer at NBC News Specials, invited me to become the network's Vatican specialist. After some preliminary conversations about what this might entail, I decided to accept—and thus began a very satisfying professional relationship and a host of new friendships.

Given my general public profile, I doubt that many people would have been surprised I had been invited to be the "Vatican analyst" of EWTN. But NBC?

Talking with Joe and others at the network, I came to the view that the people I would be working with were professionals; that they respected expertise, which was what I was being hired to provide; and that my expertise would be useful in framing NBC's coverage of Vatican affairs and John Paul II. It also seemed to me that this was a major catechetical opportunity that should not be ignored just because I viewed American politics through a different lens than most of my colleagues at 30 Rockefeller Plaza. On NBC, I'd be talking to people who weren't already convinced about the Catholic Church and indeed might be hostile to it, and I might be able to clear up things that had previously been misunderstood, about both the Church and the Pope.

My previous experiences with the mainstream media had taught me that a lot of its coverage of the Catholic Church and John Paul II was driven less by ideological bias than by a lack of real information. So my approach would be to provide real information, and my information would be based on real contacts with real knowledge, not on the niblets put out to uninformed American journalists by Vatican monsignori who would talk about anything, including matters of which they were wholly ignorant, over a cappuccino or two. And I would put that real information into an ecclesial context, not a political one—which meant that I wouldn't be parsing everything Catholic in liberal-versus-conservative terms.

Everyone at 30 Rock knew that John Paul II's jubilee pilgrimage to the Holy Land was going to be an epic event, so I was brought to Jerusalem to provide background information for the entire NBC family as well as to do on-air commentary for NBC, MSNBC, New York's WNBC, and other local NBC affiliates. On the flight over, I reread Evelyn Waugh's experimental novel *Helena*, which was good preparation for what was to follow: Waugh's novel is about the gritty reality of salvation history, and that's what John Paul was going to the Holy Land to affirm. He was not just satisfying a deep desire of his own heart, although he was certainly doing that; he was reminding the world that the God of the Bible (as he once put it) "does not look down on us from on high, but . . . became our traveling companion." This was a pilgrimage, and its primary purpose was to invite the world to look, hard, at the stuff of its redemption.

It was also a personal triumph. John Paul had wanted to spend his first Christmas as pope in the Holy Land; the traditional managers of popes said it wasn't possible, and for once he bowed to their lack of imagination. Throughout the pontificate, he asked his diplomats, time and again, "Quando mi permeterrete di andare?" (When will you let me go?) He finally got tired of the excuses as to why it couldn't be done and simply announced, as part of the run-up to the Great Jubilee of 2000, that he was going.

The very fact of his doing so made history. As I was being driven into Jerusalem on Sunday, March 19, 2000, there were two flags on virtually every lamppost, the papal flag and the Israeli flag: something many never expected to see; something some would have been happy never to see.

I hadn't been in Jerusalem in over nine years, but, with an NBC colleague who'd never been to the Church of the Holy Sepulchre and wanted to visit it, I managed to find the way there on Sunday afternoon, through Jaffa Gate and the rabbit's warren of streets in the Old City. The usual cacophony prevailed in what for Christians is the world's holiest site. As before, though, I found it the easiest place in the world to pray: and not "pray" in the sense of reciting prayers but in the sense of practicing the presence.

The next day, while the Pope was in Amman, was full of television. It was my first experience working with Chris Jansing, who would become a good friend; Chris understood that what was afoot during this papal visit couldn't be dumbed down into sound bites, so we had a real conversation during our segments together, not just an exchange of one-liners. That evening I went over to East Jerusalem with my Toronto classmate Father Michael McGarry, a Paulist priest then running the Tantur Ecumenical Institute on the border between Jerusalem and Bethlehem. The Palestinian restaurant at which we ate, Philadelphia, had an excellent kitchen and its people couldn't have been friendlier. On the way out I saw a poster in which John Paul had been Photoshopped together with Yasser Arafat; the two of them were superimposed on Jerusalem and the poster proclaimed, "Welcome to the Palestinian Holy Land"—a variant on the "Palestinian Jesus" theme that Arafat had been retailing. Some people, it seemed, were going to do politics, whatever John Paul II did or didn't do.

The meetings I had in and around the television work were fascinating, if also occasionally puzzling and even disturbing. Over breakfast one morning, I described John Paul II's efforts to get the Jewish-Catholic dialogue on a sound theological basis with a learned and kindly rabbi, a friend of Phil Alongi, one of the NBC producers;

but I also sensed that alarm bells were going off in the rabbi's head. When I asked him if that were so, and if so why, he smiled sadly and answered, "Because your sacred text is anti-Semitic." I asked what *that* meant and he cited the gospel of John. When I replied that the polemics against "the Jews" in John's gospel were the result of a bitter family quarrel and couldn't be read as if they were the ancient equivalent of a 1928 blackballing at a New York men's club, he said he found my formulation intriguing; but surely the way I read the New Testament was not the way the majority of Catholics read it?

This intelligent man's misinformation about the Catholic Church and its people was widely shared by his countrymen, unfortunately. One poll reported that 56 percent of Israelis had no idea that the Catholic Church publicly condemned anti-Semitism and worked against it. Thus it was clear, if depressingly so, that the sea change in Catholic-Jewish relations since the Second Vatican Council, which had been deepened and broadened by the Polish pope who called the Jews of Rome his "elder brothers" in the faith of Abraham, had not sufficiently registered in the Jewish state—in part, I suspected, because of the palpable anti-Zionism (and worse) of many of the Holy Land's non-Israeli Catholics.

The high drama of the visit was expected to center on the papal visit to the official Israeli memorial to the Holocaust, Yad Vashem. What would the Pope say? I already knew the answer to that hotly debated question, because on Tuesday night, March 21, I had walked through the rain to the Notre Dame of Jerusalem Center near New Gate, where the papal party was being housed. There, a friendly Vatican official slipped me a diskette containing all the prepared papal texts. I read them back at the Jerusalem Hilton, and while I was used to John Paul's ability to seize a moment and say precisely the right thing, the remarks prepared for Yad Vashem were so striking, and so appropriate, that I felt chills go down my spine.

Two days later, the Pope walked slowly and with difficulty toward the Eternal Flame in Yad Vashem's Hall of Remembrance—and I remembered something Joaquín Navarro-Valls once told me: he asked the Pope whether he ever cried, and John Paul responded, "Not outside." He was certainly crying inside as he bent his head in silent prayer over the flame, no doubt seeing the faces of his boyhood friends who became victims of Nazi genocide, and no doubt hearing again the jackboots on the streets of Kraków. Then, having quoted Psalm 31 ("I have become like a broken vessel . . . But I trust in Thee, O Lord"), he slowly and softly spoke the words that put a stop to the previous caterwauling about what-would-he-say, as he taught the entire world an unforgettable lesson: "In this place of memories, the mind and heart and soul feel an extreme need for silence. Silence in which to remember. Silence in which to try to make some sense of the memories [that] come flooding back. Silence because there are no words strong enough to deplore the terrible tragedy of the Shoah."

Our newsroom felt the impact of those words, spoken with the weight of history bearing down on John Paul and on all who heard him: normally a place of bedlam, the newsroom fell completely silent. No one spoke a word.

A few days later, I got a call from my old Wilson Center friend Menahem Milson, who had seen a lot in his life as soldier and scholar. "I just had to tell you," he said, "that Arnona [his wife] and I cried throughout the Pope's visit to Yad Vashem. This was wisdom, humaneness, and integrity personified. Nothing was missing; nothing more needed to be said."

The next flap involved papal vesture: would John Paul II wear his bishop's pectoral cross when he went to the Western Wall? Some were demanding that he not wear it, to avoid offending those for whom the cross was a symbol of Christian anti-Semitism. It seemed time to clear that up, and I thought I had the man for the job: Rabbi James Rudin of the American Jewish Committee, a friend from the Jewish-Christian dialogues that Richard Neuhaus's center in New York regularly sponsored. I called Rabbi Rudin and invited him to come on MSNBC and address the controversy. He was perfect. In "real interreligious dialogue," he said, "we respect the other for what he is and we begin the conversation from there."

Then, off camera, Jim told me a story I'd have given gold and frankincense to have known when writing *Witness to Hope*. It seems that the Great Synagogue of Rome has a strict rule against crosses in the sanctuary, to the point that ushers with sticks will rap the knees of anyone crossing their legs. Rabbi Elio Toaff, the chief rabbi of Rome, was being bombarded by requests from his congregation that he ask the Pope not to wear his pectoral cross on the historic papal visit to the synagogue that Toaff was negotiating. So Toaff went to see the Pope and told him what was afoot. To which John Paul replied, in so many words: "Look, if I were coming to your synagogue as a tourist I'd be happy to wear jeans. But I'm coming as the Bishop of Rome and the universal pastor of the Catholic Church, and to make that and all that it means unmistakable I have to dress the way I always do." Toaff went back to his congregants and announced that he and the Pope were completely agreed: the Pope *would* wear his pectoral cross. Small wonder that John Paul loved Elio Toaff—who, five years after the Jerusalem visit, would be thanked for his friendship in the Pope's last testament.

John Paul was scheduled to leave from Ben Gurion Airport on the evening of March 26; Chris Jansing and I were sitting on a balcony outside NBC's Jerusalem Hilton newsroom with the Old City and the Dome of the Rock at our backs, ready to cover the departure ceremony live. We could see the papal helicopter leave the city and head toward Tel Aviv, so we settled down, ready to begin our coverage—and were informed that MSNBC would be cutting away to Seattle, where the Kingdome, a vast concrete mushroom of a stadium and one of the worst places to play major league baseball ever built, was about to be imploded. Satisfying as it was to see the brutalist horror in which I had once watched (and covered) the Seattle Mariners reduced to dust and ashes, it did seem an odd editorial choice: collapsing Kingdome trumps Pope. Happily, the explosive charges were well placed, the lucky soul who won the lottery to push the detonator did the job with panache, and down went the Kingdome—just in time for MSNBC to cut to Lod, the airport, and John Paul's departure from a historic pilgrimage during which, as one NBC colleague put it, the squabbling children of the Middle East saw how an adult behaved.

Back Home in Poland

O N RETURNING FROM JERUSALEM I WENT BACK INTO BOOK-promotion mode, with some interesting encounters along the way. In Miami on April 1, I had a lovely conversation with my second-grade teacher (then Sister Mary Francis Borgia, SSND, transformed by Vatican II into Sister Corinne Gmuer, SSND). Three days later, I met the senior religion majors at hyperfeminist (but, in those days, still rational) Smith College for an engaging discussion on John Paul II's Theology of the Body. There were two trips to Rome in April and May to work on the documentary being made from *Witness to Hope*, four commencement addresses, and my first designation as *Doctor Divinitatis*. Then came the most moving of the overseas book presentations, during a whirlwind tour of five Polish cities between May 19 and 26.

After a signing at the Warsaw Book Fair and a book presentation at the Dominican priory in the Old Town, I went to Gdańsk. The presentation at the Basilica of St. Nicholas included a splendid concert by the Cappella Gedanensis (singing Handel chorales and a Bruckner motet I once sang as a choirboy) and a dramatic reading of excerpts from the Polish edition of the book, *Świadek Nadziei*. A bit overwhelmed, I spoke with feeling about the spiritual link I felt between my seaport hometown, Baltimore, where Catholicism in America was born, and the Baltic seaport that gave birth to Solidarity. There were presentations and signings as well in Poznań and Wrocław (where the ladies in charge of the cathedral bookstore baked me a cake, so that we had tea-and-signing). In Wrocław, I had a chance to visit briefly the sites associated with Dietrich Bonhoeffer and Edith Stein, both of whom once lived in the German Breslau.

Then came Kraków.

The book presentation and signing were held in the medieval chapter house of the Dominican priory, over the bones of seven hundred years of Polish Dominicans, and was covered by radio and television. By this point I had done dozens of *Witness to Hope* events, but the Cracovian presentation was the only one at which I teared up a bit, when I thanked my "third home" for its hospitality, its cooperation, and its gift to the world of its greatest son, John Paul II. Many of those who had helped me get to the "inside" of Karol Wojtyła were there, including a large Środowisko contingent, Halina Kwiatkowska, and Msgr. Stanisław Małysiak.

Alas, Kraków was also the site of the only public protest of the book, staged by a gang representing the hypernationalist and deeply conservative Radio Maryja, who presented me with a letter condemning the book (and me) for what were alleged to be its (and my) misrepresentations of John Paul's attitude toward Radio Marjya during his 1997 pilgrimage to Poland; the letter was signed by four academics, three of whom held the habilitation degree. I knew exactly what the Pope's attitude toward Radio Maryja was because we'd discussed it: he understood the importance of the radio's religious services for shut-ins and elderly people but was deeply concerned about its politicization and the more-than-faint whiff of anti-Semitism that the radio's politics occasionally conveyed. So he decided to ignore Radio Maryja during the 1997 pilgrimage, not criticizing it but not mentioning it, either, while commending virtually every other pastoral initiative in the country.

I reported all this in *Witness to Hope* (well sourced from those who had prepared the Pope's 1997 Polish texts); the Radio Maryja people, who displayed some of the characteristics of a cult, were unhappy; and they wanted me (and everyone else) to know it. Their attempt to take over the Kraków presentation until I acknowledged the error of my ways was politely rebuffed by my Dominican hosts, who eventually escorted the protesters out of the chapter house. It was a first sign that ancient Polish animosities and passions remained just below the crust of democratic public life—a hint of what was to come, a decade or so later, in a rather uglier form that would have deeply saddened John Paul II.

That unpleasantness notwithstanding, it was a wonderful evening, ending with dinner at Kraków's most notable—all right, only—Corsican restaurant, Paese, hosted by Henryk Woźniakoswki on behalf of the Znak publishing house, and including both Dominican friends and the Maleckis, Piotr and Teresa.

On my return home, I wrote John Paul II a long letter about the Polish book presentations and mentioned an interesting contrast: whereas in Italy many reporters had begun by asking, "Why is an American doing this?" that question wasn't raised once in Poland.

Lusitania and Oz

THE PORTUGUESE EDITION OF THE BOOK, *Testemunho de Esperança,* was published by Bertrand, a company that began as a bookstore in 1732 and later grew into a publishing house. Portuguese rights were acquired by Zita Seabra, the first European instantiation of a type I had known from neoconservative political circles in the US: the intellectually convinced Marxist who gets sobered up by hard political reality and becomes a committed democrat. Zita was the only woman in the higher echelons of the Portuguese Communist Party in the days when Henry Kissinger feared that Portugal would become a communist dictatorship. But she was so offended by the comrades' behavior when power was in their grasp that she broke ranks and, at no small personal risk, became a supporter of Mário Soares, the Social Democrat who saved Portugal from communism just before communism collapsed in Europe.

In the course of this political drama Zita rediscovered her Catholicism and became a passionate partisan of John Paul II—thus as a senior editor at Bertrand she insisted on their acquiring the book and then saw that a Portuguese translation was done in jig time. I was only able to be in Lisbon for three days in late June 2000, but the book launch there was well organized, Zita became a friend with whom I would do two other books—and I told Irving Kristol, back in Washington, that certain kinds of conversions were not only gestated at CCNY in the 1930s battles between Stalinists and Trotskyists.

Several months later, I called another New York neocon friend, Norman Podhoretz, and asked, "What's a great long novel you think I haven't read?" I was facing a flight to Australia and wanted to be prepared. Without missing a beat, Norman said, "*The Forty Days of Musa Dagh.*" When I asked him what the heck that was, he said it was Franz Werfel's best book and that I'd love it as a study of character. So I duly got it and between Los Angeles and Sydney I read two-thirds of Werfel's novel, which I finished Down Under and have been recommending to friends ever since—all of whom, without exception, ask me what the heck *The Forty Days of Musa Dagh* (a novel of the Armenian genocide during World War I) is.

Thoughtful questions were raised during the book presentations in Sydney and Melbourne, but I had more fun with the media work. Australian television and radio are, like other things Australian, contact sports. And when I discovered that the prevailing local media mores dictated that I give as good as I got, I had a fine time, saying things I likely wouldn't have dared say in a US, Canadian, or British context. This was particularly true of my exchanges with John Paul's chief (and relentless) Aussie critic, Paul Collins, a former priest whose book title, *The Modern Inquisition*, rather telegraphed his punch. Collins was a fixture on the radio service of the Australian Broadcasting Corporation, attacked me (and the Pope) with gusto, and seemed a bit taken aback when I riposted, at one point, "That's the stupidest thing I've ever heard"—after which I demonstrated from the facts precisely what I meant, in the kind of pushback he'd evidently not received before. A notable exception to the monochromatic portside tilt of the Australian media was Sydney-based columnist Miranda Devine, with whom I had an enjoyable conversation that produced a thoughtful article about John Paul II.

It wasn't all media combat in Oz. In Melbourne, I reconnected with my oldest friend, George Pell, then the city's archbishop and shortly thereafter to become Archbishop of Sydney and a cardinal. In another providential "coincidence," Pell had come to my Baltimore parish as a newly ordained priest, heading for graduate studies at Oxford, in the summer of 1967 and over a few months became close to my entire family. George's sister Margaret, then a violinist with the Melbourne Symphony Orchestra, accompanied the two of us on a visit to the Healesville Sanctuary, where the strange and wondrous local fauna were on full display. I rather liked the wallabies and platypuses, didn't see much in the wombats, was informed by the Archbishop of Melbourne that all those cute koalas were stoned by midmorning from chewing coca leaves—and could only imagine what Darwin would have written about the striking evolutionary accomplishments of the proto-rat on the island-continent.

ERASMUS, THE ETHEREAL SPANISH PYRENEES, AND A REPORT TO THE POPE

NEW YORK, PAMPLONA, AND ROME, NOVEMBER–DECEMBER 2000

TWO WEEKS AFTER RETURNING TO THE US FROM AUSTRALIA VIA Singapore and Rome—having flown to Oz via Los Angeles, I thought I might as well make the complete circuit—I gave the fourteenth Erasmus Lecture at the Institute on Religion and Public Life in New York, at the invitation of Richard Neuhaus. It seemed an appropriate occasion to expand some of the arguments I had made in *Witness to Hope* about John Paul II's approach to world politics into an appraisal of the Holy See's role in the world, and the twenty-first-century papacy's.

In my lecture, I argued that the only real power that the Bishop of Rome wields in twenty-first-century global affairs is moral power: the power of moral argument and moral witness to bend the course of events in a more humane direction, through the work of individuals (and not only Catholics) who are persuaded by those arguments and moved by that witness. The recent examples of this form of exercising moral power with real effect seemed obvious. First and foremost, there was John Paul's role in the Revolution of 1989, which had nothing to do with Vatican diplomacy in the conventional sense and everything to do with planting the "forest of awakened consciences" that Józef Tischner (who died five months earlier) had celebrated. Then there was John Paul's impact on the 1994 Cairo International Conference on Population and Development and the 1995 Beijing World Conference on Women: there, the traditional instruments of Vatican diplomacy were deployed with effect after a global campaign of moral argument and witness, blunting efforts by the Clinton administration and the UN to get abortion on demand defined as a fundamental human right.

There was a tension here, though. The Holy See's exchange of diplomatic representation with more than 170 states was a long-sanctioned feature of international law and diplomatic practice and a useful tool in safeguarding the interests of the Church and its people in circumstances where Catholics were under cultural or political pressure. Moreover, in protecting its own the Church was protecting civil society and building barriers against the totalitarian temptation. Yet in this exchange of diplomatic recognition, was there a tacit pressure to play by the normal, worldly rules of the game, a pressure that cut against the new form of papal power as moral suasion and witness? That, arguably, was one cautionary lesson to be learned from the *Ostpolitik* of Paul VI and Agostino Casaroli: playing by the world's rules could make matters worse. How could the "post-Constantinian" papacy emerging from Vatican II and the pontificate of John Paul II be both a player in the game of power and a moral witness?

No successful resolution of this ambiguity was foreseeable, I concluded. The power of papal moral witness ought to be deployed whenever possible. Yet the Holy See ought to remain engaged in the grubby business of world politics, not for its own sake but for the world's. And to what end? Not to be a player but to keep alive the notion that "politics," rightly understood, means mutual deliberation about the oughts and the goods of our common life, thus ensuring—or at least trying to ensure—that politics does not completely degenerate into an exercise of the will to power.

The day after Thanksgiving, I flew to Spain to give a lecture at the University of Navarra in Pamplona and hold a press conference for further discussion of *Witness to Hope*. My host, Dr. Alfonso Nieto of the university's faculty of communications, was the soul of hospitality, meeting me at the airport in Bilbao, driving me to San Sebastián for an exquisite lunch overlooking the Bay of Biscay, and then taking me to Pamplona, the city of the running bulls, where I spent two days. On Sunday, we drove up to Roncesvalles, one of the starting points for the pilgrimage road to Santiago, where I saw the tomb of King Sancho el Fuerte and was given an extensive tour of the Royal Collegiate Church by its pastor after we attended Mass there.

Alfonso and I then drove further up into the Spanish Pyrenees, toward the Franco-Spanish border. The ethereal quality of those forested mountains made it seem as if one could hear Roland sounding his horn through the mists. Franz Werfel and his wife, Alma Mahler, had trekked through these mountain passes to escape Vichy France after leaving Lourdes—where Werfel was inspired to write *The Song of Bernadette.* Yet the extraordinary combination of forest, mountain, and mist seemed to make Roncesvalles and the territory north of it a perfect place for an epic poem—which, of course, it was.

On November 27 I gave a press conference in the auditorium of the University of Navarra; the university president breezily informed me on the way in that, although the Basque separatists of ETA had set off a bomb in the room not too long before, no trouble was expected this time. During the presser, the inevitable question of John Paul II's possible abdication at the end of the jubilee year came up. My response was that the Pope thought of his office as a form of spiritual fatherhood and paternity wasn't something you resigned, so it didn't seem likely to me.

From Spain I flew to Rome to give papers at conferences sponsored by the Pontifical Council for the Laity and the Pontifical Council for the Family. Bishop Dziwisz invited me for lunch with the Pope on Wednesday, November 29, after the weekly General Audience. No sooner had we gotten into our seats than Dziwisz turned to me and said, "That was an interesting interview you gave in Spain on Monday—one doesn't 'resign paternity.' A good point." I thanked him for the compliment and said, "That's a nice intelligence operation you're running." The point in Pamplona, which I had made many times before, was that the Church wasn't a corporation but a family, and the Pope wasn't a CEO but a father. This somehow struck Dziwisz as fresh; John Paul gave me a whimsical look while this to-and-fro was going on.

With the US election still hanging from chads, as it were, the conversation inevitably turned in that direction. I said the important thing to ponder was not the Florida shenanigans but the fact that the country was split down the middle on moral-cultural issues; thus the Pope had been "unfortunately right," as I put it, in his *Centesimus Annus* analysis of where the next challenges lay for the democracies. I don't think John Paul heard this with any satisfaction, for he still hoped that America would be different from what he already saw as a morally and culturally disintegrating Western Europe, thus providing an alternative model for the new democracies of Central and Eastern Europe. We talked about the "Catholic vote," which I explained had far more to do with frequency of Mass attendance than any other factor, and discussed which bishops had been strong leaders in framing the moral issues during the campaign.

I brought the Pope a signed copy of *Crisis and Reform*, my friend Father Borys Gudziak's book on the history of the Union of Brest (which brought the Ukrainian Greek Catholic Church into full communion with Rome) and briefly described Gudziak's remarkable work in launching the Ukrainian Catholic University in L'viv. After we spoke about the book and the university a bit, I asked John Paul what he hoped to achieve in Ukraine the following June. "We'll see what can be done," he replied. He was obviously looking forward to the trip, told us that he had been rehearsing the Byzantine liturgies he would celebrate, and spoke at some length about intellectual life in Galicia, especially L'viv (then Lwów), during the interwar period. A true son of his father, he kept referring to L'viv by its Austro-Hungarian name, "Lemberg," or the even older "Leopolis." When I suggested that, given Ukrainian sensibilities, he'd better avoid "Lemberg" and "Leopolis" when he was in L'viv, he smiled and suggested that old habits were hard to break. Fr. Maciej Zięba, who was also at lunch, threw in the suggestion that the Pope do a drop-by in Kraków while he was in the Galician vicinity; that drew an alas-it-isn't-possible shrug from the Pope and a melodramatic groan from Dziwisz, imagining the mob scene he would have to manage under such circumstance.

Then we turned to the Great Jubilee. I asked whether it had met his expectations and John Paul replied, "It has exceeded my expectations completely." He was particularly pleased with the massive turnout for World Youth Day in Rome, where, Dziwisz noted, there had been ninety thousand French youngsters: an obvious outgrowth of World Youth Day 1997 in Paris.

John Paul was happy with the recent and quite positive statement on Christianity by several Jewish scholars, *Dabru Emet* (Speak the Truth); I explained the connection between that striking sign of a new theological seriousness in the dialogue and the work of Fr. Neuhaus and *First Things*. The Jewish-Catholic connection put Bishop Dziwisz in mind of Baltimore's Cardinal William Keeler, a leader in that conversation, and Dziwisz asked whether I was familiar with a "very interesting lecture on religious freedom" that Keeler had recently given in Lublin. When I replied, "Well, er, yes . . . " Dziwisz said that he "thought [he] recognized a few phrases."

John Paul had long since finished *Witness to Hope*. He asked about sales in the various language editions and said, once again, "It is so *big*," to which I replied, as always, "That's your fault, not mine." I mentioned that the English-language paperback edition that would be published in the spring of 2001 included a section on the jubilee. I also noted that I'd been in Jerusalem during the jubilee Holy Land pilgrimage and the Pope started joking about my "becoming a Vaticanista," to which I replied in mock horror, "That's the first unkind thing you've ever said about me."

I was the last one out of the dining room. John Paul gave me a long hug, we spoke of getting together in the spring, and he asked to be remembered to Joan and the children. As we were leaving the apartment, I noticed that, as usual, he was back in the chapel.

Via Crucis

On the evening of October 12, 2003, the Sala Clementina of the Apostolic Palace became the "studio" for a silver jubilee salute to Pope John Paul II, hosted by Poland's public television channel, TVP1. Some 150 invited guests formed the studio audience: senior members of the Roman Curia, diplomats accredited to the Holy See, men and women from the Roman Polonia. The Sala Clementina was video-linked to sites in Poland: Warsaw, Kraków, Wadowice, Częstochowa. TVP1's host, Piotr Kraśko, was joined at the anchor position in the Sala Clementina by Professor Rocco Buttiglione; Cardinals Angelo Sodano, Achille Silvestrini, and Roger Etchegaray; and me. We were told that John Paul would watch the program on a closed-circuit link to the papal apartment.

Plans changed, however, as the Pope, through the open windows of his chapel, heard the Polish children's choir entertaining the studio audience one floor below and decided to greet them. So fifteen minutes or so before the program was to go live, John Paul II was wheeled into the Sala Clementina on a large mobile chair to greet and bless the children. He then asked to meet Piotr Kraśko and those with him at the front of the Clementina, so we queued up and walked to the rear of the hall, with me at the end of the line. When I got to John Paul and took his hand, his face was so frozen by his Parkinson's disease that he couldn't even smile. As he drew me into an awkward embrace, he looked straight into my eyes and without uttering a word seemed to say, "Look what has happened to me."

I found it hard to say anything. Walking back to the front of the hall, I saw my friend Hanna Suchocka, the former Polish prime minister then serving as Poland's ambassador to the Holy See; I pointed to my wet eyes, she started to weep, and I had to get a firm grip on myself before the program began in a minute or two.

The last four years of my conversation with Pope John Paul II unfolded along a Via Crucis, a way of the cross. There were the serious discussions and moments of gaiety to which I was accustomed. But there were also times of tension, suffering, and pain: in the aftermath of 9/11; during the Long Lent of 2002, when revelations of the sexual abuse of the young ripped through the Church in the United States; in the months before the US-led invasion of Iraq in 2003; when the Pope learned that Ronald Reagan had no memory of ever being President of the United States; as John Paul went through his own dark night of suffering from the combined effects of Parkinson's and severe arthritis in his knees; when my father died. During these moments, I saw Karol Wojtyła become ever more the Carmelite he once imagined he might be: the Christian disciple who conforms his life, not without difficulty, to the crucified Christ—and who finds in the embrace of the Cross the key that unlocks the door to the Father's house.

Under the Golden Dome

IN LATE 2000 I GOT AN INVITATION FROM FRIENDS ON THE UNIVER-sity of Notre Dame faculty to come to their campus for what they hoped would be a debate about John Paul II with Father Richard Mc-Brien, the former chairman of the Notre Dame theology department and a stringent critic of John Paul and his pontificate. Fr. McBrien and I had played dueling columnists in the Catholic press for years, frequently matched on the same op-ed page. But things were cordial on the rare occasions we met; I thought it might be fun to debate him and accepted the invitation.

Dick McBrien had other ideas. He didn't want to debate me, he said. Rather, he suggested that we both make opening statements, with a chance to respond to each other, after which the floor would be open for questions. That was fine by me, and during the preliminary chat before the event, held in the library auditorium with former Notre Dame president Father Theodore Hesburgh, CSC, in the front row, Dick and I talked more about baseball than anything else.

The auditorium was packed, and McBrien and I said what we had to say from two lecterns on the stage. It was quite civil, perhaps even a little dull. Then came the questions, which illustrated something important about what was beginning to be called the "John Paul II Generation." Virtually all the queries were directed to me, every question was friendly to the Pope and the pontificate, and some were quite searching. It got sufficiently awkward that I suggested, at the end of several of my answers, "Perhaps Father McBrien would like to comment on this? . . ."

Then there was the book signing. Tables had been set up in an adjacent room so those in attendance could buy *Witness to Hope* and have it autographed, or McBrien's *Lives of the Popes* and have it auto-graphed, or both. The line in front of my table was out the door, and the line in front of Dick's table was . . . not. Dick eventually left while I was still signing, and one of my former students walked him out. He later told me that McBrien asked him, "Who were all those people?" "Most of them were the theology students," my friend replied, quelling what was evidently Dick's suspicion that ringers had been bused in.

Ted Hesburgh came up after the un-debate and said, "That was wonderful. It's exactly the kind of thing a Catholic university should do." I wasn't about to challenge Ted, whom I'd always liked, on his own turf. But to my mind the evening underscored the failure of the ap-proach to Catholic higher education that he and Dick McBrien embod-ied—and that serious students, formed by the pontificate of John Paul II, were beginning to reject. The students wanted to explore John Paul II's magisterium in depth and get to know the Pope from the inside; they weren't interested in Catholic Lite.

I felt sorry for McBrien, one of the most prominent of the theo-logians who had gone into a kind of psychological schism after *Hu-manae Vitae*, maintaining a formal connection to the Church but convinced that its supreme pastors were teaching untruths. Things just hadn't turned out the way he expected; the ratchet of ecclesiastical and theological history didn't work in only one direction—another exam-ple of the John Paul II Effect.

Abraham Lincoln in Full Pontificals

RICHARD NEUHAUS WAS IN WASHINGTON IN LATE JANUARY 2001, so Joan and I invited him, and Mike and Karen Novak, to dinner on January 21. Earlier that day, John Paul II announced a February consistory for the creation of new cardinals, one of whom was Fr. Avery Dulles—a friend of us all. So we toasted Avery's red hat, and then, just as we were sitting down at the table, the phone rang in my study. I went to answer it and there was the cardinal-designate. He absorbed the first barrage of my congratulations and then, referring to the canon that required cardinals to be bishops, said, "Thanks a lot but look, I don't have to be a bishop, do I?" A bit surprised, I said, "No. I think you just write the Pope asking for a dispensation; he'll certainly grant it, as he did for Congar and Grillmeier" (Yves Congar, OP, and Aloys Grillmeier, SJ, two elderly theologians whom the Pope had previously honored with the cardinalate). "But why are you worried about this, Avery?" I asked. "Because I'm too old to be running around New York doing confirmations!" answered John Foster Dulles's son.

At the consistory on February 21, Avery was last on the list of forty-four new cardinals, and thus all eyes were on him when he knelt before the Pope to receive the red biretta. John Paul placed the biretta on Avery's head, Avery bowed while taking John Paul's hand to kiss his ring—and the biretta fell into the Pope's lap. The Pope reimposed the biretta; Avery bowed again; the recalcitrant headgear fell into John Paul's lap again—all this being easily visible on the jumbotrons installed in St. Peter's Square for the Great Jubilee of 2000. The Pope, smiling as much as his Parkinson's allowed, handed Avery the biretta and Avery jammed it onto his head, kissed the papal ring, and got a good round of applause.

Immediately after the consistory, there was a reception for the new American cardinals in the cortile of the North American College, a large open space dotted with orange trees. Avery, feeling the effects of the post-polio syndrome that would kill him in 2008, asked for a chair to sit in while receiving those who wanted to greet him. I watched from a distance and was struck by the eerie resemblance between the new Cardinal Dulles and one of his intellectual heroes, Cardinal John Henry Newman, as painted by Emmeline Deane in London's National Portrait Gallery.

At the Mass with John Paul the next day, during which the new cardinals received their rings, Avery got the loudest applause in the cardinalatial class of 2001. His traveling party was then hosted to lunch in the atrium of the Pontifical Gregorian University, Avery's Roman alma mater. One of the toasts was a bit trying. The rector of the university began by saying how much he had learned from Cardinal Dulles, especially from his book *Models of the Church*. "I have learned from him," the rector said, "that the Church is an institution," which thought he developed for several minutes. "And I have learned from him that the Church is a mystical communion. . . ."—at which point I turned to Father Joseph O'Hare, SJ, the president of Fordham, and Fr. Neuhaus, and whispered, "Oh no, he's going to do all five of them." So Joe, Richard, and I quietly slipped outside for a postluncheon smoke, while Father Rector completed his reflection on all of Avery's models of the Church.

At 5:30 p.m. on Friday, February 23, Cardinal Avery Dulles, SJ, "took possession" of the Roman church of which he was now the titular pastor, Holy Names of Jesus and Mary on the Via del Corso. It was only the second time the church had been a cardinalatial "title" and it was an appropriate one for Avery: one of his heroes, the Jesuit saint Robert Bellarmine, preached there during the Counter-Reformation. The church was in the care of the Discalced Augustinians, and on meeting several of the fathers I got the impression that they imagined themselves to have won the red hat jackpot—surely the eminent son of a famous American family was wealthy enough to spend some of his riches on their church? Alas, their freshly minted cardinal-titular patched his shoes with duct tape, wore his clothes until they fell apart, and gave his substantial book royalties to his religious order.

The lean, craggy-faced new cardinal processed into his title wearing the miter and pectoral cross and carrying the crozier that befitted his new rank, even though he had not (to his great relief) been ordained a bishop. As congregations do, we all turned toward the aisle as the procession approached the altar—at which point Jody Bottum whispered to me, "Now we know what Abraham Lincoln would have looked like in full pontificals."

When I got back home, I mailed some souvenirs from the consistory to one of Cardinal Dulles's friends at Fordham, Father Joseph Lienhard, SJ, a distinguished patristics scholar. Joe wrote back, "Thanks for . . . sending the mementos of Avery's elevation. He looks great in a faded navy windbreaker and a pectoral cross."

Ash Wednesday fell on February 28 in 2001, so with the entire North American College community I walked up the Aventine Hill to receive ashes at Santa Sabina, the crown jewel of paleo-Christian basilica architecture and the first of the Lenten station churches. The following day Bishop Harvey called with an invitation to lunch from Bishop Dziwisz for Friday, March 2. Harvey and I went up to the papal apartment together and while we were waiting for John Paul, Dziwisz came in, apologized for the Pope's being late, and said, "We've got a problem." "What's that?" we asked. "I just went into the kitchen and discovered that there's no dessert. The sisters said, 'But it's Lent.' I said, 'Yes, but we have guests.'" "What was the resolution of this dilemma?" I inquired. "We decided to give up penance for Friday lunch," answered the papal secretary.

Both John Paul and Dziwisz asked for a rundown on sales of *Witness to Hope,* translations, and reactions. They seemed particularly interested in getting a German edition published and I promised to push harder on this front, mentioning that I had asked Cardinal Ratzinger for help the previous week. We talked a bit about the new George W. Bush administration in Washington, with the inaugural address and the president's reinstatement of the ban on US foreign aid to international abortion providers getting good marks. When John Paul asked about reactions to the new American cardinals, I said something bland about Edward Egan of New York and Theodore McCarrick of Washington before thanking the Pope heartily for giving the red hat to Avery Dulles—a possibility raised at that table during previous meals. Honoring Avery was an important encouragement for American theology, I said, and it would give the new cardinal an even more prestigious platform from which to continue his important work.

When I tried to draw John Paul out on his upcoming pilgrimage "in the footsteps of St. Paul" to Greece, Syria, and Malta, the Pope tended to deflect the questions rather than answer them directly. It was something of a sore subject, and he would have been less than human if he weren't severely disappointed by the bitter reaction in some Orthodox quarters to this effort to extend the jubilee's Holy Land pilgrimage while urging Christians both East and West to recapture St. Paul's missionary fervor.

On the way out, Dziwisz gave Harvey, Bishop Ryłko, and me copies of a large, beautifully illustrated book on the Great Jubilee of 2000, edited by another newly created cardinal, Crescenzio Sepe, who had run the jubilee. The book included the Pope's remarks at each of the sixty-four unique jubilee celebrations, and John Paul signed it for each of us. I was struck that, in this attempt to create a permanent record of the jubilee, all of the papal texts were in Italian—yet another indication that the insular locals still imagined they were working in a world language, which in fact was spoken by 0.8 percent of the world's population.

Chilled Guinness, Michael Jackson, Honorable Members, and Unhappy Tabletistas

AS I HADN'T DONE ANY PRESENTATIONS OF *WITNESS TO HOPE* IN Ireland or the UK and was curious to learn more about how the Pope was perceived there, I was grateful for invitations of to do lectures-and-signings in early March 2001. Flying to Dublin the day after lunch with John Paul, I landed at the beginning of a national panic over bovine foot-and-mouth disease and walked through several disinfectant stations before passing Irish immigration. But a greater trial awaited: having given myself a temporary pass from Lenten disciplines, I had to try seven pubs on and around St. Stephen's Green before finding one that hadn't chilled the Guinness stout to accommodate tourists. Globalization, it seemed, had its downsides.

Cardinal Desmond Connell, whom I'd met in Rome during the recent consistory, kindly invited me to the Mass of Thanksgiving he was celebrating in his cathedral on Sunday afternoon, March 4. We had a good talk the following morning, and when I asked Connell whether the Irish Church had "hit the bottom yet," he said, no, he didn't think so, but at least they could now see where the bottom was. Alas, that turned out to be too optimistic a forecast.

In addition to a book presentation and signing, I did radio and television interviews on RTE, the national network; friends later told me that it was the first time in over twenty years that someone had been allowed to say positive things about John Paul II and the Church. That was doubtless an exaggeration, but perhaps not all that much of one: the media environment was intensely hostile and anticlerical, and the most prominent Catholic voices were uniformly purveyors of Catholic Lite. Why the Irish, of all people, wanted to effect a Catholic imitation of Anglicanism and its meltdown was a puzzle I didn't solve during those days in Dublin, and haven't since.

The Catholic chaplaincy at Oxford and my friends at Orme Court and Netherhall House in London worked hard to arrange a book presentation at the venerable Oxford Union for the evening of March 6. Alas, another group invited pop star Michael Jackson for the same day at the same venue, and my somewhat embarrassed hosts were left to explain that Michael Jackson trumped John Paul II at the Oxford Union. On the way to the Catholic chaplaincy's auditorium, to which our event was moved, we passed Mr. Jackson and his posse in the High Street, but there was no chance for dialogue.

The lecture drew several hundred people and I was much impressed with the chaplain, Father Peter Newby. At dinner afterwards, I pressed Fr. Newby on the challenges of Catholic university work in a traditionally anti-Catholic and now increasingly secular, postmodern Britain. The impression I formed from his answers and others' confirmed what I'd experienced a few months earlier at Notre Dame: all-in Catholicism as preached by John Paul II was a viable proposition, while Catholic Lite was of little interest in university circles, save among the tenured.

Two friends in Parliament, Lord Alton of Liverpool and Tory MP Edward Leigh, arranged for me to address an informal meeting of members of the Lords and the Commons in the Palace of Westminster on John Paul II's social doctrine and the future of democracy. My presentation was listed on the March 7 parliamentary schedule; shortly before David Alton was to introduce me, I looked up from the dais and saw Ian Paisley, the veteran anti-Catholic bigot, poking his head in the door to see what popish tomfoolery was afoot. But Paisley, evidently satisfied that another Gunpowder Plot wasn't in the offing, took off for other mischief before I could invite him in.

That evening was the high point of my visit to the British Isles: a lecture attended by over a thousand at Westminster Cathedral, the great brick and stone Byzantine pile built after the restoration of the Catholic hierarchy in Great Britain. I'd never much liked the cathedral architecturally, but it certainly came alive that night. I spoke on the achievements of the pontificate; the questions afterwards were thought-ful (with one or two lurches into the eccentricity that is one hallmark of English Catholicism); and I got to chat briefly with Bolesław Taborski, the translator of Karol Wojtyła's plays, from whom I'd learned a great deal.

I'd done some writing over the years for the London-based Cath-olic weekly *The Tablet* and had engaged in a friendly correspondence with its longtime editor, John Wilkins. Learning that I was coming to London, John invited me to address the "Tablet Table": a monthly din-ner meeting of the magazine's editors and regular contributors, held in a local parish hall after a Mass. I accepted, not knowing quite what to expect. It was a most instructive evening.

As we were going through the buffet line, I sensed some tension, but Wilkins was affably determined to get things off to a good start, so after we ate, he gave me a friendly introduction and asked me to say a few words about John Paul II's social doctrine as a prelude to the discussion. As the latter was what everyone was obviously interested in, I spoke briefly on the Pope's insistence that a robust public moral culture was the key to the success of democracy and the free economy. Then I invited questions.

And they came. And came. Not so much questions but harsh, bit-ter indictments, one after another, as if the Tabletistas had been wait-ing for over two decades to have a shot at John Paul II and decided that I was the next best thing: sloppy seconds, American version. The tone varied from supercilious to snarky to bitter to offensively aggressive to passive-aggressive, but the common denominator was anger, erupting after years of repression. At one point there was a pause in the venting and I turned to John Gummer, a former cabinet minister and said, quite seriously, "I think I'm beginning to understand this. You all want to be Anglicans with valid sacraments." He didn't seem to find the for-mulation outlandish. John Wilkins was embarrassed, wrote me after-wards saying that I had been "the soul of courtesy throughout," and penned a puff piece on my London visit for the magazine's "Notebook" section the following week.

But as I said over a beer later that night to my friend Jack Valero, who sat through the tantrums with head bowed, I wasn't insulted, just depressed. Serious, well-informed challenge was one thing; ill-mannered Catholic Lite, smug in its certainties despite their obvious falsification over time, was something else. And these were the people running one of the most influential Catholic magazines in the world. As I wrote Cardinal Cormac Murphy-O'Connor, an important journal like *The Tablet* ought to be able to find writers who understood that the Church had moved beyond 1968 and that the real challenge for the future in Great Britain was giving life to John Paul II's New Evangelization.

The last laps of my first *Witness to Hope* tour in the UK took me to Glasgow and Edinburgh. I was given a tour of the magnificent Glasgow City Chambers before a session with Cardinal Thomas Winning in his office—over a decade and a half later, I remember him taking me to the window and quietly pointing across the River Clyde to a large new mosque. Even more memorable, though, was what Cardinal Winning said, with a tremor in his voice, while introducing me to some four hundred people in his cathedral on the evening of March 9: "I'm very grateful to the Pope. But it's not because he made me a cardinal. I'm grateful to him because he's made me a better Christian."

Ben-Hur and the Pope

ROME, MAY 2001

W HILE *WITNESS TO HOPE* WAS BEING EDITED IN EARLY 1999, I
met Catherine Wyler, a filmmaker, through a mutual friend,
Declan Murphy, former assistant to Jim Billington at the Library of
Congress. Declan thought that there should be a documentary film
based on the book and that Catherine should make it. After some discussion I agreed to work with her, another unexpected friendship was
born, and a window opened into yet another new world—Hollywood.

Catherine's father was William Wyler, winner of three Academy
Awards for Best Director and a legendary taskmaster who once asked
Merle Oberon to get a few more tears out of one eye while she was
dying in the arms of Laurence Olivier in *Wuthering Heights*. At our
first planning meeting at Cathy's home near Washington Cathedral,
I noticed something on the coffee table in her living room. "What's
that?" I asked. *That*, it turned out, was Willie Wyler's Oscar for *Ben-
Hur*; Cathy's brother had gotten Messala's chariot wheels in the disposition of her father's effects.

With Catherine as producer, we needed a director. Cathy suggested
a friend, the Emmy Award–winning documentarian Judith Dwan Hallet, who eagerly joined the project. Cathy and Judy made a formida-
bly charming—not to say daring—team when it came to dealing with
sticky issues and prickly personalities. Although Cathy had spent part
of her adolescence in Rome when her father was making *Roman Holiday* and knew something of the city's languid ways, she was new to the
Vatican. Yet she and Judy, with some help from Bishop Harvey and me,
got the interviews and background footage they wanted (including an
hour with the Sistine Chapel to themselves), while converting several

difficult personalities into friendly facilitators of the project. They also had nerve, unfolding a large Nazi banner from the ramparts of Wawel Castle at dawn one morning for what became a three-second shot in the film, setting up Karol Wojtyła's experience of the occupation in Kraków.

The challenge was to telescope an extraordinarily dramatic, not to say busy, life into a film no longer than the 116-minute format of American public television. The rough cut was over four hours, so there was a lot of editing to do. With Catherine and me kibitzing over her shoulder, Judy did it with consummate skill. I began to understand the possibilities of digital film-editing when we were looking at the re-creation of young Wojtyła's ordination to the priesthood, which Cardinal Macharski had allowed to be filmed where it had taken place, in the chapel at Francziskańska 3. But something wasn't right, and I said, "Stop. The bishop's ring is on the wrong hand." Techno-illiterate that I was, I thought the scene would have to be cut. Wrong. A little digital magic on the console behind me, and voilà!—the ring was on the right, meaning "right," hand. It was sheer magic, if a little nervous-making: here were capabilities beyond the wildest dreams of those airbrushing artists who would eliminate the suddenly disfavored from the top of Lenin's Tomb at the May Day parade.

After the rough cut had been honed down to the final product, all that remained was to dub in the script, which I worked over extensively with Judy. René Auberjonois, whom I remembered as Dago Red (the chaplain, Father Mulcahy) in the movie *M*A*S*H*, agreed to be the narrator, and I prepared for him a phonetic pronunciation guide to the Italian, Latin, and Polish terms and names in the film. Still, Cathy and Judy thought I ought to be in the studio in New York when René did the job, so up to the Big Apple I went.

René was sitting on a couch outside the recording studio when I arrived and I couldn't help myself in greeting him: "Dago Red!" He took it in good humor and was a pleasure to work with during a session that lasted far longer than the film's two hours, as René, a true professional, went back over the pronunciations and other ticklish bits time and again. The result was a film I thought could be shown and seen with pride.

The one skeptic about the film had been Bishop Dziwisz. Cathy and Judy wanted an interview with John Paul; Dziwisz nixed that and told me more than once that the project made him "nervous." I assured him it would turn out fine but his skeptical nervousness continued: until, that is, he saw the film, after which he became a great enthusiast. So much so that, when Bishop Harvey and I walked to the pontifical board for lunch on May 30, the documentary was already showing, with sound muted, on the DVD player attached to the TV set in the dining room—and the Pope was about to be driven into St. Peter's Square on May 13, 1981. Knowing what was coming next and thinking this was not the way John Paul II ought to begin his lunch, I said, twice, "Don't you think we can skip this part?" But on it went, papal valet Angelo Gugel serving fettuccine carbonara while the Pope was being shot in front of us on the small screen. Neither John Paul nor Dziwisz seemed to find this odd. Spiritual detachment? Polish sangfroid? Probably both.

We spoke again about the problems with getting a German edition of *Witness to Hope* done and the Pope suggested that I try for a Japanese edition, too; I said I'd look into it, but that the Japanese likely to be interested were probably English-capable. John Paul, Dziwisz, and Bishop Ryłko, who was also at the table, said that they'd appreciated the new paperback English edition with the material on the Great Jubilee of 2000, after which Dziwisz kept joking about "new chapters still to come." It was interesting that, whenever Dziwisz, Ryłko, or both began their "new chapters" routine, John Paul listened with an almost plaintive look on his face, as if asking, "How long, O Lord?" When the two bishops quieted down, John Paul turned to me and confessed that he'd read *Witness to Hope* twice—first in English, then in Polish.

There was some discussion about an approach to President Bush in the matter of stem cell research, an issue the administration was then considering; Dziwisz and Ryłko also said they'd appreciated the speech the president had made at the dedication of the Pope John Paul II Cultural Center in Washington. From the textual evidence, Ryłko thought that I had written it, but I explained that it was the work of Michael Gerson, the president's principal speechwriter, who had studied *Witness to Hope* closely.

We talked about what Maciej Zięba and Richard Neuhaus were up to, and then Dziwisz, out of the blue, started asking about my background. For what must have been the fourth or fifth time I spoke of Baltimore as "the Gniezno of America," but as Archbishop John Carroll's episcopate in Baltimore had been a mere two hundred years before and Gniezno (the traditional birthplace of Polish Christianity) had been a metropolitan see since 1000, I don't think my historical analogy made much of an impression. Then Dziwisz wanted to know if I'd ever been in the seminary. I said yes, I had, in high school and college, before studying theology in graduate school as a layman. The good bishop then asked, whether jokingly or seriously I couldn't tell, "Do you think you should have been a priest?" Deciding to keep it light but also wanting to make a point, I said, "Well, if I had become a priest, the Holy Father wouldn't have his biography, would he?" I then spoke briefly about what had been a challenging discernment, at the end of which I concluded that God had other things than the priesthood in mind for me—a point I followed up with a letter to Dziwisz, who wrote back thanking me for sharing my story with him.

The conversation then turned to the impending papal pilgrimage to Ukraine, and I asked the Pope whether he expected the local Orthodox leaders to replicate what he'd experienced in Greece: a lot of criticism beforehand, then a changed situation once he arrived and they sensed his respect. He simply replied, "Speriamo" (Let's hope). This got Dziwisz going and he went on a mini-jeremiad in his straightforward Vatican Italian: "La chiesa Cattolica è sempre aperta, e gli Ortodossi sono sempre chiusi. Noi li chiamiamo 'una chiesa sorella,' e loro ci chiamano 'eretici.'" (The Catholic Church is always open and the Orthodox are always closed. We call them "a sister Church" and they call us "heretics.") It was obviously a sore point with Dziwisz, whose many fine qualities did not always include the forbearance of his master. In this case, I completely agreed with him and said so.

We then talked about my experiences of the press after *Witness to Hope* and everyone seemed to enjoy the story of the "stupidest question" in Mexico City—"What does he eat?"—and my answer, "Food"—which I amplified in the telling to include " . . . especially *dolce*." The conversation became more serious when I described the interesting discussion of the Theology of the Body that I'd had at Smith College (explaining why that was a surprising venue for such a conversation), and the constant questions about John Paul's prayer life and daily routine. When I got through with the Theology-of-the-Body-at-Smith story, Dziwisz asked, "Is the Church demanding that people be heroic?" I said that I thought one of the Holy Father's attractive qualities to young people was precisely his challenge to moral grandeur and nobility—no matter how often you fail, seek reconciliation but try again and never lower the bar of expectation.

While Dziwisz went off to fetch some gifts, the Pope sighed and said, "Day off!" He certainly looked like he could use one, and with Ukraine on the horizon, I hoped he was physically up to a grueling schedule, working in multiple languages and liturgical rites in a diplomatic and ecumenical minefield. Dziwisz gave me a 2001 proof of the Vatican's five-thousand-lire coin and Ryłko asked, "What is that in euros?" To which I replied, "Well, with this and another twenty thousand lire I can go out and buy my book."

At the Sesto Quinto elevator I showed Dziwisz, who immediately showed the Pope, the galleys of my new book, *The Truth of Catholicism;* Dziwisz looked at the title page and the table of contents and cracked, "There is no need for a *nihil obstat!*" (an official certification of a book's orthodoxy). John Paul asked me to send him a copy as soon as the book was published and I promised to do so. On the elevator ride down, Dziwisz thanked me again for the film and the book, and, indeed, "Grazie per tutto." I replied in kind and was off to the North American College for the Roman premiere of Catherine Wyler's *Witness to Hope* film—which was being shown on the same screen as the Roman premiere of William Wyler's *Ben-Hur,* for in 1960 the college had the most technologically advanced screen in the city where the movie had largely been made.

New World Disorder

T HE EVER-HELPFUL MARIO PAREDES ARRANGED LECTURES ON *Witness to Hope* for me at the Pontifical Xavierian University and the Universidad de La Sabana in Bogotá in early September 2001. Elliott Abrams, my successor as president of the Ethics and Public Policy Center, had recently joined the senior staff of President Bush's National Security Council; on hearing I was going to the Colombian capital, he remarked that it was "the most dangerous city in the world" and gave me the phone number of the US ambassador, just in case. The city was in fact riddled with security; every office building seemed to have private armed guards, as did the religious house where Paredes and I stayed.

Mario and I spent an interesting ninety minutes with the papal nuncio, Archbishop Beniamino Stella, who opened the conversation by noting that I was "the one who made all the trouble with President Castro." When I asked Stella, the nuncio in Cuba before his transfer to Colombia, what that meant, he referred to El Jefe's denunciation of *Witness to Hope* in late 1999, told me that Fidel was angry at Joaquín Navarro-Valls for being so candid with me about their interactions, and said that Castro was using all this as an excuse for foot dragging on several issues involving the Church. I responded that such foot dragging was "the pathetic response of a paranoid personality." Stella did not disagree.

Stella also told us that Archbishop Giovanni Battista Re had had a fit when Archbishop Pedro Meurice had challenged the Castro regime, in front of Raúl Castro, in his welcoming remarks to the Pope in Santiago. Re evidently took Meurice aside later and said, "There was nothing wrong with what you said but this was not the occasion." To which Meurice responded, "What other occasion do you think I will have?" Game to Meurice; and it occurred to me that Re, for all his efficiency, was nonetheless the Casaroli-style papal diplomat when it came to speaking truth to power.

And there was more. Three months after John Paul was in Cuba, Stella was back in Rome and had lunch with the Pope and Bishop Dziwisz. John Paul asked, "Why did Fidel Castro invite me to Cuba?" Stella answered that it was a complicated business: Fidel respected the Pope (or what he imagined John Paul to be); he was a complex personality with a Catholic background; there were strategic considerations and there was the matter of the embargo. The Pope listened carefully and then said, "I still don't understand why he invited me to Cuba . . . "
—that is, if Castro wasn't going to follow up on his commitments to open things up. It was not a statement of naïveté but of sadness and disappointment.

The lectures at the universities went well, and I got some sense of the layout of colonial Bogotá, capital of the Viceroyalty of New Granada in Spain's Latin American empire. As in other South American venues, I was struck by the rapid transition in this megalopolis between wealth and dire poverty, shanties cheek by jowl with wealthy neighborhoods. And I wondered again what it was about Iberian Catholicism, translated to Latin America, that had failed to set the cultural foundations for stable, responsible governance and the sustained economic growth that raised all boats. Might it have had something to do with the close linkage between the Church and state power embodied in the proximity of the vice-regal palace and the cathedral in Old Bogotá?

There were direct flights to Bogotá from Newark, so I had driven to Newark International and left my car there on September 6. When I was driving out of the airport in the late afternoon of September 9, I saw the Twin Towers in the gloaming and, having taken my son to the top of the Empire State Building a few months before, thought, "I'll have to take Stephen to Windows on the World the next time we're in New York."

Thirty-six hours later, I was typing up the interview notes from my visit to Colombia when the phone rang. It was Fr. Scott Newman asking with some urgency, "Have you got your television on?" When I asked why, he simply said, "Turn it on *now*." I did so, just in time to see the second plane fly into the South Tower, which collapsed a half hour later. Shortly after, there were reports of something terribly wrong at the Pentagon, so I called the EPPC office and, as none of the senior staff were yet in, I had the receptionist tell everyone to leave calmly and go home, and put a message on the answering machine saying we would be back in business as soon as circumstances permitted. We were back the next day, with the DC National Guard stationed in front of our building, a few blocks from the White House.

On October 1, immediately after celebrating my father's eightieth birthday, I flew to Rome for five weeks. John Paul II had wanted to include a meeting of the world Synod of Bishops in the Great Jubilee of 2000, to consider the role of the bishop in the Church of the Third Millennium; but the scheduling proved impossible so the Synod was rescheduled for October 2001. I hoped to use the occasion of Synod 2001 to continue old conversations and begin new ones, with an eye to the inevitable transition beyond John Paul II and the completion of what I had begun in *Witness to Hope*.

On October 29 I had my first conversation in some time with Cardinal Joseph Ratzinger, who thanked me for *The Truth of Catholicism*, saying "we need apologetics," and then continued with a typically lucid and insightful survey of the world Catholic scene at the beginning of the new century. When I asked him what the key theological issues of the next two decades would be, he had an intriguing answer. In the West, he said, the "first problem" was a radical moral relativism born of a deep skepticism about the human capacity to know anything with confidence; that relativism also reflected a hostility to the very idea of truth, thought by the high culture to lead to intolerance and exclusivity because there was only "your truth" and "my truth." Ratzinger then made the connection to 9/11: How was a West saturated in skepticism and relativism going to defend itself against people with a profound if distorted sense of religious "oughts"? Was happy hedonism defensible? Who would sacrifice or die for this?

The cardinal was also concerned about the state of Christology, the Church's reflection on Christ himself. If Jesus is "one of the illuminators of God" but not the Son of God, "then God really is at a great distance from us"—so perhaps the West's sense of the "absence of God" was really a by-product of the "absence of Christ." On the other hand, Ratzinger continued, "if we see this Christ crucified for us, then we have a much more precise idea of God, who God is and what God does"—and this was crucial for the post-9/11 dialogue with the Islamic world, which is really over the question, "Who is God?"

Dealing with these challenges, the cardinal suggested, would mean putting the historical-critical reading of the Bible in its place as a useful tool but not an all-purpose guide: "The historical-critical approach is necessary but not sufficient," he said, and if the Bible was not read with faith, the result would be the dissection of a corpse, not an encounter with the living Word of God. Ratzinger also spoke of the need to ground the renewal of moral theology in Christology, for Christ is the model of "man fully alive." But he didn't see any theological renewal coming from his native land. "Organized Catholicism [in Germany]," he said, "is a task force for the old ideas."

Joseph Ratzinger was virtually without peer as an intellectual analyst of the contemporary Catholic scene, but my five weeks in post-9/11 Rome were also full of interesting comments about John Paul II's grand strategy for the future—the New Evangelization—from churchmen of various backgrounds.

Peruvian archbishop Héctor Miguel Cabrejos Vidarte was one of several Synod fathers who told me that the New Evangelization would be energized by saints more than by anything else, and that those saints were most likely to come from the ecclesial "margins"—renewal movements and new forms of Catholic community—rather than from the Church's formal structures.

Cardinal Desmond Connell of Dublin, like Ratzinger, thought that 9/11 marked a watershed in the history of the West, forcing urgent questions on the global agenda: Could a "world without oughts" respond to the challenge of a "world of distorted oughts"? And if the West could respond, how could it do so in a way that didn't turn "us" into "them" by violating our concept of human dignity and morality?

My old friend Cardinal Francis George of Chicago had some pungent comments on the Synod's discussion of whether the Church in the West should, following the Orthodox model, adopt a more "synodal" model of governance. Synodal governance, he said, was governance without headship; governance without headship was governance by committee; and "Jesus didn't intend his Church to be governed by a committee." Cardinal George also spoke bluntly about his first four years in Chicago, an archdiocese with a notoriously cranky presbyterate: "It's not so much that they don't want me as their bishop; they don't want a bishop, period." Evidently, he had found a note from his predecessor, Cardinal Joseph Bernardin, who had written that Chicago was "ungovernable." The cardinal also said that the recently elevated Cardinal McCarrick of Washington, known for his Democratic political sympathies, had told him on the Synod sidelines that the only way to "restore American credibility in the world" was to elect Hillary Clinton president in 2004 with Wesley Clark as her vice president—to which His Eminence of Chicago had responded, "Are you out of your cotton-pickin' mind?"

Cardinal Lubomyr Husar, Major Archbishop of the Ukrainian Greek Catholic Church, filled in some interesting details of John Paul's recent visit to his country: the continuing recalcitrance of Orthodox leaders; the positive impression the Pope had made on many ordinary Orthodox laity; John Paul's saying "I never expected anything like this" when he saw the crowds, ten deep, lining the road into L'viv from the airport; the "very strong" impact of the Pope's deliberate use of old Slavic imagery and terminology to foster reconciliation and unity.

Cardinal Joachim Meisner of Cologne argued forcefully that too many Germans "want to make the German-speaking world the norm . . . for the whole Church." Meisner also thought that there was Teutonic snobbery involved in the German disinclination to take John Paul II, a Pole, seriously as an intellectual; yet Meisner said that John Paul knew German literature better than many Germans and was always quoting Schiller and Goethe to him. He also gave me one great story, which nicely illustrated the barbed wit that John Paul II was capable of. *Polnische Wirtschaft*—"Polish stuff" or "Polish business"— had become a popular if definitely snarky put-down in Germany, and the Pope was aware of this when the Archbishop of Cologne and several other cardinals were called to Rome to sort through a gruesome financial mess. John Paul drew Meisner aside on the way to lunch and said, "So, Eminence, do you think we have some *polnische Wirtschaft* in the Vatican finances?" Meisner was speechless; when the others asked what the Pope had said, Meisner told them, "It can't be translated."

Cardinal Karl Lehmann of Mainz was a veteran of many Synods and had a certain reputation in world episcopal circles: he often fell asleep, loudly, during Synod speech making. As Cardinal George said, "I don't mind him sleeping; we all do. But he *snores*." Lehmann seemed genuinely concerned about the collapse of the German birth rate but was unwilling to concede that *Humanae Vitae* may have been right about the effects of the "contraceptive mentality"—despite admitting that Europe's demographic winter was, at bottom, a result of solipsism and selfishness. The cardinal, a leader of the Church's progressive party, did offer one suggestive image of the deleterious effects of secularization in his country: some people, he said, were discovering that "they cannot live with the silence."

There was a fair amount of pre-conclave politicking at Synod 2001. But I also detected a disturbing attitude of "Let's not worry about the Pope's health; things will sort themselves out." One would have thought that this was an opportunity for the cardinal-electors to be discussing what kind of pope they thought might best follow John Paul II. Curial dysfunction was regularly criticized, yet it often came across like complaining about the oppressive Roman heat during Ferragosto: a staple of the local scene for which no one seemed to have a remedy.

Tourism was taking a beating in Rome in the aftermath of 9/11, so Joaquín Navarro-Valls and I had the Taverna Angelica pretty much to ourselves at lunch on October 26. The savvy papal spokesman was already concerned that popular European support for the US action in Afghanistan was going to unravel sooner rather than later, which would give the politicians of the left in Germany, France, and Belgium the excuse they needed to back away from the anti–al-Qaeda coalition. Joaquín suggested that President Bush call in thoughtful European print and television reporters for video-recorded conversations that could go "over the heads" of the Euro-commentariat and speak directly to the people, as John Paul II had done before the Cairo world population conference in 1994. It seemed a sensible idea, which I passed along to friends at the White House, to no discernible effect. Navarro was also candid about the incapacities of Cardinal Sodano and the Vatican

Secretariat of State in grasping that the Euro-left was trying to portray John Paul as the chaplain of their anti-US campaign.

As for the Pope's health, Joaquín said that it had taken a bit of a downturn but that John Paul's mind was as clear as ever and that he remained "the center of all initiative." A recent attempt to crack open the door to China with a papal letter marking the four hundredth anniversary of Matteo Ricci's arrival in the Middle Kingdom and asking forgiveness for whatever offenses Christians may have committed in China in the past was the eighty-one-year-old Pope's idea: "Nobody in the bureaucracy would ever have thought of such a thing."

On the evening of November 3, my penultimate night in Rome, I had dinner with John Paul, Bishops Dziwisz and Ryłko, and Msgr. Mokrzycki. It was the eve of the Pope's name day and, following Polish tradition, the apartment was filled with flowers, with more coming up on the family elevator with me.

Despite the long haul of the Synod, John Paul was in good form, yet obviously concerned that 9/11 and its aftermath would shatter the hope he expressed at the UN in 1995: that the tears of the twentieth century would give rise to a "new springtime of the human spirit." At the beginning of dinner the Pope asked me to summarize what I thought the last month and a half meant. I said I thought it was a turning point in world history, an example of the mystery of evil at work through the corruption of an already defective monotheism, a possible moment of moral sobering-up in the US, and a very complex mess from a strategic and international-political point of view. All of this, I continued, was a moral challenge as well as a political challenge, and while the first duty of a responsible government was the security of its citizens, President Bush's September 20 speech indicated that American military action against al-Qaeda and its Taliban facilitators would be conducted according to just war principles and not as a matter of vendetta or revenge. It was essential for everyone to understand that what was at stake here was not simply the security of the United States but the very possibility of any world "order." I also pointed out that Osama bin Laden was a very rich man and that it didn't help clarify what we were all facing when it was said that terrorism was the product of poverty—the line being taken at the UN by Archbishop Renato Martino, the Holy See's permanent representative there.

Each of these points was the subject of discussion among John Paul, Dziwisz, Ryłko, and me; three times during the back-and-forth, the Pope punctuated the conversation with a heartfelt, if somber, "God bless America." The United States had been wounded; John Paul, whose affection for America ran deep, knew that, and in quoting Irving Berlin he was trying to convey his understanding and his sympathy.

We then talked about upcoming World Youth Day 2002 in Toronto, and while there had been some chatter during the Synod about postponing it because of 9/11, it was clear that John Paul wouldn't hear of it. I completely agreed and said that WYD 2002 was more important than ever as a countersign to al-Qaeda, the Taliban, and the world that publicly vibrant and assertive religion wasn't necessarily violent religion.

The question of a German edition of *Witness to Hope* had been resolved, and my dinner companions were happy about that. John Paul said he was reading the book in Polish for a second time; I asked him why, and he said I helped him think about things he otherwise wouldn't have the opportunity to reflect upon. When I mentioned that I'd been in Warsaw in October, there was some joking about the relative merits of the Polish capital and Kraków, with none of the devout Cracovians present suggesting the superiority of the former. As for the city he loved so well, and those he loved who lived there, I could see that, as John Paul dealt with some of his correspondence over dessert, several of the responses to name-day greetings were signed "Wujek."

The Pope seemed reluctant to say goodbye; we did so three times, the first including a blessing for Joan, the children, and "all my American friends." (At one point in the conversation, Bishop Ryłko had asked whether one of those friends, Richard Neuhaus, was a *parochius,* a parish priest, in New York. I said he was, at Immaculate Conception Church—to which Ryłko replied, with a laugh in which the Pope and Dziwisz joined, "Parochius sui generis.") Bishop Dziwisz regifted me a cake that had obviously just arrived for the name day, saying "This is for your wife." Not knowing quite how I was going to get a cake back to the United States, I didn't think Joan would mind if I took the liberty of regifting the regift to the faculty dining room at the North American College.

THE LONG LENT

ROME, PORTUGAL, TORONTO, AND GERMANY, 2002

IT WAS RICHARD NEUHAUS WHO FIRST CALLED IT THE "LONG LENT": the crisis caused by revelations of clerical sexual abuse in the United States, which broke out in January 2002 and continued throughout the year (and beyond). It certainly felt that way. Day after day, stories of grave clerical sins and episcopal misgovernance hammered the Church in America, demoralizing a Catholic community beginning to experience the fruits of the John Paul II Effect, especially in seminaries and among younger priests. Day after day, US Catholics wondered why the Pope and the Vatican didn't do something dramatic to stanch the bleeding. My experience of this disaster involved three expeditions to Rome, two to try to help senior Vatican officials and John Paul II understand what was going on, and one to begin sifting through the debris.

In mid-February 2002, with the crisis in flood tide, I went to Rome to co-chair an academic conference and spent many hours outside that event trying to understand the Roman perception of the crisis, while filling in what blanks I could from my own experience and analysis of it. Before I arrived, I'd asked a friend in the Curia whether anyone in real authority in the Holy See "got it." His reply: "No." My conversations with various Roman officials taught me that my friend's response was too simple; some did get it, or were beginning to get it, although there was a long way to go before the creaky bureaucratic machinery of the Holy See "got it" comprehensively.

Some old friends, including Cardinal J. Francis Stafford (who had dealt with these problems forthrightly when he was Archbishop of Denver), understood that this was fundamentally a spiritual crisis: a manifestation of grave sin that could not be addressed solely in bureaucratic, legal, or therapeutic terms. That one of the chief villains, Father John Geoghan, had been treated at a Catholic facility for troubled priests without any of the therapists making recommendations about the reformation of Geoghan's spiritual life spoke volumes about the disaster the therapeutic culture had wrought in American Catholicism.

But if there was at least some capacity to recognize that a spiritual crisis underlay the abuse crisis, there was little willingness to acknowledge, much less address, one aspect of that spiritual crisis: the fact that homosexual predation had played a large role in these crimes of abuse, which would become ever more clear as the investigation of the abuse continued. That the general breakdown of clerical discipline since Vatican II involved the homosexual exploitation of the young was not something with which senior officials in Rome were willing to wrestle in the first months of the crisis.

During this February Roman work period I began to sense that there was a serious information gap between Rome and the United States. US Catholics imagined the Vatican was experiencing the crisis as they were, in real time, and that simply wasn't the case. The Vatican and the Pope were months behind the information curve, thanks to incapacities in Rome and in the nunciature in Washington.

This information gap and the institutional sluggishness that caused it came into dramatic focus two and a half weeks after I left Rome. On March 21, Cardinal Darío Castrillón Hoyos of the Congregation for the Clergy held a press conference to present John Paul II's annual Holy Thursday letter to the priests of the world. Castrillón's presser was an unmitigated disaster. Not only did the cardinal fail to mention that John Paul II had been a vocal advocate of the reform of the priesthood and seminary formation for two decades and more, Cardinal Castrillón also failed to point out that the relatively few cases of clerical sexual abuse in the 1990s suggested that John Paul's reforms were having an effect. John Paul's description of sexual abuse as a manifestation of the "mystery of evil" in the world had caused a furor; Castrillón did not say that this described the crisis with complete accuracy and in a way that reflected the terrible experiences of the victims of abuse. He also failed to emphasize the Pope's grief over the victims and over the abusers' betrayals of the priesthood, whose nobility as a vocation he had upheld and lived. Rather, Castrillón blamed the furor on the obsessions of the world media and went on to suggest that, what with a crisis in the Middle East, the Pope had other things to worry about. An opportunity for clarification was thus turned into a fiasco.

The catastrophe of the Castrillón press conference persuaded me that I should return to Rome immediately after Easter to try again, this time armed with materials I was determined to get to John Paul II—articles by men and women he trusted, analyzing the crisis in the theological terms in which he understood it but also arguing that serious measures were required if the crisis were to become an opportunity to advance the New Evangelization through a deeper reform of the priesthood, the seminaries, and the American episcopate. Otherwise, the evangelical grand strategy the Pope had proposed for the Church of the twenty-first century and the third millennium was going to be gravely impeded.

I began by going over the whole tawdry mess with Bishop James Harvey during an overnight stay at Castel Gandolfo, in the capacious apartment he used in the Villa Barberini as Prefect of the Papal Household. Over the next week, I met with officials of various curial offices, including the Secretariat of State, the Congregation for the Doctrine of the Faith, and the Congregation for Bishops. Knowing that repetition was essential to cutting through bureaucratic lethargy and the fog of incomprehension, I repeated the same basic message time and again: the crisis was not a media invention and there were serious problems that must be addressed; the Pope had to be directly engaged with the US bishops' conference leadership, urging them to take effective action. That, I hoped, would reinforce what the conference leadership was telling John Paul. In the midst of all this, Cardinal Bernard Law, who had become the symbol of the entire crisis, arrived in Rome, prepared to step down. Yet because the Pope and the senior officials of the Curia were three months behind the information curve, they couldn't hear Law's offer as anything other than a desperate gesture, which it was not; it was a well-considered and courageous offer, and Law should have insisted that he knew the situation better than John Paul and the Curia.

While that drama played out, I sent John Paul and Bishop Dziwisz the dossier of materials I brought with me, convinced from my conversations that such analyses of the gravity of the crisis, its sources, and the likely remedies were not being forwarded from the Washington nunciature with the sense of urgency that would get them taken seriously.

Bishop Dziwisz invited me for dinner on April 17, which I had to decline because of conflicting commitments to the University of Dallas and my daughter Monica (then doing her Rome semester at the Due Santi campus), and to colleagues who were arriving for yet another academic conference I was to co-chair. We hoped to find another opportunity for a meal, but amid the chaos—the US cardinals were called to an emergency meeting with curial officials and the Pope to discuss the crisis—that never happened. Which was likely for the best, because at Dziwisz's suggestion I sent John Paul a lengthy letter that gave a more detailed summary of the crisis than would have been possible over a meal: an analysis and a set of recommendations I hoped would help frame the discussions with the American churchmen he was about to meet.

The letter was built around what I called six essential points:

1. The crisis was real and it was the Church's crisis.
2. The crisis of clerical sexual abuse was fundamentally a spiritual crisis, a manifestation of inadequate conversion to Christ.
3. The three expressions of clerical sexual abuse included pedophilia strictly speaking (a disordered sexual attraction to children), the age-old problem of priests in irregular and sinful relationships with women, and, most prevalently, the abuse of teenage boys and young men.
4. The crisis of clerical sexual abuse had been fed by a culture of dissent in the Church, in which men who lived lives of intellectual deception—pretending they accepted Church teachings with which they disagreed and that they had no intention of promoting—learned to live lives of deception in their sexual conduct as well.
5. The key to transforming this crisis into a moment of renewal and reform for the Church was leadership, which could only come from evangelical, pastoral, courageous bishops who responded to

these problems like apostles, not managers, and who taught the
faith boldly and by the example of their lives.

6. The Holy See had to address the question of when a bishop's
credibility had become so weakened that he can no longer govern his diocese effectively; far more scandal was being created by
inept episcopal leadership than by the Church's frank admission
that a man, even if not personally guilty of willful irresponsibil-
ity, had lost his capacity to teach and govern.

I closed on a personal note:

*Holy Father, you have honored me over the years with your
friendship and by giving me the opportunity to write your biography. . . . Yet . . . nothing I have ever written [to] you has been
more important than this letter. The great achievements of your
papacy are, in the United States, in jeopardy; yet those achievements have also laid the foundation for the reform we now need.
Help us, Holy Father, to make that reform happen.*

At the same time that I was writing John Paul, I was consulting with
the English section of the Secretariat of State on a draft of the remarks
the Pope would make at the impending meeting of American cardinals
and the Curia. There was a tug-of-war over the language; the superiors
were raising the usual bureaucratic cautions and were concerned about
being too specific; the men I was working with were pushing back. I
thought the statement needed a "money quote"—and after no little difficulty the final draft included the sentence I thought would be in the
first paragraph of every story and at the top of every newscast: John Paul
stating bluntly that the people of the Church must "know that there is
no place in the priesthood for those who would harm the young."

By the time I got back to Washington on the evening of April 22, I
was sick of the whole business. But there was no respite, as the media
frenzy over the cardinals' meeting in Rome continued unabated for
days. On Friday afternoon, April 26, I tried to escape for a few hours
at my son Stephen's baseball game, and while sitting in a lawn chair
watching Our Lady of Good Counsel take on Paul VI, a thought

occurred: stop grumbling and write a book. So between innings I called Loretta Barrett, told her that I was going to write a book on the crisis, and suggested that she find a publisher—quickly.

It turned out to be the best therapy possible. I wrote *The Courage To Be Catholic: Crisis, Reform, and the Future of the Church* in three and a half weeks. Loretta brought the manuscript, and me, to Elizabeth Maguire at Basic Books; Liz became a good friend as well as editor and publisher, and the book was published in record time, in late August.

While I was writing *Courage* I received a letter from Bishop Dziwisz in response to what I had written John Paul when we couldn't meet in April. As he put it about the timing problem, "Everything worked out fine. In fact it was probably better that the Holy Father was able to see your important words in writing. . . . He has asked me to personally convey his gratitude and appreciates the time and effort you took to analyze, explain, and give valuable insights on the present day crisis. It may well have been the Holy Spirit guiding us all at that very moment. Your daughter's play and our schedules adjusted accordingly were for the good."

I wrote back on May 5, thanking Dziwisz for his understanding and his kind words but reiterating my concern that the nuncio in Washington, Archbishop Gabriel Montalvo, did not "grasp the magnitude of the problem, its origins, or the great effort at reform that must be made if this crisis is in fact to become a moment of opportunity." In a recent address, the nuncio had described the crisis as one caused by a few disturbed and aggressive people looking for money and by media hostility toward the Church. There were elements of both in play, I wrote, but to read the situation primarily through those lenses was "deeply flawed."

On June 4 I delivered the annual Alexis de Tocqueville Lecture at the Catholic University of Portugal in Lisbon, speaking on "two ideas of freedom"—Isaiah Berlin's and St. Thomas Aquinas's—at the invitation of my friend João Carlos Espada. The following morning, João arranged for me to discuss John Paul II's social doctrine with what he described as "two-thirds of the country's GNP" at a luncheon meeting. The timing was not optimal, for Portugal unexpectedly lost to the United States in World Cup soccer that morning—a true shame, I told my shocked and depressed audience of Portuguese business and political leaders, because not that many people in America cared about the World Cup. It was intended as consolation and I hope received as such.

Joan arrived that evening, and after I did a little press work to help promote *The Truth of Catholicism* in its Portuguese edition, we explored Lisbon with Zita Seabra, a knowledgeable guide, before renting a car and heading out to see what could be seen in three days. The Fátima basilica site was a bit too much Tiananmen Square for my tastes, but it was striking to see the crown on Our Lady in which John Paul II had put the bullet recovered from Agca's assassination attempt. Most impressive were the earthen huts outside the city in which the young Fátima visionaries had lived: small one-story homes preserved as they were at the time of the apparitions in 1917. There was a palpable sanctity about the place that had been less tangible at the basilica.

On our last day in Lisbon, we spent some time on the waterfront along the Tagus, with its colossal monument to Henry the Navigator and other Portuguese explorers who set off from that river, not knowing where they were heading but believing they had a religious and patriotic duty to do so. I was already wondering whether any of that moral energy was left in Old Europe; so, evidently, was John Paul II, who was preparing an apostolic letter asking the same question.

The 2002 Tertio Millennio Seminar on the Free Society in Kraków gave Richard Neuhaus, Maciej Zięba, and me the opportunity to fly to L'viv and the Ukrainian Catholic University for three days. On Saturday, July 13, we drove with Fr. Borys Gudziak to a summer camp the university sponsored so that interested high school students could spend two months immersed in English; I thought of my old friend Bohdan Bociurkiw, who had died in 1999, and wished that he could have lived to see the sight. The following day, before we returned to Kraków, we visited several historical sites in L'viv that kept alive the cultural patrimony first preserved by the great twentieth-century leader of Ukrainian Greek Catholicism, Metropolitan Andrey Sheptits'kyi, at whose grave in St. George's Cathedral we had prayed shortly after our arrival.

The day after the seminar concluded I did one of Karol Wojtyła's favorite treks, up Leskowiec in the Beskid Mały Mountains, with Piotr and Teresa Malecki. In the clean, bracing air of the Carpathians, the

Long Lent of 2002 seemed far away. But it wasn't, as I was returning to the US and the publication of the book in which I tried to make sense of it all from a religious and theological point of view. More happily, there was also World Youth Day 2002 in Toronto, where I worked with NBC throughout the papal visit.

There were many memorable moments in WYD 2002, including a showing of *Witness to Hope*, the film, as part of the program, but the real drama came on Sunday. The weather in the early morning was vile, with rain and high winds. Up at 4 a.m., I was driven to the Mass site, Downsview Park in the northern part of the city, by an NBC car. The network television crews were stashed in a four-story-tall tubular steel structure with a clear view of the massive field and the papal altar, and the NBC section of this not-altogether-reassuring platform was on the top floor. Keith Miller and I were the NBC team, and at one point everything almost came to grief. There was plastic sheeting on the side of the platform behind the cameras and similar sheeting behind Keith and me, theoretically protecting us from the elements as we stood with our backs to the site. Someone decided to open the sheeting behind Keith and me to improve the shot, just as a gust of wind blew into the platform. The sheeting behind the cameras acted like a plastic sail, and the whole thing started tilting ominously. Keith and I continued our on-air conversation while technicians and cameramen with box cutters ripped open the "sail" behind the cameras before the platform crashed to the ground, taking us with it.

Providentially, the weather began to clear just as John Paul II arrived. He was driven into the Mass site from the nearby helicopter landing pad by Popemobile, with Bishop Dziwisz, as usual, in the car with him. The muddy roadway took them just beneath our platform and I leaned out and waved, looking rather soggy from the rain. As in Camagüey three and a half years before, John Paul II and his secretary looked up, pointed to me, and laughed.

Thanks to the hard work of Dr. Manfred Spieker of the University of Osnabrück and translation subventions from the German cardinals, *Witness to Hope* was finally published in German in the fall of 2002. Cardinal Joachim Meisner wanted me to do a book presentation in Cologne before I did press work at the annual Frankfurt Book Fair, so I spent October 7 and 8 in the Rhineland's largest city. After arriving and getting settled in an archdiocesan guest house, I asked for directions to the convent where Edith Stein spent her first years as a Discalced Carmelite. A brisk walk got me to the Cologne Carmel in time for evening Mass; afterwards, I knocked on the convent door and asked if the Mother Superior was available. Sister Ancilla a Maternitate Mariae was, and after I introduced myself and we established that my surname did not indicate fluency in German, she called in another of the sisters, Sister Verina a Corpore Christi, who had impeccable English. We had a fine talk for a half hour or so about Edith Stein's experiences in Cologne and John Paul II's sense of her importance; then the Mother Superior excused herself for a moment. She returned with several books on Edith Stein and the Cologne Carmel—and completely bowled me over with the gift of a relic.

There are no first-class relics of the martyr, whose ashes were scattered at Auschwitz II-Birkenau, but the Carmelites had found the wedding dress in which St. Teresa Benedicta of the Cross made her final vows, almost miraculously preserved after the city's destruction during World War II. Half the dress was used to make the chasuble worn by John Paul II when he beatified Edith Stein in Cologne in 1987; the other half was cut into very small patches that were then framed in glass reliquaries, one of which has rested in my study, with an icon of the saint, ever since.

The only two translations of *Witness to Hope* for which I wrote special forewords were the Polish edition, for obvious reasons of gratitude, and the German edition, because I wanted to make some points—chiefly, that the German-speaking world was missing John Paul II's intellectual significance because it peremptorily dismissed him as a premodern mind, when in fact he was a thoroughly modern thinker with a distinctive critique of modernity. That foreword ought to have been the basis for the press work I did in Cologne and Frankfurt, but with the exception of a few Catholic journalists, the scribes were more interested in my views on whether John Paul should retire, on the Long Lent in America, and on George W. Bush.

After another month of talks about *The Courage To Be Catholic*— including a memorable evening at Boston College at which one prominent Jesuit theologian frankly admitted that he and others thought the magisterium of the Church taught falsely on issues like contraception and the ordination of women to the priesthood—I flew to Rome to follow up on my work there in February and April, to brief John Paul on the German presentation of *Witness to Hope*, and to see what I could do to keep the lines of communication open between the Vatican and the Bush administration on the deepening crisis in Iraq.

The last was greatly facilitated by the friendship I had formed with the US ambassador to the Holy See, R. James Nicholson, and his wife, Suzanne. Jim was a West Point graduate who, after active-duty military service, studied law and became a successful real estate developer in Colorado; Suzanne was a talented painter whose charming watercolors graced the Nicholsons' Christmas card every year. Jim and Suzanne came to Rome after Jim's term as chairman of the Republican National Committee and quickly set the gold standard for the work of future US representatives at the Vatican.

Throughout the fall of 2002 and the spring of 2003, Jim bent every effort to prevent the breakdown of communication between Vatican and White House that had occurred before the 1990–91 Gulf War. This was neither easy nor simple, for at both ends of the telephone line there were misperceptions and flawed assumptions. But things would have been worse without Jim's persistent efforts to keep the principals in conversation with each other so they could at least know and understand, if not agree with, each other's positions.

My conversations with curial officials over nine days suggested that the learning curve on the Long Lent remained far too shallow. The Boston drama came to a first point of resolution while I was in Rome, when the Pope finally accepted the resignation Cardinal Law first offered in April. But I was told by knowledgeable officials that several key curial superiors, including Cardinal Darío Castrillón Hoyos, Prefect of the Congregation for the Clergy, and Cardinal Giovanni Battista Re, Prefect of the Congregation for Bishops, still didn't grasp the nature and magnitude of what was afoot and continued to blame the mess on the media and the lawyers; one of Re's collaborators described the atmosphere at the highest level of the congregation as "ecclesiastical denial"—an idée fixe that all these things *can't* be true. That continuing incomprehension, plus the usual bureaucratic torpidity, meant that Cardinal Law's successor was not named immediately, so a new beginning for the long-suffering archdiocese was delayed again.

On the night of December 19, Bishop Dziwisz called Bishop Harvey and asked him to invite me to the papal apartment for lunch the next day. Dziwisz also wanted to know what Harvey thought about my public commentary on the Long Lent thus far. Harvey told him about *The Courage To Be Catholic*, said he agreed with it, admitted that it included criticism of some bishops, but added that numerous other bishops supported my position. Not knowing what to expect, I arrived at the Portone di Bronzo at 1:10 on December 20, only to run into an incompetent porter, unshaven and glassy-eyed, who snickered when I told him that I was there for lunch with the Pope and called a Swiss Guard, presumably to throw me out. Fortunately, an elderly porter I'd gotten to know over the years came in and straightened things out, so I got to the apartment on time. Dziwisz greeted me warmly, joking about a recent *Daily Express* photo of what he called the "priceless" Pope surrounded by the millionaire soccer stars of Real Madrid, and took me into the usual waiting parlor. There I found Bishop Ryłko, who told me that he'd bought a copy of *The Courage To Be Catholic* in the United States in September, read it immediately, and thought it well done.

This was a great help at the table, as Ryłko proceeded to give John Paul and Dziwisz a brisk summary of the book, its analysis, and its prescriptions, in Polish, while I added detail. No one balked at the analysis, with the Pope listening intently and Dziwisz asking probing questions. One of the most controversial sections of the book was its linkage of the breakdown of clerical discipline to the "culture of dissent" that had taken hold in some US Catholic quarters after *Humanae Vitae*; I told the lunch company what had recently happened during the discussion after my lecture at Boston College, which rather illustrated the point. I then said that, while my friends and I would continue to defend the Church's teaching, and the current generation of seminarians and younger priests had remained strong throughout the crisis, we simply had to have more bishops capable of articulating what John Paul had called, in his April meeting with the US cardinals, "the fullness of Catholic truth."

There was agreement that too many bishops had fallen into the habit of talking about these terrible crimes and grave sins in excessively psychological terms; I said it was crucial that bishops speak the Church's language, and thus "change the context of the conversation." To drive home the point one more time, I concluded by saying that, while there were things that I and others could do—I mentioned Richard Neuhaus's commentaries in *First Things,* which Dziwisz always read carefully—"only you can give us the bishops we need." This led to Dziwisz musing that perhaps Richard should be made a bishop. I said Richard certainly would say what needed saying; Ryłko chipped in that "he is very courageous; he writes what he believes is true no matter what the cost."

We talked a bit about my experiences in presenting *Witness to Hope* in Germany, and I promised to send John Paul the special foreword I had written to the German edition. The Pope then pressed me on whether there would be a Chinese edition of the book: I explained some of the difficulties but said I'd keep working on it. John Paul certainly knew by then that he wasn't going to get to China, given his health and the recalcitrance of the government. Perhaps he thought getting the book there would be a kind of literary embassy to a place in which he badly wanted to bear witness, strengthen the persecuted Church, and do what he could to advance a reconciliation between the underground Church and the officially recognized Church, many of whose bishops had privately declared their fidelity to the Successor of Peter.

The conversation then turned in an unexpected direction, with the Pope asking me how President Ronald Reagan was doing. I said that friends of the former president had told me that Mr. Reagan simply had no memory of being President of the United States for eight consequential years. Hearing this, John Paul II looked stricken, and the sorrow on his face seemed to suggest he was imagining something even worse than his own infirmity—a situation in which he couldn't reflect on his life because he had no memory of it. A long silence was broken by the Pope asking me to get a message to Nancy Reagan, assuring her of his prayers, which I promised to do.

We also spoke about the mounting crisis with Iraq, and while John Paul, Dziwisz, and Ryłko were clearly not persuaded that Saddam

Hussein had to go, there was no resistance to my assertion that President Bush was a morally serious man who would take whatever decision he took with the proper sense of responsibility.

We then returned to the Long Lent, with the Pope saying that he wanted to read my book; having brought two copies with me, I inscribed one to him and the other to Dziwisz as lunch was finishing. There were Christmas presents for the family, including a strange, highly modernistic German pectoral cross (without chain) for me. After the usual *baci e abbracci,* John Paul went to his chapel and Dziwisz, wanting to talk more, walked me out of the apartment the long way, through the formal library. The Long Lent, he said, was a "horrible situation," and I repeated my mantra about the imperative of strong bishops. When the papal secretary asked me, of the American hierarchy, "Who are the leaders?" I mentioned Cardinal Francis George of Chicago and Archbishop Charles Chaput of Denver. At the door I got a bear hug that almost crushed my glasses on Dziwisz's shoulder.

THE IRAQ CRISIS

MY ROMAN CONVERSATIONS IN THE IMMEDIATE AFTERMATH OF 9/11 convinced me that the cast of mind I dubbed "functional pacifism" now dominated the Holy See. The Vatican formally accepted the just war tradition as the normative framework for a Catholic analysis of war and peace. But there was little serious just war thinking inside the Leonine Wall, and the results of that conceptual vacuum were not encouraging. The just war tradition itself was regularly misconstrued and misrepresented by Vatican officials, adding to confusion among politicians and in the media. The urgent just war questions being raised by the rise of global jihadism were not being explored, and the issue of what might constitute a "just cause" for the proportionate and discriminate use of armed force under twenty-first-century circumstances was never seriously examined. Moreover, Vatican diplomats and other senior Catholic officials seemed locked into the conviction that the United Nations had exclusive moral as well as legal *compétence de guerre,* which was something the UN didn't even claim for itself.

What this meant in practice was that senior officials of the Holy See had become "functionally pacifist": to their minds, a just war under modern circumstances was virtually unimaginable. That this thought had not occurred to the jihadists, or to various bloody-minded dictators around the world, made no discernible difference to the analysis of the new world disorder one heard in many Roman circles— which was not so different from what one heard in Western Europe as a whole. For there, as Joaquín Navarro-Valls had warned, the immediate post-9/11 commitment to resist jihadism quickly melted away.

In the world media and on the Euro-left, this had led to something else Navarro feared: John Paul II was being interpreted as a kind of trophy chaplain to what styled itself a "peace movement" but was in fact an anti-American-power coalition, whose raucousness I had observed on the streets of London in mid-February. As Navarro rightly insisted, John Paul understood his role in world politics in different terms than those hollering "No blood for oil." His task, as he saw it, was to keep pressing all parties toward a diplomatic resolution of their differences while recognizing that the decision as to when those efforts were futile, even counterproductive, was not his to make. That struck me as exactly right, as I tried to explain to friends in the Bush administration who sometimes read the Pope exclusively through the prism of his diplomats' statements.

These confusions and misperceptions came to a head in the period immediately preceding the invasion of Iraq in March 2003 by an international coalition led by the United States and Great Britain. January, February, and March 2003 will not, I think, be remembered as high points of modern Vatican diplomacy. The Vatican "foreign minister," Archbishop Jean-Louis Tauran, so helpful to me in preparing *Witness to Hope*, said time and again that the world must vindicate the "force of law, not the law of force"—a trope that ignored the hard facts that law is never self-vindicating and that the man who created the Iraq crisis, Saddam Hussein, was an international outlaw by any standard. Tauran and others also kept using, and deprecating, the term *preventive war*, as if military action in response to an imminent threat was never admissible in just war thinking—which was surely not the conviction in the classic just war tradition. Cardinal Angelo Sodano, the secretary of state, admitted in late January that the term *preventive war* was "ambiguous"; but he stunned me, and others, by warning against "getting bogged down in the question of whether or not the war [i.e., a possible attack on Iraq to enforce UN resolutions] is moral." Pragmatic considerations, in the cardinal's view, were of more consequence than ethical analysis.

Amid this cacophony, I thought the best thing I could do—in addition to bringing whatever insight I might have to the US debate—was to support Ambassador Nicholson in his efforts to keep Vatican officials and the relevant officials in Washington in open and serious conversation with each other. The problems on this front became intolerably severe in early February 2003, in the immediate aftermath of Secretary of State Colin Powell's February 5 speech to the UN Security Council. The voluble Archbishop Renato Martino had left the UN to become President of the Pontifical Council for Justice and Peace, from which perch he continued to opine on UN affairs. Thus the day after Secretary Powell's speech, Martino said in a Reuters interview that he found Powell "vague and unconvincing" and wondered "why those who want to make war do not take into account the serious consequences"—before admitting that he hadn't read the speech.

This was beyond the pale, so I wrote a two-page letter to Bishop Dziwisz, which he received on February 7. It was unacceptable, I said, for a senior Vatican official to accuse an American secretary of state, not least one "whose long desire for a non-military resolution of the conflict with Iraq is a matter of public record," of duplicity and to do so on the basis of impressions. I then addressed Martino's suggestion that moral frivolity was the order of the day in Washington, quoting Martino on "those who want to make war" being obtuse about "the serious consequences." This was verging on slander, I wrote, for it assumed a level of recklessness and moral blindness that was deeply offensive. It also contradicted the Pope's lifelong insistence on the moral responsibility of the laity.

Archbishop Martino was noticeably less noisy in the weeks immediately following, although he did return to form on St. Patrick's Day, comparing George W. Bush to the Pharaoh of the Exodus. I wrote Joaquín Navarro, saying that I understood there was little he could do but asking whether he didn't think that "calmer language" could be found to express the Holy See's concerns. He admitted that "it is indeed a difficult moment . . . for everyone."

With the first phase of the war winding down, I had a long conversation on May 21 with Archbishop Martino's replacement at the UN, Archbishop Celestino Migliore, who would become a friend in the years ahead. Neither of us was interested in revisiting the arguments over the deposition of Saddam Hussein. Our common concern was the poverty of thought in Catholic circles that was evident in the debate over the Iraq War, and we explored what we might try to do about that together. Then Mount Martino erupted again, and the President of the Pontifical Council for Justice and Peace announced at the Gregorian University that "freedom and the restoration of law have never been achieved by force or war." I wrote Migliore that this struck me as a curious argument for an Italian of Martino's generation to make, "freedom" and "law" having been restored to Italy by Allied troops during World War II. "This is precisely the kind of gross exaggeration," I wrote, "that has many friends of the Holy See wondering just what is going on." Why did Martino, in order to defend the notion of the rule of law in international affairs, "feel it necessary to make statements that have no foundation in reality?"

At my invitation, Archbishop Migliore offered a thoughtful public response to the twenty-sixth Thomas Merton Lecture, which I delivered at Columbia University in October 2003 and which was later published in *First Things* under the title "World Order: What Catholics Forgot." In April 2004, with help from Archbishop Migliore and Father Kevin Flannery, SJ, the Gregorian's Dean of Philosophy, I organized an international conference in Rome on the Church and world affairs in the twenty-first century. In planning that conference, no one suggested that we invite the President of the Pontifical Council for Justice and Peace, who by then had become Cardinal Martino.

Dark Night and Silver Jubilee

THE SUMMER OF 2003 WAS THE LAST OF THE "DARK NIGHTS OF THE soul" that recur in the life of a spiritual Carmelite like John Paul II. The weather was infernally hot, even at Castel Gandolfo. The Pope had been promised an operation to relieve the pain in his arthritic knees, but the doctors decided that, given the Parkinson's disease, they couldn't risk putting their patient under general anesthesia, so the operation was called off and the pain continued. The "new springtime of the human spirit" for which John Paul had hoped in 1995 seemed to drift farther beyond his (or anyone else's) reach: even as the tempo of military operations slowed in Iraq, the war in Afghanistan continued and the difficulties of the transition to a normal society in Iraq intensified.

In late August, I received an e-mail inviting me to participate in Polish public television's October commemoration of John Paul II's silver jubilee, to be anchored from the Vatican. As the e-mail was somewhat garbled and I wasn't sure how seriously to take it, I faxed Bishop Dziwisz and asked his advice. He quickly replied that "it would be appreciated" if I participated in the program: a polite way of saying "Get over here." So I flew to Rome only to be shocked and saddened by the evident pain in which the Pope was living, when we met briefly in the Sala Clementina before the program went on-air.

Several other events were folded into the weeks surrounding the twenty-fifth anniversary of John Paul II's election, which was formally marked at a Mass in St. Peter's Square on Thursday evening, October 16. The Pope spoke movingly of having "experienced the divine mercy in a particular way" on the day of his election, as he trembled at the thought of the responsibility that would be his. Three days later, on October 19, Mother Teresa of Calcutta was beatified at another Mass in the Square. The Mass featured one of the more bizarre innovations of Master of Pontifical Liturgical Ceremonies Piero Marini: during the Great Amen, what appeared to be smudge pots were ignited in a variation of the Hindu *arti* ceremony, in which wicks soaked in ghee are offered to one or more deities—in this case, presumably one. But Marini's curious adaptations of the Roman Rite were of less concern to me than the fact that the Pope was having great difficulty breathing: at one point, Cardinal Joseph Ratzinger, one of the principal concelebrants, quietly took over the audible recitation of the Eucharistic Prayer when John Paul was out of breath.

John Paul II's last consistory took place on October 21 and included several men whom I had come to know: above all, George Pell, but also Jean-Louis Tauran and Marc Ouellet. With the consistory filling out the College of Cardinals for the next conclave, and given the Pope's obvious physical difficulties, Rome was rife with papal election rumor mongering, most of it nonsensical but some of it amusingly implausible. I did some NBC work during the anniversary Mass and the consistory with my fellow survivor of the tottering camera platform in Toronto, Keith Miller. Among other things, that gave me the opportunity to quash the more lurid tales swirling through Rome while discussing the nature of sanctity in the modern world, which Mother Teresa embodied in a singular way.

President Bush invited me to be part of the official US delegation at the Pope's silver jubilee, but I responded that, as I would be working with NBC, it was best that I decline so as not to get wires crossed. Jim and Suzanne Nicholson nonetheless invited Joan (who came for the beatification of the great woman her parents had helped in Calcutta) and me to the buffet dinner they hosted for the US delegation on October 18. Everyone at Villa Richardson that night was deeply concerned about John Paul's health, and as I hadn't had an opportunity to see him yet, beyond that brief encounter in the Sala Clementina, I couldn't do more than suggest that he would soldier on. We were, it seemed, rapidly approaching the end of an epoch.

T. S. Eliot and a Good Story Ruined

IN EARLY NOVEMBER 2003, ARCHBISHOP JAMES HARVEY (AS HE HAD been since late September) told me that Archbishop Dziwisz (who was bumped up a rank at the same time) was asking whether I was still in Rome and saying that the Pope was sorry he'd missed me in the crush of the papal jubilee, the Mother Teresa beatification, and the consistory. This was another signal to catch a plane, so I came to Rome for a week in mid-December, with Dziwisz inviting me to dinner on Monday evening, December 15.

When I arrived at the Bronze Doors the Swiss Guard at the desk called upstairs and asked for Dziwisz; he wasn't immediately available, so the guardsman asked for Msgr. Mokrzycki, who was also not to be found; he then asked for one of the household nuns, who said, "I'm not expecting anyone for dinner." At which I smiled and said, "Maybe she isn't, but they are." After a few minutes it got sorted out and I was directed to the family elevator in the Cortile Sesto Quinto. Archbishop (since October 4) Ryłko arrived at the same time, so we went up to the papal apartment together. As if to indicate that no damage had been done by the forthright exchange of views before the invasion of Iraq, the banter started immediately when Archbishop Dziwisz came in and I observed, by way of congratulation, "So, we now have two *arch*bishops." Yes, Dziwisz said, "we have two archbishops but you are *niente* [nothing]." "Not yet," I replied. Dziwisz then gave me a newly published volume of John Paul's major philosophical works, *Karol Wojtyła: Metafisica della Persona* (The Metaphysics of the Person) before taking Ryłko and me into the dining room, where the Pope was already seated at his place and seemed happy to see me.

John Paul looked much better than he had in October; his face wasn't frozen as it had been then, his color was good, he spoke easily and swiftly in Polish, and his breathing difficulties were, for the moment, resolved. A letter from Joan, asking prayers for a sick friend, was by his plate and the first thing John Paul said was that he'd offer Mass for her the following day.

As had become customary over the past three years, we spoke briefly about the various language editions of *Witness to Hope*; the Pope seemed particularly interested in reactions to the German edition and everyone was grateful that the redoubtable Bishop Joseph Zen in Hong Kong had agreed to get a Chinese edition done. It was a shock to learn that the publishers of the different editions hadn't sent copies to the papal apartment, so I promised to put a box together and send everything to Archbishop Dziwisz as soon as I got home.

Then we began discussing John Paul's new poem, *Roman Triptych,* which had been published in September. I asked the Pope whether he would write any more poems and got a very emphatic response: "No, è finito!" (No, that's over!)—at which Dziwisz muttered, with a slight roll of his eyes, "Per oggi . . . " (For today . . .). I then told John Paul that he'd "ruined a good story," meaning the tale of his having broken his pen when he finished writing what was assumed to be his last poem, "Stanisław." That got me an expressive papal shrug and whatever sort of a wink John Paul could still make.

The Pope then asked about the family and I mentioned that Gwyneth would be married the following August. That set off a round of banter among John Paul, Dziwisz, and Ryłko, asking whether "Professor Weigel was ready to be a *nonno* [grandfather]," to which I replied, "Not quite yet."

My Christmas gift was T. S. Eliot's *Collected Poems, 1909–1962,* and when the Pope unwrapped it and read the title, the old actor immediately said, "Eliot: *Murder in the Cathedral*"—which, Ryłko noted, had once been performed at Wawel Cathedral, the climactic scene being staged in the sanctuary. When Ryłko asked whether my bishop, the globe-trotting Cardinal Theodore McCarrick, was in good health and I replied that "I really don't know; we don't see him in Washington all that much," knowing looks went around the table. Saddam Hussein had been captured the day before and Dziwisz said something about how awful he looked; I suggested that's what you look like when you've murdered thousands of people, which got expressive grunts from the entire company but no further discussion.

At 8:30 the Pope, looking tired, announced "Basta!" (Enough!), so after saying grace I went around the table to say good night, going down on one knee as the Pope was still in his chair. His face was far more expressive than in October and he held my hand for a long time, looking deeply into my eyes. Twice, he asked to be remembered to Joan and the children, which I assured him I would.

I walked over to Archbishop Harvey's apartment and said that, while I admired the great witness John Paul was giving through his suffering, "I could have wished for a different ending." To which the Prefect of the Papal Household replied, "But isn't that another sign of his greatness? That he's willing to submit himself to public humiliation daily out of dedication to the mission?"

"I Proved Them Wrong!"

ALTHOUGH I DIDN'T SEE JOHN PAUL II AGAIN FOR A FULL YEAR, the first eleven months of 2004 were full of events that grew out of *Witness to Hope* and my subsequent work as the "witness to the witness." On two occasions, at Princeton in February and at a Frassati Society meeting in Indianapolis in September, I spoke about the pontificate and the Pope's hope for the New Evangelization to large audiences of young adults. Both were impressive in their enthusiasm, and the questions raised at Princeton were so striking that I wrote John Paul about them. In May I gave the fourth annual Tyburn Lecture, on Catholic social doctrine as shaped by the magisterium of John Paul II; the lecture was held at London's Tyburn Convent, a cloistered Benedictine house of perpetual Eucharistic adoration that houses a memorial to the Catholic martyrs of the Reformation in the UK. In July, after the Kraków summer seminar, I climbed up to Rusinowa Polana in the Tatras with Piotr and Teresa Malecki, replicating another favorite Karol Wojtyła trek. Over pierogi in a wooden-hut restaurant at the high point of a scenic mountain meadow, we signed a postcard for the Pope, and I added "Środowisko honoris causa" in parentheses under my signature; Piotr and Teresa later told me John Paul had found my honorary membership in the group appropriate.

There were two family occasions in those months in which John Paul participated, if at a distance. On August 14, my older daughter, Gwyneth, married Robert Susil; the Pope sent an *autografo*, a personally signed blessing, for the occasion. Then on October 19, my father died after a rapid descent into dementia. On October 20, I wrote John Paul, who was always eager to know what was going on in the lives of others and with whom I felt compelled to share the story of my father's last hours. I told the Pope that my father had died the night before, on the Memorial of the North American Martyrs; that I read the gospel accounts of the Resurrection to him a few hours before he died; and that my brother had been with Dad at the very end, holding his hand and praying him home to the Lord. Two days later, when I returned home from the Vigil service, I found a fax from the nunciature in Washington with a message from John Paul for all who would attend the Mass of Christian Burial at the Cathedral of Mary Our Queen in Baltimore the next day:

> *I was deeply saddened to learn of the death of your father, George Shillow Weigel, and I assure you of my prayers for you and your family during this difficult time. I join you and all those present at the Mass of Christian Burial in commending the soul of this husband and father to the merciful love of our Savior, Jesus Christ. To all who mourn George in hope of the Resurrection, I cordially impart my apostolic blessing as a pledge of peace and strength in the Lord.*
>
> **Ioannes Paulus PP. II**

It was a thoughtful gesture from a man who knew something about fathers and sons.

I flew to Rome on December 7 to give a lecture at the Gregorian University that had been postponed because of my father's death, and to see John Paul II at what had become our customary pre-Christmas dinner.

From my tour of the papal apartment in 1997 I knew that John Paul II liked large coffee-table books of photographs, so I brought him a large photo album of the national parks of the United States for a Christmas present. When I came to the Vatican for dinner with the Pope on December 15, Archbishop Dziwisz saw me into the dining room with Archbishop Ryłko, and then disappeared on an undisclosed mission. After we shook hands, the Pope, his pastor's memory sharp as ever, asked, "How is your mother?" I was touched and amazed. It had been almost two months since my father's death and the Pope had many things on his mind, including his own debilitating fragility; yet the first thing he wanted to know was how Mom was doing. I thanked him for the message to the funeral Mass and said that my mother would be very glad to hear at Christmas that he'd asked for her.

I then brought the wrapped gift to John Paul, along with a Christmas card from my family. He insisted on opening both right away, and after the wrapping paper was removed the Pope started looking through the book. Finding Rocky Mountain National Park in the table of contents, he turned to those pages, got that look in his eye, and then showed there was still fire and humor inside his increasingly frail body: "Denver. Hmm. World Youth Day, 1993. Hmm. The bishops of the United States said it couldn't be done. *I proved them wrong!*"—the last sentence punctuated by pounding his index finger onto a photo of the Rockies. He then opened the Christmas card, noted that there was a new name—my son-in-law Rob Susil's—and asked Msgr. Mokrzycki for a pen. Laboriously, for the better part of two minutes, he wrote on the card, "God bless all your family! John Paul II."

Although the Pope looked somewhat better than I expected, the conversation was difficult as his hearing had gotten worse. So everything I said was translated into Polish by Archbishop Ryłko, which seemed easier for John Paul to hear. We spoke as usual of mutual friends in Kraków, with a little banter about my having becoming "Środowisko honoris causa"; as always, the Pope perked up when the discussion turned to his favorite trekking sites in the Tatras. There was considerable satisfaction expressed over President Bush's reelection, which, like others in Rome, John Paul and Ryłko seemed to read through the prism of Rocco Buttiglione's recent trials.

Rocco had been nominated as justice minister of the European Community but was rejected on obviously anti-Catholic grounds, the false charge being that he, an orthodox Catholic, could not justly administer human rights laws with respect to homosexual persons. It was a vicious canard but it killed the nomination, and my dinner companions seemed to find in Bush's reelection evidence that the United States was not as Christophobic (to borrow Jewish legal scholar Joseph Weiler's neologism) as Europe. It was also clear from this part of the conversation that the key people in the pontificate knew that a President John Kerry—a pro–*Roe v. Wade* Catholic—would be bad news for the Church in America.

The Pope asked again about a Chinese edition of *Witness to Hope*, which I reassured him was in the works, as was a Ukrainian edition. We talked a bit about Gwyneth and Rob's wedding, the Kraków summer seminar's longevity (which John Paul much appreciated), and my next book, *The Cube and the Cathedral*. I'd brought a spiral-bound copy of the page proofs for John Paul, who seemed very pleased with the dedication: *Amicis Crocoviensibus Meis in Corde Europae* (To My Cracovian Friends in the Heart of Europe)—both for the content and the Latin, a language he loved and whose demise he regretted.

At 8:40 p.m. the Pope declared dinner finished; it was almost like the old days, with him slapping the arms of the chair and getting up following grace after meals—except that he could no longer get up. I walked around to his side of the table, went down on one knee for his blessing, and said, of the rest of his story, "Holy Father, I promise you that, if you don't bury me, I'll finish what I started." We looked into each other's eyes; I kissed his ring (for the first time, I think); and then we parted, for what turned out to be the last time.

Fourteenth Station

IN EARLY 2005, WITH THE ABLE ASSISTANCE OF MY COLLEAGUE Carrie Gress, I completed work on a three-hundred-page briefing book for NBC News to guide coverage of the death of the Pope and the election of his successor: biographical details on John Paul II, the ritual of a papal wake and funeral, explanations of conclave procedures, vignettes from previous conclaves, a glossary, and a profile of each member of the College of Cardinals. With a platform position secured on the lawn of the Pontifical Urban University above St. Peter's Square, things seemed to be in order for what all involved in NBC's planning knew was coming sooner rather than later.

The last act of the drama began on February 1, 2005. I was driving to Annapolis to lecture at the US Naval Academy when my cell phone rang. It was Phil Alongi, head of NBC News Specials in New York, calling with a rumor that John Paul II had just been taken to the hospital. I pulled over to the side of US Route 50 and called Archbishop Harvey, who confirmed that the Pope had been taken to the Policlinico Gemelli but had no other details. My Naval Academy talk was interrupted several times by calls from 30 Rockefeller Plaza, relaying one rumor after another; I finally said I would be out-of-pocket for the next forty-five minutes until I finished my lecture and answered questions.

My commitment to the midshipmen completed, I was driving back home when Phil called again and asked me to go to the NBC bureau in northwest Washington. I stayed there until close to midnight before going home for a few hours of sleep and then returning to the bureau in the morning, staying until late that evening. By February 3 it was clear that the Pope was not in imminent danger of death and things calmed down for a few weeks as the Pope returned to the Vatican. Then the entire media circus repeated itself on February 24–25, when John Paul was taken back to the Gemelli for a tracheotomy, returning to the Vatican on Sunday, March 13.

A week after the Pope's second trip to the hospital, I flew to Rome to help finalize NBC's preparations for the funeral Mass and the conclave to follow—and to test out the apartment near the Vatican I would use during those days, which was kindly offered to me by Mother Mary Quentin Sheridan, whose Alma Mercy sisters were given it by a benefactor, John Ambrose. On the evening I arrived I was to have dinner with Archbishop Harvey, but rather than meeting as usual at the Sant'Anna Gate to the Vatican he said he'd meet me at the apartment, four blocks away on the Borgo Pio. When I came downstairs to meet him, I understood why: he had a large shopping bag for me, and therein lay a tale.

Cardinal Jan Schotte had died on January 10 without leaving a will. There were many personal effects to sort out and, as usual, the problem landed in Archbishop Dziwisz's lap. Dziwisz, in turn, told Archbishop Harvey to see to it. While figuring out what to do with some furniture and thousands of books, Harvey made a fortuitous discovery. It seemed that the late cardinal, while stationed in Washington in the 1960s, had developed a taste for bourbon—and there were three prime examples of Kentucky's finest left in the deceased's apartment. Harvey, knowing my taste for bourbon and my friendship with Schotte, figured that I might as well be the intestate eminence's beneficiary in the matter of these goods, which he was delivering into my care. I received them gratefully and stashed them in out-of-the-way corners of the apartment, thinking they might prove handy in the not-too-distant future and not wanting to subject other guests to temptation in the interim.

It was the fourth week of Lent, so on Tuesday I joined the station church pilgrims from the North American College at San Lorenzo in Damaso, the proto-Vatican where St. Jerome helped Pope St. Damasus I compile the first Roman martyrologies—a fitting place to ponder the life of the martyr-confessor struggling for breath and speech in the Policlinico Gemelli. On Wednesday, the stational Mass was at St. Paul

Outside the Walls. There, I had a brief talk with the Polish ambassador to the Holy See, Hanna Suchocka, who said of the Pope, "This is his Via Crucis and the press doesn't understand that." But my NBC colleagues did, and their seriousness of purpose reflected that understanding. Our personnel preparations were completed by my introducing the senior producers to various Roman friends whose commentary I thought would enhance our coverage. I also discussed conclave possibilities with several colleagues in the Roman media and had a long session in the Borgo Pio apartment with Cardinal George Pell, pondering the epic pontificate that was manifestly drawing to a close and the post–John Paul II future.

In the early afternoon of March 9 I was walking up to the Sant'Anna Gate and a lunch meeting with Monsignor Peter Wells of the Secretariat of State when I ran into Archbishop Ryłko. We spoke briefly of the Pope's condition and then he asked, "Does Stanislao know you're in Rome?"—meaning Archbishop Dziwisz. I said no, I hadn't called as I didn't want to add to the confusion at the hospital, which the press had turned into a bedlam. Ryłko suggested that, if I wanted to visit the Pope in the Gemelli, I should just call Dziwisz. I thought a moment and said, "Thank you, but I think not. It would just be another burden. Tell the Holy Father and Archbishop Dziwisz that I'm thinking of them and praying for them."

John Paul and I had had a good last meeting on December 15. There was no need to say anything more. We were united in a solidarity that didn't require immediate physical presence.

I flew back to Washington on March 13 and two days later had lunch with Mike Gerson and Pete Wehner in the White House mess; these two senior aides to President Bush were great admirers of John Paul II and wanted to know what was actually going on, as they were helping prepare the statements the president would make when John Paul died. The Pope returned to the Vatican and the death watch continued, even as he underwent physical therapy to prepare himself for giving his blessing, aloud, from the papal apartment window on Easter Sunday. Good Friday, March 25, produced the iconic photograph of John Paul II's last days: the Pope, watching the traditional Via Crucis at the Roman Coliseum on a TV set in his chapel, shot from behind while embracing a large crucifix. I spent several hours the next morning explaining to various segments of the *Today* program that, no, the shot wasn't framed that way because the Pope looked too awful; the shot embodied what he had been saying for over twenty-six years, which was not "Look at me" but "Look at Jesus Christ." Throughout the morning, Katie Couric could not have been more sympathetic in posing the question and letting me answer it in something more than a sound bite.

On Easter Sunday, I called Piotr and Teresa Malecki in Kraków and asked what they thought of the drama playing itself out in Rome, where the Pope had been unable to speak that morning yet blessed the crowd again and again, silently. Piotr had known Karol Wojtyła since 1948, when a young priest befriended a nine-year-old boy who'd lost both parents during the war; he thought for a moment and said, "I think they're finally beginning to understand him."

Shortly after that conversation the thought came to me—"He's going to die on Divine Mercy Sunday." There was no rational reason for this; I had no special knowledge of the medical situation. But I was suddenly certain that the drama would end, as it should, on the day John Paul II gave the entire Church as a way of healing the wounds of the twentieth century and as a reminder of what was essential for a nobler human future.

With the Pope sinking, I spent most of the late afternoon and evening of March 31 at the NBC studio. About 11 p.m., 30 Rock called and said I should go home, as a mobile studio was being sent to my house. By the time I got to North Bethesda, the crew was setting up in my living room; I showed them where the refrigerator, the pantry, and the bar were, invited them to help themselves, and said that I was going to bed for four hours.

On Friday morning I did various *Today* show "hits" from my living room. At 10:30, Phil Alongi called to say they were bringing me to New York by car and that I should be ready to leave in an hour. Joan had thoughtfully packed my bags a week earlier, thinking that I was going to have to move quickly when the time came, and after Carrie Gress brought some materials I needed from my office, I left for New York and went straight to work on arrival, talking with science correspondent Robert Bozell about the way this was going to end medically (on which I had been briefed by my brother, a physician), making various appearances on MSNBC, and getting to the hotel on Central Park South close to midnight.

At 3:15 a.m. on April 2 my mobile rang; it was an overnight producer at NBC, saying that Joaquín Navarro-Valls would be holding a press conference at 11 a.m. Rome time, and would I please be ready to leave at 4:15 for a remote studio—even 30 Rock was closed at that hour—in case any commentary was required. None was, so I went back to the hotel, had breakfast, and returned to 30 Rockefeller Plaza, bags in hand. After various MSNBC appearances, I was feeling the need for sustenance and asked Elena Nachmanoff, who was in charge of my NBC contract, if she could find a corned beef on rye for me. She came through handsomely, and after inhaling half a massive sandwich from the Carnegie Deli I went to Phil Alongi's office, hoping to take a nap on his couch.

No sooner had my head hit the cushion that substituted for a pillow than another producer came in, told me John Paul would die shortly, and hustled me down to the set of *NBC Nightly News*, where Brian Williams was in the anchor chair. Brian and I had worked well together before and he expressed his sympathy for my personal loss before we began the broadcast. When the news came through that John Paul II had died at 2:37 our time, we went into an hour and a half of live coverage, talking with eminent personalities around the world after Brian asked me for some personal reflections. I said that while I, like millions of others, felt a little orphaned by John Paul's death, I was also powerfully struck by its providential timing, just as the Church began to celebrate Divine Mercy Sunday, which was so prominent a theme in John Paul's life and pontificate. It was a life of incredible drama, I continued, beyond the imagination of any Hollywood scriptwriter. Yet there was a common thread in it—his rock-solid confidence in God's guidance of his life. That confidence, I concluded, made him the freest man in the world.

One striking comment on our broadcast came from Henry Kissinger. Over the previous weeks, I had said in several interviews that I thought the Pope embodied the human drama of the second half of the twentieth century in a singular way, as Winston Churchill had for the first; Kissinger went me one better and said that it would be hard to imagine anyone with a greater impact on the entire twentieth century than John Paul II. Zbigniew Brzezinski took a different tack, suggesting that Karol Wojtyła's life spoke to a global yearning for spiritual truth at a moment when much of Western culture was feeding the world stones.

I felt drained when I walked back into the control room after the special report concluded. Several producers and technicians embraced me and thanked me, one saying, "We know what that cost you." I asked for a fifteen-minute break to call my family, and did so from the 50th Street entrance to 30 Rock. It was the one time I choked up.

Brian, his producer, and I were leaving that night for Rome via London, so I went to a 6 p.m. memorial Mass that was hastily organized at nearby St. Patrick's Cathedral before being put into an NBC car and sent out to John F. Kennedy Airport in a driving rainstorm. On the way, Fr. Scott Newman called from Greenville, South Carolina, and said, "I've just had the most remarkable three hours of my priesthood." Fr. Newman had left our television coverage to go to St. Mary's Church and hear regularly scheduled Saturday afternoon confessions. Six people who hadn't been to confession in decades were so moved by John Paul's death that they came to church to receive the Sacrament of Reconciliation. As Fr. Newman said, "It's only been four hours since he died and the grace is already pouring out."

Jogging through Heathrow to catch our connecting flight to Rome, I scooped up whatever newspapers and magazines I could to get the immediate reactions and was touched to see Billy Graham describing John Paul as "unquestionably the most influential voice for morality and peace in the world over the past one hundred years." (The next day, I ran into Dr. Graham's daughter coming down from the *Today* set; we talked briefly about the providential coincidence of Cardinal Karol Wojtyła having given permission for Billy Graham to preach in St. Anne's Collegiate Church in Kraków, just before he left for the conclave that would elect him pope.)

When we got to Rome, I was driven by NBC car to the Borgo Pio apartment, chatting with the driver about the extraordinary crowds already beginning to arrive. One of the Mercy sisters met me, got me into the apartment, and gave me the keys; I'd just started to unpack when my Italian mobile rang and it was Joe Alicastro, calling from our "studio" and "newsroom" on the top floor of the great *parcheggio* built inside the Janiculum for the Great Jubilee of 2000. "Welcome to Rome," he said. "Get up here right away. We need you." Slightly stunned, I said, "Joe, remind me, we're doing television, right?" "Of course we're doing television," he replied. "Are you nuts?" To which I said, "No, but I look like hell, so could I shower and shave before coming over?" The kindly Joe agreed.

After taping a segment for Monday's *Today* program, I had a late dinner with Phil Alongi and others on the NBC team at Da Roberto, a block from my quarters. After dinner, I did justice to Jan Schotte's bourbon and went to bed, looking forward to my first decent night's sleep in four days. It was warm, so I opened the windows in the apartment's front bedroom, thinking I'd get a nice breeze in the back bedroom, where I was sleeping.

That was not a good idea. I went to bed about 12:30 a.m. and fell asleep at 1:00. Five and a half hours later, I was wide awake, thanks to a racket coming through the open front windows. I jumped out of bed and stormed through the apartment to the front bedroom windows. Then my jaw dropped. The entire Borgo Pio was a solid mass of humanity, from the Vatican down to the Castel Sant'Angelo, and from one side of the street to another; thousands of people were anticipating where the queues would form to view John Paul II's body, which would be taken from the Apostolic Palace to St. Peter's that evening. The doors to the apartment building opened toward the street, and I wondered just how I was going to get out—or if I was going to be able to get out.

That speculation was interrupted by a phone call from Archbishop Harvey. I'd called him the night before: I wanted to pay my respects to John Paul; given NBC obligations, I didn't have time to wait in a long line; what could he do? As usual, Harvey knew exactly what to do, and when he called Monday morning he said that one of his staff, Monsignor Alfred Xuereb, would meet me at the Sant'Anna Gate at 10 a.m. and I would be taken to the Sala Clementina, where the late Pope was temporarily lying in repose on a catafalque.

I somehow got out of the building and worked my way through the dense crowd to the Sant'Anna Gate, marveling at the courtesy of those I asked to let me pass—another example of what Fr. Newman called the "grace pouring out." Msgr. Xuereb and I found each other and I was taken into the Apostolic Palace and put at the front of the queue outside the Sala Clementina. When the door to the audience hall opened, I walked to the foot of the bier, said a brief prayer, and then looked at the man whose life had so changed my own.

For the first times in years there were none of the facial distortions and frozenness caused by Parkinson's disease. He was no longer stooped and bent. As I saw him there, his back straight and his face calm and at peace, I couldn't help thinking of him as a newly elected pontiff, climbing steps two at a time, bantering with crowds, tossing babies in the air, kissing the halt, the lame, and the ill; or as a heroic bishop, celebrating Mass in a field in frozen Nowa Huta on Christmas Eve, defying godlessness and its proponents; or as a daredevil skier careening down a mountain in the Tatras. Inside his left arm was the silver pastoral staff he had taken over from Paul VI—the modernistic crucifix he waved to the crowds at his inaugural Mass like a great sword of faith; the cross he waved at the crowds of pious Catholics in Managua over the jeering Sandinista rabble. He was clad in red pontifical vestments with a gold miter, yet he was also unmistakably Karol Wojtyła, for he also wore the battered red-brown loafers that caused over a quarter-century of distress to the traditional managers of popes.

After ten minutes of revery I prayed again for the repose of his soul, whispered, "Well done; thank you," and left to try to bear witness to the witness during the televised liturgical drama in the days ahead.

Archbishop Piero Marini drew his share of criticism as Master of Pontifical Liturgical Ceremonies, but no one who cared about the catechetical opportunity presented by John Paul II's death could object to the ceremony Marini designed for the transfer of the Pope's body on Monday afternoon from the Sala Clementina to a catafalque in front of Bernini's great bronze *baldacchino* and the high altar of St. Peter's. Vatican television had set up cameras along the lengthy route—which traversed the Apostolic Palace and the Raphael *stanze*, through the Sala Ducale and the Sala Regia, down the Scala Regia, out the Bronze

Doors, and into the Piazza San Pietro, before turning toward the ba-silica itself—so we had a live feed of the procession. I had a copy of the special missal Marini had prepared for the papal exequies, so even as our live coverage followed the rule we had agreed on long before—let the pictures and the drama tell the story—I translated fragments of the psalms and canticles as requested by Brian Williams and briefly de-scribed the rooms and hallways through which the procession passed. The singing of the Litany of the Saints, I noted, was like going through a family photo album; this was the family of the Church in glory, being called to come to the aid of one whom many of us expected would soon be numbered among the saints—and who had been at the center of the global Catholic family for more than a quarter-century.

It was a deeply moving ceremony and wonderful television. That it was televised at all suggested that at least something had been learned from the greatest of papal communicators: the people of the Church should be present, even if by television, at the last rites of the universal pastor of the Church.

The next three days were consumed by television work and final preparations for the live broadcast of the funeral Mass on Friday morn-ing. The obituary columns I was asked to write by the *Wall Street Journal* and *Newsweek*, and my own Catholic press column, had been filed weeks before, so it was possible to concentrate on the TV work—and marvel at the crowds that kept pouring into the city, effectively doubling its pop-ulation in four days. Something unprecedented was happening; it was impressive and moving, but it also raised an urgent logistical question.

Despite my having every press credential and security pass imag-inable, it was going to be impossible on the day of the funeral to get across the Via della Conciliazione, which lay between the apartment I was living in and NBC's platform for our broadcast: the crowd would simply be impassable, despite Roman officials' attempts to draw people away from the Vatican by setting up jumbo TV screens at the Circus Maximus and other sites. So on the night of April 7, I took a long walk down the packed Conciliazione—noting the priests hearing confes-sions in doorways on either side of the boulevard that runs from the Tiber to the Piazza San Pietro—and tried a route I hoped would take me around the crowd the following morning.

Back in the apartment, I called Piotr Malecki. We had spoken briefly on Sunday and I asked whether he, Teresa, and other Środowisko members would be coming to Rome for the funeral. They were too upset to think about it then, Piotr said. Days later, when it was impossible to get a hotel room in or near the city, they decided to come and, thinking correctly that they'd be sleeping outdoors, wore their old Wojtyła-style camping clothes. They'd called Archbishop Dziwisz and he'd come up with tickets. So I explained my apartment situation to Piotr and invited him and Teresa and anyone else they cared to invite to come up to the apartment for tea after the funeral Mass, saying we'd find each other by cell phone after the Mass was over.

At 5 a.m. on April 8, I left the apartment and walked away from the Vatican, past the Castel Sant'Angelo and down the Tiber to the garish Palazzo di Giustizia, where I crossed the river on the Ponte Umberto I. I then retraced my route on the other side until I recrossed the river on the Ponte Principe Amedeo Savoia Aosta and walked to the base of the Janiculum; from there, I could get to the lawn of the Pontifical Urban University and our platform for broadcasting the funeral Mass. It took fifty minutes and along the way I saw more Polish flags than I'd ever seen in one place before, including Poland, but I managed to avoid getting trapped.

That, however, was not Brian Williams's fate. Fearing that the anchor would not be able to get from his hotel on the Via Veneto to our platform on the Janiculum, NBC somehow managed to get Brian a room for Thursday night, April 7, at the Hotel Columbus on the Via della Conciliazione. There was only one problem: he couldn't get out of the hotel and up to our platform overlooking St. Peter's Square, thanks to the crush on the Conciliazione. The burly Italians Phil Alongi hired to act as errand runners now had a new mission: exfiltrate the anchor from the Columbus and get him up to us. I sketched an escape route out the back of the hotel on a paper napkin and off the runners went, to return safely about forty-five minutes later with the anchor in tow. As the Duke of Wellington said of Waterloo, it was a near-run thing.

I was proud of our three and a half hours of live coverage of what Brian aptly called, at the very beginning, "the human event of a generation." The commentary filled in what needed to be explained or amplified, but as we had agreed beforehand, we let the Mass tell its own story. There was no chattering about the many famous personalities present. Brian gave me the time necessary to explain what needed explaining about the rite in a catechetical way: thus I was able to describe the baptismal significance of the white veil placed over the Pope's face by Archbishop Dziwisz just before the casket was closed, linking it to the white robe of the newly christened and the pall covering the casket at every Catholic funeral. The solemnity of the vast crowd (estimated to be between three-quarters of a million and a million, just around the Vatican) somehow came through the broadcast and helped set the proper tone—this was a mega-event, but of a different sort.

There were deeply touching moments over those three-plus hours: seeing the plain cypress casket for the first time as it was carried out of the basilica; watching the pages of the Book of the Gospels, placed on the casket of the man who had announced the New Evangelization, blow gently in the breeze; the beautiful homily of Cardinal Joseph Ratzinger, with its call to John Paul to bless us all from the window of the Father's house. But the most striking moment during the funeral Mass of John Paul II was not in the missal.

The night before, as we were going over things one last time in our NBC "newsroom," I said that we should be alert for cries of *magnus* or *magno*—"great" in Latin or Italian—at the end of the Mass; it was not a risky prediction, as I had been told by friends that they intended to do just that, and I didn't think they were the only ones. That electric moment came right after the distribution of Holy Communion was completed and Cardinal Ratzinger chanted the post-Communion prayer. It began with applause, and then the voices came—"Magnus!" "Santo subito!" "Magno!"—and continued for a few minutes, as I explained that this was something that hadn't happened since the funeral of Pope St. Gregory the Great. Canonizations in the first millennium, I said, were often spontaneous acclamations by the people of the Church. That was what happened in 604 at the death of Gregory I, and something similar was happening here: the people of the Church were proclaiming their conviction that this was a life of heroic virtue, and that, like Leo I and Gregory I, John Paul II should be known as "Pope St. John Paul the Great."

After the cries of "Magnus!" and "Santo subito!" stopped, the Mass continued with one of Marini's innovations: chanted prayers of commendation in Greek by the Eastern-rite cardinals and bishops present. Since these somewhat exotic churchmen were not well known in the West, the lengthy chant gave me the opportunity to explain the rich diversity of the global Catholic family and to pay tribute to the largest of the Eastern Catholic Churches, the Ukrainian Greek Catholic Church, which had lived underground for decades during Soviet times. Then it was over but for one more emotional moment. As the casket reached the entrance to the basilica, those carrying it, the Sediarii, turned around so that, in the mind's eye, the deceased was facing his people, and indeed all who had come to pay him their respects, one last time. The last scene in the drama needed no verbal overlay.

An hour or so after John Paul II had been buried in the Vatican basilica's grottos, Piotr Malecki and I made contact by cell phone and arranged to meet in front of the Hotel Columbus a half hour later. Some seventy Środowisko men and women had arrived in Rome the previous day and spent the night on a street near the Vatican. On arriving at the basilica, they discovered that the tickets Archbishop Dziwisz got for them were not far out in the Square but up on the Sagrato, directly behind the heads of state and government. It was a perfect Dziwisz touch: Karol Wojtyła's oldest friends, dressed in outdoor gear, as the first mourners at his funeral Mass, save for those whom protocol required be seated in the front rows.

Piotr and I finally spotted each other on the Via della Conciliazione; he was with Teresa, her sister Maria (the widow of John Paul's old friend Krzysztof Rybicki), and Karol Tarnowski, another Kraków philosopher and longtime Wojtyła friend. They looked not too much the worse for wear and we went to the Borgo Pio apartment for tea, *vino bianco*, cookies, and the inevitable tears. But not too many.

Piotr's insightful comment the week before the Pope's death—"I think they're finally beginning to understand him"—had been borne out by what we had all just experienced. As I said during the NBC coverage, the world is full of talk about "the global community"; well, here was real global community, and it was gathered and formed by Christian faith, not by political or economic forces. John Paul II cemented the principle of solidarity into the foundations of Catholic social doctrine by his magisterium, especially in *Centesimus Annus*. He had also empowered solidarity, the human experience, during the Nine Days of June 1979 on which the history of the twentieth century pivoted. Now, present in a different way, he created solidarity in a vast throng drawn from all over the globe, through an act of worship.

There were no tears to be shed over that. There was, rather, a profound sense of gratitude for having known such a man—and the reassuring conviction, born of Easter faith, that he was now where he always wanted to be.

Mission
Continued

In July 2007, Fr. Maciej Zięba, with whom I was teaching in Kraków during what had been renamed the Tertio Millennio Seminar on the Free Society, gave me a dossier of documents in which he thought I "might be interested." That was an understatement.

What Fr. Zięba brought were copies of official documents from the Polish secret police (the Służba Bezpieczeństwa, or SB), various organs of the Polish communist government, and the East German secret police, the Stasi, recording the comrades' attempts to impede the work of Karol Wojtyła before and after he assumed the Office of Peter. The documents had been culled from Poland's Institute of National Remembrance and the Stasi Records Agency by Andrzej Grajewski, a Polish historian interested in the Cold War efforts of Eastern bloc intelligence services to penetrate the Catholic Church and to worm their way into the Vatican. Grajewski made copies of documents he thought might interest me as I continued to explore the life and times of Pope John Paul II.

The documents Fr. Zięba left with me were a gold mine—SB reports on Cardinal Wojyła to the Polish Communist Party politburo; Polish decrypts of ciphered cables sent from Rome to the Polish foreign ministry, reporting on diplomatic contacts with the Vatican;

reports from the Polish Ministry of Religious Affairs on its own Vatican conversations; General Wojciech Jaruzelski's memo to the politburo on his negotiations in Rome prior to John Paul's third Polish pilgrimage in 1987; and four Stasi analyses of John Paul II's potential impact on the Cold War from the crucial first months of the pontificate. Before I became the beneficiary of Dr. Grajewski's meticulous research and generosity, I had studied the Soviet secret police materials on the *Ostpolitik* of Paul VI and on John Paul II analyzed by British intelligence expert Christopher Andrew in a groundbreaking book, *The Sword and the Shield: The Mitrokhin Archive and the Secret History of the KGB,* published while *Witness to Hope* was in press. But I certainly never expected to see memoranda prepared for the notorious head of Stasi foreign intelligence, Markus Wolf, using information and speculations from moles in the Vatican, or detailed reports of the SB's efforts to understand (and undermine) Karol Wojtyła. As I worked through these materials, discussed the communists' endless anti-Wojtyła/John Paul II projects with Grajewski, and dug into scholarly analyses of materials newly available from other communist security service archives, my concept of what I should do in keeping the promise I made to John Paul II at our last meeting changed.

Originally, I thought a second volume would tell the John Paul II story from 1999 until the Pope's death, ending with a more comprehensive evaluation of his life and accomplishments than was possible in *Witness to Hope.* Now, it seemed that I should preface the completion and evaluation of the John Paul II story with a much more detailed examination of the *Ostpolitik* of Paul VI, Wojtyła's battle with Polish communism in Kraków, and John Paul II's efforts to work for the liberation of Central and Eastern Europe amid the communist penetration of the Vatican that was one result of the *Ostpolitik.*

Then my plans were altered further.

While analyzing the materials I'd been given by Andrzej Grajewski and others, I was invited to be an official witness for John Paul's II's beatification cause—an experience that would lead me to rethink the evaluative section of my second biographical volume, the book that would eventually be published in 2010 as *The End and the Beginning: Pope John Paul II—The Victory of Freedom, the Last Years, the Legacy.*

Professor Jerzy Gałkowski of the Catholic University of Lublin told me in 1997 that "adventures weren't unusual with Karol Wojtyła." In my case, those adventures continued for more than a decade after the publication of *Witness to Hope* and for five years after the Pope's death. There was more to be learned and a deeper understanding to be gained.

A Gold Mine of Secrets

A QUARTER-CENTURY AFTER THE COMMUNIST CRACK-UP IN CENTRAL and Eastern Europe, the contradictions with which the Marxist-Leninist project was riven are still not well understood in the West. A prime example involves communism and religion.

Lenin founded the world's first officially atheistic state; the Soviet regime he created maintained a colossal academic and propaganda apparatus to advance the cause of state atheism; communist regimes, led by the USSR, were the greatest persecutors and murderers of Christians in history. Yet for all that they mocked religious conviction as fantasy, the communists seemed curiously unpersuaded by their own dismissive attitude toward faith.

The same regimes that scorned those unscientific religious primitives also expended enormous financial and human resources trying to "disintegrate" religious communities (as the Polish SB put it), thus showing themselves terrified by religious conviction and religious institutions. And the particular focus of communist fear and animus was the Catholic Church. No less a figure than Yuri Andropov, longtime head of the KGB and successor to Leonid Brezhnev as leader of the USSR, was convinced that the Catholic Church and the Vatican were conducting ongoing, dangerous ideological sabotage against communism in general and the USSR in particular. Marx may have believed religion an opiate; for Andropov and similarly ruthless spymasters like the German Markus Wolf and the Pole Konrad Straszewski, the Catholic Church was a sinister enemy with which there could be no compromise.

That communism was permanently and determinedly at war with the Catholic Church was not well understood in the Vatican of Pope

John XXIII and Pope Paul VI. These men and their diplomats thought the deep freeze in Soviet-Vatican relations and in relations between Church and state in the Soviets' Warsaw Pact satellites was in part the Church's fault. From that premise, they concluded that a thaw was possible, were the Church to dial down its rhetoric. This led to the Vatican *Ostpolitik* of the 1960s and 1970s.

None of this made sense to me when I was writing *The Final Revolution*. It made even less sense when I was preparing *Witness to Hope*. The documentary evidence that I worked with in writing *The End and the Beginning* helped demonstrate from primary sources the truth of what I had argued in the two previous books: the *Ostpolitik* was a failure that John Paul II was quite right to jettison, if in his own unique and shrewd way.

On meeting him, few would imagine Andrzej Grajewski a keen student of the darkest secrets of the Cold War. A mild-mannered historian whose day job involved writing for the Polish Catholic weekly *Gość Niedzielny* (Sunday Visitor), Grajewski was a tenacious researcher—and even more important, a judicious judge of evidence. For the world that produced the previously classified documents he shared with me was a wilderness of mirrors: a world of maximum feasible tawdriness in which it was important to retain the capacity to be shocked while maintaining a clinical distance from the shock in order to analyze motives and impacts.

With the help of three capable translators—Paula Olearnik, Szymon Malecki, and Father John Rock, SJ—I was able to discuss with Grajewski the Polish and East German documents he'd culled from the relevant archives and shared with me. Those conversations did not alter the basic story line in *The Final Revolution* and *Witness to Hope*. But they allowed me to tell the story of communism's war against Karol Wojtyła, and his victory over the comrades, in new depth and with numerous striking illustrations previously unknown or unreported. The details are in *The End and the Beginning*, but several key skirmishes and battles in what was all war, all the time stand out.

The first was the SB's attempt to blackmail John Paul II during the negotiations over his second Polish pilgrimage in 1983. The plan involved a forged diary, said to be authored by a former employee of the

Archdiocese of Kraków, Irina Kinaszewska, in which Mrs. Kinaszewska (deceased by 1983) claimed a sexual relationship with Cardinal Wojtyła. This tawdry caper was frustrated when the SB officer in charge of planting the diary in the apartment of John Paul's old friend, Msgr. Andrzej Bardecki, got stinking drunk, crashed his car, and tried to talk his way out of a bad situation by blabbing to the police about who he was and what he was doing—from which point the whole plot unraveled. At first blush, this particular "active measure" looked like something out of the Keystone Kops. But when it turned out that the same SB officer who crashed his car, Grzegorz Piotrowski, was one of those who beat Fr. Jerzy Popiełuszko to death a year later, another lesson came into focus: the moral tawdriness of the communist effort to disintegrate the Church and the Pope went hand in (iron) glove with physical brutality.

Grajewski's studies and our exploration of them also confirmed what I had long suspected: that the *Ostpolitik*'s search for a modus vivendi with communist regimes resulted in the Vatican's being seriously penetrated by Eastern bloc intelligence services, beginning with covert operations and the suborning of moles during the Second Vatican Council.

The most interesting nugget from those days involved Cardinal Stefan Wyszyński. During Vatican II, Wyszyński, whose deep Marian piety was also an icon of Polish anticommunist resistance, urged the Council to issue a document on the Blessed Virgin Mary. Working with Catholic collaborators among theological specialists in Mariology (some of whom were even given SB code names), the Polish secret police sponsored a "Memorandum on Certain Aspects of the Cult of the Virgin Mary in Poland": a putatively scholarly paper suggesting that Wyszyński's Marian piety was heretical, which was distributed to all the bishops at Vatican II. The memorandum was accepted as authentic by virtually all the journalists covering the Council, in part because it fit neatly into the "good liberals versus bad conservatives" Vatican II story line beloved of the media. And it had an effect, if a temporary one, on the Polish primate's standing among his brother bishops and in his contest with the curial officials pushing the *Ostpolitik*.

Andrzej Grajewski's professionalism was displayed in the respect he showed for the competence of some of the SB's most accomplished agents in and around the Vatican. The most striking of these was Edward Kotowski (code name PIETRO), who was sent to Rome in 1978 and over the next five years developed several levels of open and clandestine contacts through a combination of the skills that make for a superior secret intelligence operative: linguistic capabilities, personal charm, a tremendous memory, and a capacity to tell his superiors the truth. Thus while PIETRO was an especially capable opponent fully involved in the SB's efforts to impede or blunt the effect of John Paul II's 1983 pilgrimage to Poland, it was also Kotowski who, after returning to Poland, told General Jaruzelski in 1989 that the jig was up and that the regime had to recognize the legal personality of the Church—thus opening the door to the legal reemergence of Polish civil society from under the rotting carapace of the Communist Party state.

During the Cold War, the East German Ministry for State Security, the Ministerium für Staatssicherheit, or Stasi, was generally regarded as the most competent, and thus the most dangerous, of the Warsaw Pact secret intelligence services. Grajewski's documents and the information he gave me about Stasi penetration of the Vatican did nothing to diminish that reputation. These people, I quickly came to see, were quite professional and completely ruthless. Yet for all their professionalism, their worldview impeded their analysis. The reports to Stasi foreign intelligence chief Markus Wolf were full of accurate detail about what was afoot inside the Vatican, but the analysis was often skewed by the tendency to view everything about John Paul II through a political lens—such as his first encyclical, *Redemptor Hominis*, which was thoroughly misconstrued by the German moles in Rome. The Stasi reports grasped the reasons for John Paul's insistence that the Church did not do politics, but they missed his larger strategic goal, which was to redefine the battleground between Catholicism and communism, shifting the contest from the realm of diplomacy to the realm of conscience, conviction, and cultural resistance. These Stasi memoranda thus illustrated a fundamental principle in Espionage 101: the data may be solid, but it's only useful when the analysis through which it's filtered is based on accurate premises and assumptions.

A year after giving me the initial cache of Polish and East German materials, Andrjez Grajewski and I met in Katowice to review another crucial document he had acquired: a November 1979 "Decree of the Central Committee of the Communist Party of the Soviet Union." That decree and its appendix gave orders to various Soviet state organs about actions to be taken against Pope John Paul II. The document was interpreted in some quarters as a direct order to kill the Pope, which it was not (no such order would likely have been written down). Rather, it was a call for "active measures" against the Pope and the Church, including a full range of covert activities: spreading disinformation about John Paul as a "conservative" who threatened world peace (a trap in which many Western journalists and Catholic commentators were ensnared); provocations; and intensified efforts at information gathering from within Church circles, including the Vatican. The decree also called for closer cooperation with those Vatican circles in favor of "peaceful relations," meaning those still pushing the old *Ostpolitik*.

The appendix went on to express grave concern about the effects of John Paul II's election and program, not only in Poland and other Catholic areas of the Warsaw Pact but within the Soviet Union itself, explicitly identifying Lithuania, Latvia, western Ukraine, and Belarus as regions that could be destabilized. Poland was not neglected, however, for one part of the appendix described it as a Catholic salient from which "to carry out the strategic policies of the Vatican" against the Soviet bloc.

Perhaps the most striking thing about this document—which was labeled "absolutely secret"—was the threat analysis. The struggle for the future was still described in the old dyad of socialist social order versus Western imperialism. But the mortal threat to the former was not the ex officio leader of the "imperialists," US president Jimmy Carter. The threat to the Soviet imperium was John Paul II.

While I was digging into these materials with Andrzek Grajewski, I got into contact with Martin and Annelise Anderson, then completing work on their book *Reagan's Secret War*. The Andersons shared with me a previously classified White House memorandum of conversation on Reagan's working lunch with Cardinal Agostino Casaroli, two days after martial law was declared in Poland in December 1981. It was a revealing document.

Casaroli initiated the conversation on the Polish crisis by accepting General Jaruzelski's claim that he had acted under Soviet pressure and to forestall a Soviet invasion, claiming a "personal knowledge" of the Polish general as the basis of his judgments. A day before Polish troops killed nine striking workers at a mine in Katowice, Casaroli seemed confident that the Polish army would not take violent measures against nonviolent strikers.

Against Reagan's argument that the forces of freedom should take full advantage of the attempt to crush Solidarity to underscore the case for freedom, Casaroli replied that "it was unrealistic to think that one East European country could be extensively liberalized on its own," for "no country could be far ahead of the others"; the cardinal then claimed this was John Paul's view, which it certainly was not. At one point, Casaroli even said that, while "the events in Poland were unfortunate," they were also "predictable," given what Polish officials had told him about "the lack of worker discipline" since the rise of Solidarity.

When Reagan spoke of a "terrible hunger" for God in the Warsaw Pact, Casaroli said that that might be true in some circles, but that young people were "insensible to God." The cardinal then repeated twice that the time was "not ripe" for "major change" in Central and Eastern Europe (at which point Reagan's personal representative to the Vatican, William Wilson, shrewdly observed that they would probably only know in retrospect when the time was ripe for real change). The memorandum, read between the lines, also suggested that Casaroli bought the caricature of Ronald Reagan as a warmongering cowboy, telling the president that the world relied "on his judgment and wisdom"—that is, Casaroli looked to the United States to cool tensions with the Soviet bloc in the wake of martial law in Poland.

Throughout a ninety-minute conversation, Ronald Reagan was the voice of John Paul II's morally driven approach to world politics while Cardinal Casaroli played the role of the worldly-wise practitioner of realpolitik. The president believed in the power of moral witness to change things; the cardinal secretary of state took the measured, "realistic" view. The president wanted to help John Paul's global campaign for human rights by condemning repression publicly; the Vatican diplomat argued for muted voices.

All of which confirmed that, whatever else was misguided about the Stasi, SB, and KGB analyses of life inside the Vatican, the claim that there were "Vatican circles" deeply disturbed by John Paul II and his approach to world politics was well founded. I got a further sense of just how well founded from an unexpected source.

Achille Silvestrini, Cardinal Casaroli's longtime deputy for the *Ostpolitik*, was one of the two curial cardinals who refused to speak with me when I was preparing *Witness to Hope*. I thought I understood Silvestrini's reluctance. As principal keeper of the Casaroli flame, he was likely unhappy with the analysis of the *Ostpolitik* in *The Final Revolution*, thought that I would propose more of the same in my papal biography, and thus played hard to get. It was all the more surprising, then, when, during the October 2003 Polish television broadcast for John Paul II's silver jubilee, Cardinal Silvestrini greeted me like a long-lost friend and invited me to meet with him. I took him up on his offer and we met twice in 2008.

The parlor in his apartment was a memorial to the Italian sub-tribe to which he belonged: the denizens of Brisighella, near Ravenna, which had produced two other modern-day cardinals in addition to Silvestrini, the brothers Gaetano and Amleto Cicognani. Near a large picture of the two prelates and the walled medieval town was a bookcase featuring all five volumes of the canonical progressive account of the Second Vatican Council, edited by Giuseppe Alberigo. That, and the fact that Silvestrini wore the bishop's ring that Paul VI had designed for the Council fathers rather than the cardinal's ring given him by John Paul II, readily positioned the cardinal on the ecclesiastical map.

Our meetings were entirely friendly—although the follow-up session in November 2008 was only possible because Hanna Suchocka sat me at the same table with Silvestrini at a dinner party and he could no longer evade my reminders that he'd agreed to meet a second time. Despite the cordiality, I had the sense at both our meetings that he was playing Mr. Magoo, effecting an innocence and diffidence belied by his experience and by his constantly thumbing through a well-marked copy of Cardinal Casaroli's memoir and defense of the *Ostpolitik*, *Il Martirio della Pazienza* (The Martyrdom of Patience).

There were, however, moments in our conversations that were genuinely helpful. In my writing I had occasionally noted the striking fact that the Cuban Missile Crisis coincided with the opening days of

Vatican II: a conjunction of events I thought might have badly shaken John XXIII and Casaroli. When I asked him about this, Silvestrini confirmed that the 1963 encyclical *Pacem in Terris* (Peace on Earth) "had its origins" in the experience of those days, when the Vatican judged that a "new voice was needed." Further, he tacitly conceded the extreme cautiousness of the Casaroli approach to communist governments and the Solidarity movement by saying, with the hint of a smile, that John Paul II had "less prudence" in such matters—meaning more willingness to push for change. He agreed with my suggestion that the Soviets regarded John Paul II as a threat to their entire enterprise, not just to their grip on Poland: a view Silvestrini may well have formed at the outset of the pontificate through his contacts in the Italian Communist Party. And he described John Paul's 1980 letter to Soviet leader Leonid Brezhnev as a "personal initiative" that would have been discussed with Cardinal Casaroli but didn't emanate from him—another important indicator of John Paul's independence and boldness.

Practiced diplomat that he was, he complimented me on my books and asked me to sign his copies of the Italian editions of *The Final Revolution* and *Witness to Hope*. Yet Achille Silvestrini remained the true Casaroli acolyte. John Paul II's election, he claimed, was only possible because of the *Ostpolitik;* but he never acknowledged the cardinals' criticism of that policy during the interregnum after the death of Paul VI. Despite the massive documentary evidence I had seen that the *Ostpolitik* led to the serious penetration of the Vatican Secretariat of State by Warsaw Pact secret intelligence services, Silvestrini never conceded that the Vatican tried to deal with moles and leaks, saying only that there were "concerns" but "no concrete evidence" of penetration (and this despite admitting that he and others were warned about agents in place by Western intelligence). He persistently defended the work of his own deputy, Luigi Poggi, whom the Grajewski documents showed to be one of the most gelatinous Vatican diplomats in dealing with the hardball players in the Polish communist leadership. Moreover, he still insisted that the idea of putting a papal nuncio into Poland in the mid-1970s—Poggi—was a sound one, despite the virtual certainty that this would have cut the legs out from under Cardinal Wyszyński in his dealings with the Polish communist regime.

Not unlike Cardinal Casaroli in his December 1981 lunch conversation with President Reagan, Silvestrini conveyed the impression that the chief operators of the old Vatican *Ostpolitik* regarded the Solidarity movement as a distraction, a gaggle of pious, idealistic amateurs making trouble for the diplomatic professionals—which was, of course, a world removed from John Paul II's notion of Solidarity as a unique embodiment of Catholic social doctrine. And, again like Casaroli, Silvestrini was willing to cut Wojciech Jaruzelski a lot of slack over the imposition of martial law, even after it was clear that there was no serious threat of a Soviet invasion of Poland in December 1981.

I was grateful for Cardinal Silvestrini's time and courtesy but frustrated by his unwillingness to engage me robustly or to deal seriously with the accumulating scholarly consensus that the *Ostpolitik* had few accomplishments and in fact had done a lot of damage. My conversations with the main protagonist of the Casaroli heritage confirmed me in the judgment that the default positions in the Vatican diplomatic service, especially among the Italians, were not materially changed by the pontificate of John Paul II and its powerful demonstration of the potency of papal moral witness.

Beatification and a
Life Reconsidered

P OPE BENEDICT XVI'S DECISION TO WAIVE THE NORMAL FIVE-YEAR
waiting period for opening a beatification and canonization cause
for John Paul II was a wise response to the calls that rang out across
St. Peter's Square on April 8, 2005—"Santo subito!" There would be
no instant canonization, but the process of investigating the case for
John Paul II's beatification and eventual canonization could begin
immediately. For the process to be credible, however, a certain kind
of postulator (in effect, a project manager) was needed: someone who
understood the late Pope and appreciated his thought and his virtues
but who wouldn't be stampeded or rushed; someone familiar with the
new method of assessing possible saints' causes that John Paul created;
someone who knew Polish and Italian, the two languages in which
most of the extensive documentation in this cause would be found. As
it happened, the right man was at hand.

Monsignor Sławomir Oder, a priest of the diocese of Toruń, had
stayed in Rome to work for Cardinal Camillo Ruini and the Vicariate
of Rome after completing doctoral studies in canon law at the Pontifical
Lateran University. I found him very impressive as we got to know each
other. He was smart and precise; he had a good sense of humor and wasn't
overawed by what Vatican wags call the *pezzi grossi,* the big shots; he had
worked on a previous cause, so he knew the procedural ropes. Above all
he was a good priest who insisted on serving as pastor of a Roman parish
because, he said, too many Roman priests are merely bureaucrats.

We first met in 2006, when Oder wrote and asked me if I
could share with him a copy of the memoir fragment, *Curriculum*

Philosophicum, that John Paul II had given me in 1996—a first indication of the postulation's meticulousness, as the only reference to that document was buried in the dense forest of endnotes at the end of *Witness to Hope*. I'd been given *Curriculum Philosophicum* on the understanding that it was for my eyes only, so I thought it best to check with Cardinal Dziwisz; he encouraged me to cooperate fully with Oder, so I sent a copy along to my new correspondent with apologies for its somewhat tattered and annotated condition.

Some months later, Msgr. Oder got back in touch and asked me to be an official witness for the beatification/canonization cause. This was unexpected. So I went to Oder's office in the Lateran Palace, former home of popes, to discuss the matter during a December 2006 Roman work period. He explained that he wanted to solicit opinions from a wide range of knowledgeable sources, that I would be sworn to confidentiality under the rubric of the "pontifical secret," and that I should be prepared to put aside several hours for oral testimony before a canonical judge, whose questions would be based on a questionnaire developed for the cause. That seemed fair enough. Then, after reviewing the questionnaire, I asked whether it wouldn't make more sense for me to offer my testimony in written form, after having sworn the required oath. Oder readily agreed.

Without violating the "pontifical secret," I can say that the extensive questionnaire—more than 120 questions—began with some throat-clearing about the witness (me) and then proceeded to more than sixty historical and biographical questions about the subject, which took me a bit aback. So I called Oder and asked, "Do you really want me to answer these biographical questions? I've already written a thousand pages on them." He laughed and said that, in response to those questions, I could make reference to the appropriate pages and chapters in *Witness to Hope*—because "your book is the bible in this office." That was reassuring, so I set to work on the rest of the questionnaire. It was a marvelous experience in that it compelled me to rethink John Paul II's life and pontificate through a new prism: the virtues.

I'd written a lot about Karol Wojtyła as a Christian disciple, because that dimension of his personality seemed to me the foundation of all the rest. But I had never "read" his entire life and pontificate through the optic of the theological virtues—faith, hope, and love—and the cardinal virtues of prudence, justice, courage, and temperance. That was what the balance of the questionnaire asked me to do. I found the experience so intriguing that I adopted the "virtues" framework in the evaluative third section of *The End and the Beginning*.

I submitted my testimony in December 2006 but my conversation with Msgr. Oder continued. In the course of several meetings, I learned that the Positio, the formal record of John Paul II's cause, was composed of four massive volumes, the first of which was a "small biography" (to which *Witness to Hope* was appended). The second and third volumes of the Positio were compilations of testimonies from over a hundred witnesses, among whom were more than two dozen laypeople; their remarks, Oder observed, were frequently the most interesting. The first three volumes of the Positio would eventually be available for scholarly research. The fourth volume, *Quaestiones Selectae* (Special Questions), would remain under the pontifical secret.

Which fact brought me back to the murky and sometimes brutal world of the secret intelligence services. In one conversation, Msgr. Oder told me of some recent nonsense in the Italian press to the effect that, during World War II, Karol Wojtyła had taken part in the assassination of two Gestapo agents. That struck me as impossibly out of character, to which Oder replied, "Obviously." But the postulation office spent six months tracking down the story and preparing a rebuttal for inclusion under those "special questions." Then an idea occurred to me about the possible origin of such a calumny and I said to Oder, "Markus Wolf?" He thought it quite possible. The worst of the bad guys never quit, it seemed.

The formal investigative process included testimony from serious critics of John Paul II, including the schismatic followers of Archbishop Marcel Lefebvre. Their large dossier accused the Pope of just about everything in the Lefebvrist parade of horribles—but not, it seemed, liturgical abuses, thus confirming what John Paul II had said: the Lefebvrist rejection of Vatican II was primarily a matter of the Council's endorsement of religious freedom, its openness to interreligious dialogue, and the new emphasis it placed on a Church engaging the world.

Criticism from schismatics paled into insignificance, however, when our conversation about the opposition to the cause coincided with a discussion of exorcisms that could be attributed to John Paul II—a delicate subject I had raised with Cardinal Stanisław Dziwisz, appointed Archbishop of Kraków by Benedict XVI, in 2008. Dziwisz told me frankly that, in 1978, he thought that what Catholic tradition referred to as "demonic possession" was one form or another of mental illness. But after several experiences of situations in which a deep, calming change was worked in a highly disturbed person by an encounter with John Paul II that included the Pope's praying with or over the afflicted person, he no longer thought of Satan as a metaphor; Satan was real and at work in the world. Msgr. Oder, a most measured man, agreed: "I can feel his power sometimes. . . . He hates him [John Paul II]." It was not the kind of comment one typically hears over lunch; I promised my Polish friend that I would pray for his protection.

The catalog of "favors received" through the intercession of John Paul II was strikingly appropriate, in that so many seemed to reflect the late Pope's pastoral priorities: couples enabled to conceive children; family reconciliations; "returns to God," conversions, and recoveries of faith; difficult pregnancies brought to term. I smiled at the number of students who wrote the postulation office, reporting happy results on fearsome exams. Even more touching were the letters from those reporting that they found employment after praying for John Paul II's help.

But the most moving of all were the letters Msgr. Oder showed me in a small cubbyhole next to his office. There, in a variety of languages, were letters addressed, "Pope John Paul II / Heaven." I almost teared up, but then I laughed and said, "You mean the people who can't get my electric bill from one side of the county to the other can manage to deliver these here?" Oder and I agreed that it was, like so many more serious and urgent "favors received," a miracle.

A PROMISE KEPT

WRITING THE SECOND VOLUME OF MY JOHN PAUL II BIOGRAPHY occupied a considerable amount of my time in 2008 and early 2009, not least because of the challenges involved in helping readers traverse the twilight-zone world of communist secret intelligence services and their attempts to penetrate the Vatican and impede the Pope's work. In structuring the book, I decided to follow the format I had adopted for *Witness to Hope*, beginning each chapter of the historical sections with a timeline of events and a tone-setting vignette from John Paul's life, before proceeding to the narrative. The book opened with a prologue that summarized *Witness to Hope* in eighteen and a half pages and then continued in three parts. "Nemesis" retold the story of the battle between communism and Karol Wojtyła / John Paul II, now amplified by the Grajewski materials and other new documentation. "Kenosis," the theological term for emptying oneself in imitation of Christ's self-emptying (Philippians 2.7), took up the story where *Witness to Hope* left off and told the tale of John Paul's last four and a half years. "Metanoia," a biblical term for Christian conversion, was the lengthy evaluation of the man and the pontificate that could not be done in the first volume, for obvious reasons.

I took the idea for the new book's title, *The End and the Beginning*, from "East Coker," the second part of T. S. Eliot's *Four Quartets*, in which the poet speaks of ends connected to beginnings: which seemed true of the arc of John Paul II's life and reflective of the book's somewhat odd structure—a revisiting of Wojtyła versus communism before the finale of the John Paul II story and the long evaluation. It was perhaps too clever and didn't sharply signal that this was the sequel to *Witness to Hope*—which many people thought had already told the whole story. Published in the United States in the fall of 2010, *The End and the Beginning: John Paul II—The Victory of Freedom, the Last Years, the Legacy* eventually appeared in Spanish, Italian, Ukrainian, Polish, and German editions, with a Chinese edition to follow.

The Polish edition appeared in 2012, and I spent a week in Warsaw, Lublin, and Kraków promoting it at various media and public events. There were excellent discussions of John Paul II's Polish legacy at the Dominican priories in Warsaw and Kraków and an engaging luncheon at the presidential palace in Warsaw, hosted by President Bronisław Komorowski and attended by the great Tadeusz Mazowiecki. Throughout the week, though, I was struck by how poorly John Paul II's intellectual project had been received and internalized in Poland, with the exception of my Polish Dominican friends, a few other scholars in Lublin and elsewhere, and a scattering of journalists, politicians, and laypeople. Poland's emotional attachment to the late Pope was massively evident the year before in Rome, at his beatification. But John Paul's vision of a public Church that was not a partisan Church, a Church that shaped public life by forming culture through the evangelization and catechesis of the people, was not much in evidence in twenty-first-century Poland, sadly. That impression was a portent of difficulties to come in Polish public life.

Seeing *The End and the Beginning* was not quite the intensely emotional experience that opening the box with the first copies of *Witness to Hope* had been. It was a blessing and a satisfaction to have been given the time to keep the promise I made to John Paul on December 15, 2004. I was grateful for the cooperation I'd received from so many interlocutors and colleagues in preparing the book. I thought the first section, drawing on those hitherto unknown or unremarked Stasi, SB, and KGB documents, made a real contribution to the study of an important period of modern history—and were a useful reminder to the generations that knew not Joseph (Stalin) of what the Cold War had been about, why it had to be fought, and why it was so important that the forces of freedom won.

Yet something was different, and the difference was obvious.

This time, there would be no "good country dinner" at Castel Gandolfo, no reminiscence with my subject about the things we had been through together, no shared laughter, no silent bear hug or prayer in the chapel at the end. That reunion would have to wait for another dinner party, what the Book of Revelation calls the Wedding Feast of the Lamb, in another location: the New Jerusalem.

Lessons in Hope

T HE CROSS BENEATH WHICH I WROTE *WITNESS TO HOPE* AND *The End and the Beginning* is a framed reproduction of Marc Chagall's *White Crucifixion*. Slightly below it and to the right is an icon of the Black Madonna of Częstochowa. These two works of art watched over me during the decades of research and writing that led to the two volumes of my John Paul II biography. As icons do, they also make present spiritual realities: in this case, the lessons in hope I learned from the saint whose life changed mine, in ways I could never have anticipated during a dinner of consequence in December 1995.

The *White Crucifixion* has long struck me as the most evocative religious painting of the twentieth century. Painted shortly after the Nazi Kristallnacht in 1938, its Christ is unmistakably Jewish, clothed on the cross in a *tallith*, a traditional prayer shawl, with Pilate's inscription in Hebrew over his bowed head. Instead of the mourning angels common to renderings of the Crucifixion, he is surrounded by three Jewish patriarchs and a matriarch; beneath him is a ceremonial seven-branched candelabrum; and around him swirl the lethal ideological madnesses of the mid-twentieth century, symbolized by Jews fleeing burning synagogues and revolutionaries following the red flag.

The great historian Jaroslav Pelikan read the *White Crucifixion* as, in part, Chagall's rebuke to those Christians who imagined they were doing the will of God by persecuting Jesus's people, the People of Israel. Yet Pelikan went on to note that this very Jewish Rabbi Jesus is also the Church's Lord Jesus: a son of Israel who is the universal savior in his Jewishness, not outside of it. In that sense, the *White Crucifixion*, read through the prism of Easter faith, embodies the answer to the question so sharply posed at Auschwitz and the gulag camps, during the Ukrainian Holodomor, and in the killing fields of Cambodia: Where is God? To which the Christian reply is, God is here, in the person of his Son, bearing the world's sin and overcoming it through obedient suffering undergone for love of the world.

The Virgin Mary is not a figure in Chagall's rendering of Calvary, which is one reason why I placed that icon of the Black Madonna beneath the *White Crucifixion*, as John Paul II had placed a similar icon beneath the cross in the chapel of the papal apartment. For John Paul, Mary was the preeminent disciple, the woman of faith whose articulated yes at the Annunciation, and whose silent yes in receiving the body of her Son in the familiar composition of the *Pietà*, is the model of all discipleship: the humble yet liberating acceptance of the divine will as one's own. So to contemplate the Black Madonna beneath the *White Crucifixion* is to make an act of faith in the providential governance of history and an act of hope in the future.

Where is God? God is here, in the midst of the human condition, redeeming his creation through radical, self-giving love. God is here, even when humanity is at its worst, so that fear and hatred and death don't have the final word. God is here, even when, to human eyes, the Holy One seems silent or indifferent. God is here, and God's creative and redemptive purposes are going to win the day, ultimately.

John Paul II lived by that conviction, embraced his suffering because of that conviction, and died in that conviction. That is why his life was a witness to hope. And that is why the lessons he taught me were, above all, lessons in hope.

In the days before his canonization, when it came time to try to say something fresh thing about him, it occurred to me that Karol Wojtyła was a man who refused to accept what I called, in the *Wall Street Journal,* the "tyranny of the possible." His faith in the providential governance of history was so deep, and his belief in the power of human solidarity was so strong, that he could discern possibilities where others could only see fixed and unchangeable realities: like the Berlin Wall, or the seeming indifference of the young to the Gospel, or the irrelevance of the Catholic Church to an authentic liberation of humanity in the twenty-first century and the third millennium.

More than a decade after his death, with his hope for a "springtime of the human spirit" being frustrated in world politics and his call for a Church of missionary disciples being ignored by Catholics still litigating the Sixties, it can seem that this refusal to accept the tyranny of the possible was itself quixotic, a reflection of Polish romanticism. But such cynicism would be a betrayal of the lessons in hope that he taught.

The Church and the world may be heading for a difficult patch in the middle decades of the twenty-first century. Recognizing that is a requirement of Christian realism. But submitting to those difficulties as something inexorable and irresistible is a betrayal of Christian hope. To know both those things and to try to live responsibly in the tension between them is to have learned something important from Karol Wojtyła, Pope St. John Paul II.

Acknowledgments

M ANY FRIENDS HELPED ME CHECK MY RECOLLECTIONS WHEN I didn't have a written record of an event or needed counsel in tracking down a stray piece of information. It's a pleasure to acknowledge their kind cooperation: Clare Duffy, Andrzej Grajewski, Archbishop Thomas Gullickson, Ed Gund, Judith Dwan Hallet, Candice Hughes, Father Tomasz Jaklewicz, Fr. Roger Landry, Joan Lewis, Luis Lugo, Teresa Malecka, Piotr Malecki, Bishop James McCarthy, Ed Meese, Keith Miller, Zbigniew Nosowski, Cardinal Edwin O'Brien, Msgr. Sławomir Oder, Mario Paredes, Rodger Potocki, Father Ronald Roberson, CSP, Brad Roberts, Gwyneth Spaeder, Father Tomasz Szopa, Joan Weigel, John Weigel, Tracy Wilkinson, Henryk Woźniakowski, Catherine Wyler, and Fr. Maciej Zięba, OP.

Stephen White excavated boxes of my materials from the archives at the Ethics and Public Policy Center and kept its Catholic Studies Project humming while I was writing. EPPC is the best possible professional home for a project like this, or indeed any other, and I thank my colleagues for their support and friendship.

I should also like to thank the board and staff of the William E. Simon Foundation, which sponsors my chair at EPPC, for their stalwart and generous support. Best thanks, too, to the other philanthropic partners of EPPC Catholic Studies.

This is my sixth book with Basic Books and the third I've done while Basic has been led by the wonderful Lara Heimert. My gratitude to Lara and the Basic staff, an author's dream team, is longstanding and most sincere.

It's a pleasure to dedicate this book to my wife, Joan, in abiding gratitude for helping make much of what's recounted here possible, and to our grandchildren—William, Claire, and Lucy Spaeder—so they'll have an idea of what their Papa was up to before they came on the scene.

G. W.

North Bethesda—Kraków—Allumette Island—Rome
February–November 2016

Index

Daniel Sheehan Photography

George Weigel is a *New York Times* bestselling author and one of the world's leading authorities on the Catholic Church. Weigel is Distinguished Senior Fellow of Washington's Ethics and Public Policy Center, where he holds the William E. Simon Chair in Catholic Studies, and lives in North Bethesda, Maryland.